THE
HISTORY OF
VENEZUELA

THE
HISTORY OF
VENEZUELA

H. Micheal Tarver
and
Julia C. Frederick

 ST. MARTIN'S GRIFFIN NEW YORK

Micheal Tarver dedicates this book to Maria Auxiliadora Petit de Márquez and to the memory of Guillermo Márquez Arenas and Orlando Jordán Petit. Julia Frederick dedicates this book to John Frederick.

THE HISTORY OF VENEZUELA
© H. Micheal Tarver and Julia C. Frederick, 2006.

Published by St. Martin's Press Griffin.

ISBN-13: 978–1–4039–6260–7 paperback
ISBN-10: 1–4039–6260–X paperback

Library of Congress Cataloging-in-Publication Data is available from the Library of Congress.

First published in 2006 by Greenwood Press.

10 9 8 7 6 5 4 3 2 1

Contents

Preface   vii

Timeline of Historical Events   ix

1   A Petroleum Republic   1

2   Venezuela to 1600   19

3   The Colonial Era (to 1810)   31

4   Movements toward Independence (1810–1830)   49

5   The Age of *Caudillismo* (1830–1989)   61

6   Restoration and Rehabilitation (1899–1935)   77

7   The Emergence of Modern Venezuela (1935–1958)   85

8   The Return of Democracy (1959–1963)   101

9   The Institutionalization of Democracy (1964–1973)   115

10   Venezuelan Boom and Bust (1974–1988)   123

11   Chaos, Futility, and Incompetence (1989–1998)   139

12   The Bolivarian Revolution (1999–2005)   151

Notable People in the History of Venezuela   161

Glossary of Selected Terms   171

Bibliographic Essay   177

Index   181

Preface

This work is the culmination of Micheal Tarver's twenty-year fascination with the Republic of Venezuela. During the period from his first visit to the country in the mid-1980s to his most recent visit in 2005, the South American nation has undergone major transformations. The country offers its visitors such a wide variety of cultures, languages, political ideologies, historical landmarks, and excitement that one never tires of going back. In the pages that follow, the authors hope that the richness of Venezuela and its people can be fully appreciated.

For the ease of our readers, Spanish words have been translated the first time they are used. The glossary also provides additional information on the various terms used throughout the text. The first time an individual is mentioned in the text, his or her birth and death dates are given in parentheses. With monarchs, only the dates of rule are given; with presidents, both birth and death dates and dates of govern are given, depending on the context.

This work would not have been possible without the support and assistance of several individuals. Micheal Tarver would like to acknowledge the intellectual support of his friends and colleagues at Arkansas Tech University, the Universidad de Los Andes, and McNeese State University.

He would also like to recognize the contributions of Jack Thomas, Wes Cady, and Robert Butler, who guided him through the various stages of his intellectual enlightenment. He would also like to thank Luis Loaiza Rincón for his contribution to the discussion of President Hugo Chávez Frías and Sarah Colwell for her gracious patience and assistance throughout this project. Julia Frederick would like to thank her husband, John Frederick, for his patience and support of her continuing exploration of Latin American history, and Micheal for allowing her to join him on this project. Finally, both authors wish to thank Carlos Márquez for his incalculable assistance with this project. This book could not have been completed without his hard work and tireless efforts. The authors are indebted to him for his gracious contributions.

Timeline of Historical Events

1492   Spanish reconquest of Granada. First voyage of Cristóbal Colón (Christopher Columbus) to the New World.

1493   Columbus's second voyage.

1494   Treaty of Tordesillas is signed between Spain and Portugal.

1498   Columbus's third voyage. Columbus discovers Tierra Firme and names it Tierra de Gracia; the area corresponds to the territory today known as Venezuela.

1500   World map of Juan de la Cosa, first known map showing New World.

1501–1502   East coast of South America surveyed by Amerigo Vespucci.

1502–1504   Columbus's fourth voyage.

1503	Royal license issued allowing for the enslavement of Carib Indians. Establishment of the *Casa de Contratación*.
1504	Death of Queen Isabel of Castile and León, "the Catholic."
1506	Death of Columbus.
1507	World map of Martin Waldseemüller, first known map using the name "America."
1509	From Española (Hispaniola), Alonso de Hojeda leads an expedition to the Venezuelan and Colombian coast.
1510–1540	Initial period of exploration and colonization.
1510–1567	Founding of cities begins.
1510–1810	Colonial period.
1512	Leyes de Burgos, the first code regulating Spanish treatment of Indians. Franciscan and Dominican missionaries reach Tierra Firme, on eastern coast of Venezuela.
1512–1515	Original exploration and settlement off Venezuela's eastern coast, especially on pearl-rich island of Cubagua.
1516	Death of King Fernando V of Castile and León, "the Catholic." Accession of Carlos I to the Spanish throne (Carlos V of the Holy Roman Empire after 1519).
1519–1595	Decimation of indigenous population.
1522	Papal Bull Omnimoda entrusts the evangelization of New World Indians to regular clergy.
1524	Creation of the Consejo de Indias.
1525	Introduction of African slaves into Venezuela.
1526	Founding of settlement of Nueva Cádiz on island of Cubagua, the first settlement on what would eventually become Venezuela.
1527	Founding of city of Coro, the first permanent settlement on Tierra Firme, by Juan de Ampíes.

1528	King Carlos I authorizes the establishment of the first *cabildo* in what is now Venezuela, on the island of Cubagua.
1528–1556	Venezuela ruled by Welser governors.
1529	Founding of the pueblo de Maracaibo, the first settlement on the shores of Lake Maracaibo, by Juan de Alfínger. This settlement was later reestablished under the name of Nueva Zamora Laguna de Maracaibo by Pedro Maldonado in 1574
1531	First bishopric of colonial Venezuela is established in Coro.
1532	Encomienda system is established in colonial Venezuela.
1538	Founding of Santa Fe de Bogotá.
1542	Promulgation of the Nuevas Leyes de Indias, which reformed Spanish government in the New World and modified the encomienda system.
1549	Royal ban on the use of Indians in encomiendas for labor.
1556	Abdication of King Carlos I. Accession of Felipe II to the Spanish throne.
1559	Sale of notarial offices begins in Spanish America, with the approval of the Crown.
1567	Founding of city of Caracas by Diego de Losada.
1580–1640	Spanish and Portuguese empires united under Felipe II.
1588	Defeat of Spanish Armada.
1598	Death of King Felipe II.
1628	First Jesuit college established in Venezuela, in city of Mérida.
1636	King Felipe IV approves the transfer of the Bishopric of the Province of Venezuela, from Coro to Caracas; although this transfer would not become official until 1656.

1641	Founding of the Real Seminario de Santa Rosa de Caracas.
1681	Recopilación de las Leyes de los Reinos de la Indias (Compilation of the Laws of the Kingdoms of the Indies) is published.
1687	Encomienda system is abolished in Venezuela.
1700	Death of Carlos II, last of the Hapsburg rulers of Spain.
1701	Accession of Felipe V to the Spanish throne.
1701–1714	War of Spanish Succession.
1721	Founding of the Real Universidad de Caracas, and made Pontificia by papal bull in 1722
1728	Founding of Compañía Guipuzcoana de Caracas.
1739	Establishment of Viceroyalty of Nueva Granada.
1746	Death of King Felipe V. Accession of Fernando VI to the Spanish throne.
1750	Birth of Francisco de Miranda, the Precursor.
1759	Death of King Fernando VI. Accession of Carlos III to the Spanish throne.
1764	American ports open to single ship trade.
1767	Jesuits expelled from Spanish dominions.
1776	Establishment of the Intendencia de Ejército y Real Hacienda in Caracas.
1777	Establishment of the Capitanía General of the United Provinces of Venezuela.
1778	Spain's Free Trade Act is promulgated, allowing for free trade among Spanish colonies.
1781	Rebellion of the comuneros del Socorro in Nueva Granada.
1783	Birth of Simón Bolívar, el Libertador.
1786	Establishment of the Real Audiencia de Caracas.
1788	Death of King Carlos III. Accession of Carlos IV to the Spanish throne.
1790	Birth of José Antonio Páez, first president of Venezuela.

1795	José Leonardo Chirino–led uprising breaks out in Coro.
1797	Spain is forced to allow its colonies to trade with neutral countries. La Guaira uprising breaks out, led by Manuel Gual and José María España.
1803	Creation of the Archbishopric of Caracas.
1806	Francisco de Miranda attempts but fails to incite rebellion in Venezuela.
1808	Abdication of King Carlos IV. Accession, exile, and abdication of King Fernando VII. Napoleonic occupation of Spain. José Bonaparte is installed on the Spanish throne as José I by his brother Napoleon. First printing press arrives in Venezuela.
1810	Caracas *cabildo* breaks relations with Spanish government and establishes itself as the proper Venezuelan government on April 19, until Fernando VII is returned to the Spanish throne.
1811	Declaration of Venezuelan independence from Spain on July 5. Two days later, the Act of Independence is approved.
1811–1812	First Republic or Patria Boba.
1812	Constitution of Cádiz.
1813	Napoleon expelled from Spain.
1813–1814	Second Republic. Campaña Admirable. War to the death. Bolívar's entry into Caracas. Bolívar proclaimed el Libertador.
1816–1819	Third Republic.
1819	Congress of Angostura. Battle of Boyacá. Creation of República de Colombia or Gran Colombia.
1820–1830	Attainment of independence.
1821	Battle of Carabobo.
1823	Proclamation of Monroe Doctrine.
1825	End of Spanish rule in South America.
1830	Dissolution of Gran Colombia. Death of Simón Bolívar.

1830–1835	First presidency of General José Antonio Páez.
1830–1848	Period of Conservative Oligarchy presided over by General José Antonio Páez.
1835–1836	Revolución de las Reformas.
1839–1843	Second presidency of General José Antonio Páez.
1847–1851	First presidency of General José Tadeo Monagas.
1851–1855	Presidency of General José Gregorio Monagas.
1855–1858	Second presidency of José Tadeo Monagas.
1858	President José Tadeo Monagas is overthrown.
1859–1863	Federal War.
1861–1863	Dictatorship of General José Antonio Páez.
1864–1865	Provisional presidency of General Juan Crisóstomo Falcón.
1868	Revolución Azul overthrows General Falcón.
1870–1877	Septenio, first presidency of General Antonio Guzmán Blanco.
1879–1884	Quinquenio, second presidency of General Guzmán Blanco.
1884–1886	First presidency of General Joaquín Crespo.
1886–1888	Bienio or Aclamación, third presidency of General Guzmán Blanco.
1892–1897	Second presidency of Joaquín Crespo.
1899–1908	Dictatorship of General Cipriano Castro.
1902	Anglo-German-Italian blockade of Venezuelan coastline.
1908–1935	Dictatorship of General Juan Vicente Gómez.
1914	Mene Grande oil field discovered in Venezuela with the drilling of the Zumaque-1 oil well.
1914–1918	World War I; Venezuela remains neutral.
1918	Massive oil exploitation begins.
1926	Oil becomes Venezuela's number one export.
1928	Students rise up against Gómez at UCV campus.

1935–1941	Presidency of General Eleazar López Contreras.
1936	Appearance of first contemporary political parties in Venezuela.
1939–1945	World War II.
1941–1945	Presidency of Isaías Medina Angarita.
1945–1948	Trienio.
1947	In December, Rómulo Gallegos is elected president in the first universal, direct, and secret elections held in Venezuela.
1948	Presidency of Rómulo Gallegos.
1948–1952	Junta Militar de Gobierno.
1952–1958	Dictatorship of Marcos Pérez Jiménez.
1958	Revolución del 23 de enero. Pérez Jiménez is overthrown. Junta de Gobierno is established. Rómulo Betancourt is elected constitutional president.
1959–1964	Presidency of Rómulo Betancourt.
1964–1969	Presidency of Raúl Leoni.
1969–1974	Presidency of Rafael Caldera.
1973	Venezuela benefits from oil boom and its currency peaks against the U.S. dollar.
1974–1979	Presidency of Carlos Andrés Pérez.
1975	Steel industry is nationalized.
1976	Petroleum industry is nationalized.
1979–1984	Presidency of Luis Herrera Campíns.
1983–1984	Oil prices fall, mandating cuts in state spending.
1984–1989	Presidency of Jaime Lusinchi.
1989–1993	Presidency of Carlos Andres Pérez. Administration is hampered by economic depression, which mandated an austerity program under the direction of the International Monetary Fund.
1989	Social and political upheaval against the government's spending cuts, including deadly riots, the declaration of martial law, and general strikes.

1992   Two golpe attempts against President Pérez. The
            February attempt was led by Lieutenant Colonel
            Hugo Chávez Frías, who would later become presi-
            dent. The November uprising is led by small number
            of general-staff officers in the navy and army. Chávez
            is jailed for two years before being pardoned.

1993   President Carlos Andrés Pérez is impeached and
            removed from office on charges of corruption. Ramón
            José Velásquez becomes interim president.

1994–1999   Presidency of Rafael Caldera.

1994   President Caldera pardons Lieutenant Colonel
            Hugo Chávez Frías.

1996   Carlos Andrés Pérez is imprisoned after being found
            guilty of embezzlement and corruption.

1998   Hugo Chávez Frías is elected president.

1999   New constitution is drafted and promulgated.

2000   Hugo Chávez Frías elected president under new
            constitution for a six-year term.

2001   Main business association calls one-day strike in
            protest against Chávez's controversial economic
            reforms, especially a new land law.

2002   Chávez appoints (February) new board of directors
            for Petróleos de Venezuela (PDVSA) in a move to gain
            greater control of the agency. This move is opposed by
            the PDVSA executives, and in April, trade unions and
            Fedecámaras declare a general strike in support of
            PDVSA dissidents. Approximately 500,000 people
            rally (April 11) in support of the general strike and the
            PDVSA protest. National Guardsmen and pro-Chávez
            gunmen clash with protesters, with more than 10 peo-
            ple killed and 100 injured. In a move to minimize pub-
            lic knowledge of events, Chávez shuts down national
            media coverage of the violence. The military high
            command rebels and demands that Chávez resign.
            Armed forces leaders announce (April 12) that Chávez
            had resigned and been taken into military custody.
            Military leaders name Pedro Carmona, one of the
            strike organizers, as head of transitional government.

Two days later, Chávez returns to office, after the collapse of the interim government. An opposition strike (December) cripples the oil industry, while organizers continue to demand that Chávez resign. The lengthy strike eventually leads to fuel shortages.

2003   Nine-week general strike ends (February), with most businesses reopening. Chávez administration and opposition leaders agree (May) to a deal—brokered by the Organization of American States—which sets a framework for a referendum on Chávez's rule.

2004   Several people killed and many injured in clashes between opponents and supporters of President Chávez after National Electoral Council announces (March) that there are 1.1 million signatures whose validity is in dispute. In June, election officials issue statement that the opponents of President Chávez have gathered enough signatures to force a referendum. President Chávez wins August referendum on whether he should serve the remaining two and a half years of his term.

2005   President Chávez continues to take a stance of antagonism toward the United States, especially in his dealings with Cuba, North Korea, and China. Global oil prices continue to rise and the Bolívar continues to be devalued, allowing the Chávez government to acquire more and more of its national currency per barrel of oil. The continued devaluation of the Bolívar fosters national inflation.

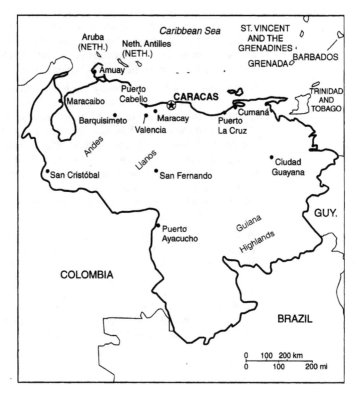

Map by Bookcomp, Inc.

1

A Petroleum Republic

The tropical *República Bolivariana de Venezuela* (Bolivarian Republic of Venezuela), situated in the northern portion of South America, is a country rich in history, natural resources, and culture. Emerging from the consolidation of six separate colonial provinces that existed in northern South America, Venezuela currently consists of 23 states, 1 federal district, and 11 federal dependencies, which collectively include 72 islands located in the Caribbean Sea. This mythical land of *El Dorado* is the birthplace of such noted figures as Simón Bolívar, Andrés Bello, Arturo Michelena, and Rómulo Gallegos. In addition, this modern republic is home to the second oldest lake, the tallest waterfall, and one of the largest petroleum reserves in the world. Rich in ecological and anthropological diversity, Venezuela produces what many consider to be the finest *cacao* in the world.

GEOGRAPHY

Long before the term "geopolitical" existed, the geography of Venezuela determined its politics. Today, the tropical nation dominates the northern coast of South America. Its 912,050 square kilometers (352,100 square miles) of total area lie between 0° 8′ and 12° 11′ north latitude and 60° and

73° west longitude. Venezuela is the sixth largest country in South America and has an estimated population of slightly more than 25 million people. Eighty-nine percent of the country's population lives in urban areas, even though Venezuela remains one of the world's least densely populated countries. Venezuela is made up of 882,050 square kilometers (340,560 square miles) of land and 30,000 square kilometers (11,600 square miles) of water. The tropical paradise has a coastline of 2,800 kilometers (1,740 miles), along the Caribbean Sea to the north and the Atlantic Ocean to the east.

The geography of Venezuela can be easily divided into three zones: (1) the Mountains and Caribbean Coastal region; (2) the *Llanos* and Orinoco River Delta region; and (3) the Guayana region.

Mountains and Caribbean Coast

The Mountains and Caribbean Coast region includes the Maracaibo Lowlands, an oval depression in the northwestern area of the country. The lowlands are surrounded by mountains on three sides and are open only on the north to the Gulf of Venezuela and the Caribbean Sea. At the center of this flat depression lies Lake Maracaibo, fed by rivers from the surrounding mountains. Geologists believe that Lake Maracaibo is the second oldest lake in the world, formed about 36 million years ago. It is the largest lake in Latin America (13,210 square kilometers; 5,100 square miles), extending 160 kilometers (100 miles) north-to-south and 110 kilometers (68 miles) east-to-west. The lake contains shallow water with swampy shores, never reaching a depth of more than 34 meters. Once filled with freshwater, the lake's ecology has been damaged by a channel that was cut for shipping in 1950. The easing of the ship passage brought salt water into the northern portion of the lake, where the water has become brackish and is now unsuitable for drinking or irrigation. Until the twentieth century, the humidity of the lowlands made it rather unhealthy and unproductive, except on the mountainsides, where coffee could be grown. After World War I, this region became the most productive oil field in Venezuela. Despite its industry, this region remains sparsely populated.

To the east of Lake Maracaibo and south of the Paraguaná Peninsula lies an elevated area of valleys and mountains called the Segovia Highlands. This area is a transitional zone between the Caribbean coast and the mountains of the Andean *Cordillera* (mountain range) to the south. Rising in elevation from 500 to 1,700 feet near the city of Barquisimeto, the sparsely populated highland contains the gentle rolling and semi-arid valleys of the states of Falcon, Lara, and Yaracuy. Along the coast, a climatic anomaly alleviates the tropical warm air brought toward the coast, forcing it to subside when it hits the lower sea temperatures along the shore. This situation creates a drier coastal area and creates savannas in the highlands and the naturally formed *Médanos* (sand dunes) of Coro, in the state of Falcón. Goat herding is common in the scrubland, and sugarcane and coffee are grown along the flanks of the mountains.

Emerging from the western spine of South America, the Andes mountain chain divides in Colombia with one system swinging abruptly eastward from Colombia, and continuing eastward for another 720 kilometers (447 miles) along the Venezuelan coast to the Araya and Paria Peninsulas. From here, the mountains disappear into the Caribbean Sea.

The Andean mountain region of Venezuela can be divided into four smaller ranges. The first range is the steep mountain chain of the *Sierra de Perijá*, which forms the border between Colombia and the western shores of Lake Maracaibo. This range also creates a distant backdrop for the city of Maracaibo. Historically, the growers from western Colombia followed the rivers down the mountains and into the lake to export their coffee via the Caribbean. Today cocaine traffickers follow the same route.

South of the lake, another Andean range, known as the *Cordillera de Mérida* or *los Andes Merideños* or *Sierra Nevada de Mérida*, pushes northward along the eastern side of Lake Maracaibo toward the city of Barquisimeto. The steep peaks of the *Cordillera de Mérida* tower above the surrounding mountains, rising to 5,007 meters (16,430 feet) above sea level at the majestic Pico Bolívar. This cool highland basin holds many of Venezuela's earliest cities and includes the modern states of Trujillo, Mérida, and Táchira, as well as portions of the states of Barinas, Lara, and Portuguesa. The fertile region surrounding Táchira, Mérida, and Trujillo supported colonial sugarcane and indigo, and the production of easily transported coffee rejuvenated the region in the nineteenth century. Today, the area also produces staple crops such as corn, wheat, barley, and potatoes. In addition to agriculture, the mountains contain mineral wealth in the form of coal.

The western *Cordillera de Mérida* ends briefly in the Boconó Valley before it begins again in a third mountain range called the *Cordillera de la Costa* (coastal range). This range forms elevated basins or *altiplano* regions whose altitude alleviates the climate of the tropical latitudes. The *Cordillera de la Costa* is commonly split into two main portions: a central section, the *Tramo Central*, and an eastern section, the *Tramo Oriental*. The central range encompasses the states of Yaracuy, Carabobo, Aragua, Vargas, Miranda, the Federal District, and sections of Cojedes, and Guárico; the eastern range includes the state of Sucre, the northeastern portion of Anzoátegui, and the northern areas of Monagas.

This coastal, or littoral, chain along the northern coastline hosts the majority of Venezuela's cities and population in the Valencia and Central Basins. The highlands of the Valencia Basin rise abruptly from the coast to the Segovia highlands. Above 100 feet, the areas receive regular rainfall allowing for the production of sugar, coffee, cotton, corn, rice, vegetables, and cattle. The main city is Valencia, which lies east of the shallow waters of Lake Valencia. Agricultural production has deforested the area, silted in the lake's original outlet, and polluted its waters. Already low, the waters have receded, creating swamps and marshes along the shores.

Another basin located within the littoral range is the valley of Caracas. Situated at 960 meters (3,150 feet) above sea level, Caracas is separated from the Caribbean by the *Serranía del Litoral*, but a small pass allows access to the coastal port of La Guaira, where the Andean slopes finally reach the sea. As Venezuela's capital, the city hosts over four and a half million inhabitants, many of whom are employed by the government.

Although Venezuela's mountains do not contain any active or recently extinct volcanoes, violent earthquakes, or *terremotos*, have troubled the region for centuries. For example, in 1530 a quake destroyed the fortress at Cumaná; in 1812, another heavily damaged Caracas, La Guaira, Barquisimeto, and Mérida; and in 1894 most of Mérida was destroyed by seismic activity.

Llanos and Orinoco River Delta

South of the Andean mountain region, the broad elevated *llanos* (plains) stretch eastward into the Orinoco River delta along the modern states of Barinas, Apure, Cojedes, Guárico, Anzoátegui, and Monagas. These prairies are primarily savannah grasslands crisscrossed by a web of rivers, which divide the region into islands of sparse population. In 1548 the colonists released cattle and horses into the *llanos,* and by the 1600s these wild herds reportedly numbered over 140,000. Because modern-day Venezuela was comprised of several different provinces until 1777, actual numbers for that time are impossible to know. However, some estimates place the number of cattle as high as four and a half million, thanks to the management of the semi-nomadic *llaneros* (plains cowboys).

Further east the *llanos* fall slowly into the deltaic plains of the Orinoco River. Orinoco is a Warao (also known as Guarauno, Guarao, and Warrau) Indian word meaning "a place to paddle." The river is created by streams from the western slopes of the *Sierra Parima,* which form part of the boundary between Venezuela and Brazil. The river's source is in Venezuela at the southern end of the *Sierra Parima,* near Mount Delgado Chalbaud in

the Guayana Highlands. The river flows through Venezuela for about
2,740 kilometers (1,700 miles) and enters the Atlantic Ocean near the island
of Trinidad. With its tributaries, it is the northernmost of South America's
three major river systems (Amazon, La Plata, and Orinoco).
The river is especially important for the inhabitants of Amazonas,
Venezuela's largest state. From Amazonas, the river flows westward
one-third of its length, at which point it splits in two branches. One of its
branches, the *Brazo Casiquiare*, eventually flows into the Amazon River,
via the Negro River. The Orinoco is the third largest river system in South
America and contains some 200 tributary rivers, including the Apure and
Caroní. Heavy spring and summer rains swell the river, flood the *llanos*,
and carry dirt and alluvium to the delta. The delta is home to approximately one thousand villages of the Warao Indians, who remain along the
river, living in homes built on pilings and fishing in the manner of their
ancestors.
While the Orinoco delta contains many distributory channels, most
have to be dredged to allow the passage of oceangoing vessels. Following
World War II, the petrochemical industry developed around the oil deposits at El Tigre (Anzoátegui). The swift rapids of the Caroní descending
from the Guayana Highlands have created a rich hydro-electric region for
Venezuela's cities and industries.
The *llanos* and Orinoco River Delta region is comprised of the states of
Apure, Barinas, Portuguesa, Cojedes, Guárico, Anzoátegui, Monagas, and
the greater portion of Delta Amacuro.

Guayana

South of the Orinoco River region is the third major geographical zone,
Guayana. This zone includes the Guayana (Guiana) Highlands in the
eastern part of the region. Although the Guayana region is comprised of
only three states (Delta Amacuro, Bolívar, and Amazonas), the zone contains approximately 45 percent of Venezuela's total land area. The highlands descend into the jungles of the *Brazo Casiquiare* and the Amazonian
arm of the *Río Orinoco* in the state of Amazonas. As mentioned previously,
the Orinoco is especially important for the inhabitants of Amazonas.
The state is the homeland of several Amerindian tribes, including the
Yanomami (also called Yanamamo, Yanomam, and Sanuma), Piaroa (also
called Kuakua, Guagua, and Quaqua), Pemón (or Pemong), and Guajibo
(also called Guahibo and Wahibo).
The region of the Guayana Highlands is dominated by ancient blocks of
mineralized, metamorphic rock plateaus. Their worn surfaces are dissected

by the tributaries of the Orinoco, especially the Caura, Paragua, and Caroní rivers. Erosion has left numerous strange rock formations called *tepuis*, especially near the *Gran Sabana* (Great Savannah). One of these bluffs is home to *Salto Angel*, Angel Falls, the highest waterfall in the world at 979 meters (3,212 feet). The highlands are rich in iron ore, manganese, bauxite, and gold, but their soils are infertile and erode easily. Most of the highlands are isolated except for a few roads, and they remain Venezuela's least populated region.

In summary, Venezuela's geography contains three regional islands of population and production. Its vast unpopulated territories still host native populations, and its mountains are the favored spots of eco-tourists. In the east, the Paria Peninsula brings tourists into Venezuela during the carnival season, a trait shared with neighboring Trinidad. In the west, the petroleum reserves of Lake Maracaibo provide the nation with a crucial source of revenue. The modern nation of Venezuela hosts a rich array of resources and a growing economy.

THE PEOPLE

Venezuela's 25,017,387 inhabitants (July 2004 estimate) are a very diverse mix of ethnic groups, including Spanish, Italian, Portuguese, Arab, German, African, and numerous indigenous tribes.[1] Religious affiliation breaks down as 96 percent Roman Catholic, 2 percent Protestant, and 2 percent other. Approximately 93 percent of the population over 15 years of age can read and write, with males and females in almost equal percentages. The country has a population growth rate of 1.44 percent, a birth rate of 19.34 births per 1,000 people, a median age of 25.2 years, and a death rate of 4.9 per 1,000 people. The population's age breaks down as 30.5 percent between the ages of 0 and 14; 64.5 percent between the ages of 15 and 64; and 5 percent older than 64 years of age. The male/female sex ratio is 1.02. The life expectancy among the Venezuelan population is 74.06 years, with males having a noticeably lower average (71.02 years) than females (77.32 years). The infant mortality rate is 22.9 deaths per 1,000 live births and is higher among males than females.

Venezuela is home to a multiethnic society that speaks 40 different languages. In addition to the predominant Spanish language, the inhabitants speak the native tongues of 28 different ethnic groups of indigenous people, as well as Catalan-Valencian-Balear, Portuguese, Corsican, English, Inga, Latvian, Arabic, and Chinese. The 1999 Constitution (Title I, Art. 9) stipulates that indigenous languages can be used by natives for official business throughout the nation.

CULTURE

Architecture in the Venezuelan provinces never reached the grandiose heights of other Spanish colonies in the New World, such as Mexico, Perú, and Ecuador. Religious and civil buildings followed the simplest forms of Spanish architectural models. It wasn't until the era of the great *caudillos*, especially Antonio Guzmán Blanco (1829–1899), in the latter part of the nineteenth century, that Venezuelan architecture began to emulate the scale and opulence of its European counterparts. This move became a way of legitimizing and adding European prestige and embellishment to government regimes. However, it wasn't until after the oil bonanza of the twentieth century that Venezuela's architectural flair found its expression in the bold contemporary design projects aimed at modernizing the urban landscape of the city of Caracas, especially in the 1950s. Caracas is today one of the most architecturally modern cities in the world.

Venezuela has a long literary tradition that dates back to the sixteenth century, when Spaniards began to write their impressions and accounts of life in the young colony. José de Oviedo y Baños (1671–1738) is considered Venezuela's first writer, having gone to colonial Venezuela at age 14. Throughout the remainder of the sixteenth and most of the seventeenth centuries, literary output was still strongly influenced by Spanish canons and primarily limited to either descriptive narratives pertaining to exploration and the establishment of administrative foundations or the creation of religious works. In fact, prior to 1811, Venezuela had not produced a mature literary tradition, in comparison with more culturally developed Spanish colonies such as Mexico and Perú. In part, this can be attributed to the fact that Venezuela did not have a printing press until 1808, when printers Matthew Gallagher and James Lamb brought a printing press to colonial Venezuela from the nearby British colony of Trinidad. In October of the same year, the colony's first periodical publication, the *Gaceta de Caracas*, made its debut.

Chronicle narrative and various styles of poetry continued to be the predominant literary forms in the late seventeenth and most of the eighteenth centuries. The nineteenth century's independence movement gave rise to political literature, including seminal works such as the autobiography of Francisco de Miranda (1750–1816). The poetry of Andrés Bello (1781–1865) helped to set a tone of erudition and further define the intellectual identity of the emerging nation. Among his works were *"Alocución a la poesía"* ("Allocution to Poetry") and *"Silva a la agricultura de la zona tórrid"* ("Ode to Agriculture of the Torrid Zone"). The philosophical and political writings of Simón Bolívar (1783–1830) also significantly shaped the intellectual consciousness of a Hispanic American identity. The first important literary genre in Venezuela was *Criollismo*, the uniquely Venezuelan version of nineteenth-century romanticism, exemplified by such works as *Peonía* (Peony), written by Manuel Romerogarcía (1861–1917), the first truly Venezuelan novel. Other noted Venezuelan writers of the nineteenth century were Rafael María Baralt (1810–1860) and Juan Vicente González (1810–1866); their writing constituted the beginnings of a style of prose increasingly reflective of Venezuela's autochthonous experience.

Following the consolidation of the independence movement, Venezuelan literature began to find a more sophisticated and diversified voice. Most of nineteenth-century Venezuelan literary narrative was concerned primarily with the struggle for independence, the emergence of "yellow liberalism" as the predominant social ideology, and the eventual rise to power of Antonio Guzmán Blanco. Antonio Guzmán Blanco carried out important educational reforms based on the ideals of mandatory, free, and secular instruction, reinforcing the ideals of free thought. In the nineteenth century, José Gil Fortoul introduced a more scientific approach to historical writing and research. In so doing, he moved away from what had been until that point a more prevalent romantic notion of superficial, partial historical writing.

It wasn't until the emergence of such notables as José Rafael Pocaterra (1889–1955), Teresa de la Parra (pseudonym of Ana Teresa Parra Sanojo) (1889–1936), and Rómulo Gallegos at the turn of the twentieth century, however, that a truly "Venezuelan" literary style reached full maturity. The poetry of Andrés Eloy Blanco (1896–1955), especially his "*Canto a España*" ("Ode to Spain"), garnered for him the title of Venezuela's most popular poet. Additionally, the works of Arturo Uslar Pietri (1906–2001), such as *Las Lanzas Coloradas* (Red Spears), and of Rómulo Gallegos (1884–1969), among others, further refined the essence of twentieth-century Venezuelan prose through the exploration of regional themes. Among Gallegos's most celebrated literary works are *Doña Bárbara*, a metaphor representing the struggle between the indomitable fury of nature and the will of man and a work that cemented Gallegos's reputation as the supreme exponent of Venezuelan lifestyle and popular traditions, and *La Trepadora*, a study of the attainment of personal power.

In pre-Hispanic Venezuela, the visual arts were well developed. Archaeologists have documented prehistoric finds in the western region of the country that include *cuencos* (bowls) of one or more feet and a variety of decorative motifs, commonly accompanied by figurines seated on four-legged stools and winged ornamentation. The northwestern coastal region is rich in geometrical and polychrome ceramics from the area of La Pita and El Cañito, as well as flutes and anthropomorphic figures. Around the area of Barquisimeto, burial sites with votive jewelry objects and *cuencos* with annular (ring-shaped) and tripod bases have been found. In Quibor, *cuencos* similar to those found in Barquisimeto have been unearthed, but the Quibor bowls have more prominent feet and more colorful geometrical decorations. In Boconó, *cuencos* and *jarras* (pitchers) have been found with annular or tripod feet, both with and without engobe. Engobe refers to a technique whereby slip (a suspension of ceramic materials and water) and glaze colorants are applied and then scratched off to create a decorative shape. These bowls and pitchers often had decorative incisions or modeling accompanied by human figurines. Two other sites in the northwestern coastal region that yielded artistic artifacts are Coro and El Mamón, the latter having styles that show a Caribbean influence.

The area around Lake Valencia contains evidence of two distinct artistic styles and eras. The earlier phase, La Cabrera, is represented by large *jarros* and *vasijas* (pots), with two spouts, smooth surface, and natural color. The latter Valencia phase is represented by diverse ceramic forms, broad in shape, and especially feminine figurines with eyes in the shape of coffee beans, and clear sexual differentiation. Also found in the area of Valencia is the only known geoglyph (a figure or shape produced on the ground by the clearing of stones or the building of stone alignments). The figure, known as *La Rueda del Indio* (Indian's Wheel) features two legs, is armless, and has a large head with three concentric circles bearing antennae. In addition, several petroglyphs (prehistoric carvings or drawings on rocks) have been found along the Chirgua River, carved with figures and faces.

The northeastern coastal area is a much less explored region. The most important archaeological site in the region is at Guaraguao, where Siboney (an Arawak-speaking Indian culture from the Caribbean) influences have been found. In the Orinoco River region, finds at Los Barrancos document influences from the Guayana region. Ceramics found in this area are decorated with stylized and geometric incisions. The sites at El Ronquín contain two types of ceramic textures: smooth and polished and non-smooth. In the *llanos* region, remains have been exhumed in urns or in elevated knolls alongside or near roadways. Finally, in the Amazon region, near Puerto Ayacucho, is the *Piedra Pintada* (Painted Stone) Natural Monument. This site contains Venezuela's largest petroglyph, a 164-foot-long snake, believed to be approximately 3,000 to 5,000 years old.

Following the artistic styles of the pre-Columbian petroglyphs, cave paintings, and ceramics, Venezuela's visual arts became influenced by Spanish religious painting and sculpture. The work of colonial Venezuela's artists grew with continued demand from other colonial centers throughout Spanish America. Important examples of Venezuela's colonial painting are *Our Lady of Light* (1760) and *Our Lady of the Rosary* (1767) by Juan Pedro López and *The Immaculate Conception* (1798) by Antonio José Landaeta. Following the independence movement, historical themes that reinforced the patriotic ideals of nation-building overshadowed religion as the dominant artistic inspiration. The originator of the new patriotic genre was Juan Lovera (1776–1841), whose historical paintings chronicling Venezuela's independence struggle led to his being dubbed "*El pintor de Próceres*" ("the painter of illustrious heroes"). Patriotic themes were best exemplified by the works of two of Venezuela's foremost painters: Martín Tovar y Tovar (1827–1902) painted *Battle of Carabobo* (1887) for the ceiling of the Elliptical Hall of Antonio Guzmán Blanco's Federal Palace (today's capitol building) and created renditions of the *Battle of Boyacá* (1894) and the *Battle of Junín* (1894) also for the Elliptical Hall; Arturo Michelena's (1863–1898) works include an iconic depiction of *Miranda in La Carraca* (1896) and the *Last Supper* (1898). The twentieth century brought a succession of modernist trends, although it wasn't until the advent of Kinetic art in the 1960s and 1970s that Venezuela's artists found their own niche of international acclaim, with the works of such luminaries as Carlos Cruz Diez (b. 1922) and Jesús Soto (b. 1923).

With the arrival of the first pianos in 1756, the opera was introduced to colonial Venezuela, although operatic productions often met with the Church's stern censure. Formal musical training made its debut in Venezuela in 1783, the year father Pedro Palacios y Sojo (1739–1799) founded the first school of music in Chacao (present-day Caracas). This school became the colony's foremost center for musical instruction, contributing to the formal training of such colonial composers as José Angel Lamas (1775–1814), author of the "*Popule Meus*" ("O My People"); Cayetano Carreño (1774–1836), composer of "*Misa de Requiem*" ("Requiem Mass"); Pedro Nolasco Colón, composer of "*Pésame a la Virgen*" ("Condolences to the Virgin"); and, most significantly, Juan José Landaeta (1780–1812), believed to be the composer of "*Gloria al Bravo Pueblo*" ("Glory to the Brave"), which would become Venezuela's national anthem by decree of President Antonio Guzmán Blanco in 1881. At the turn of the twentieth century, the talent of pianist and composer Teresa Carreño (1856–1917) helped to define Venezuela's musical legacy. Among her most memorable works are "*Himno a Bolívar*" ("Hymn to Bolívar") and "*Saludo a Caracas*" ("Homage to Caracas"). She went on to become Venezuela's most celebrated composer, and her musical legacy stands as the finest and most mature example of Venezuelan musical composition.

Venezuelan popular music traditions have evolved as a blend of Spanish, African, and indigenous contributions, finding inspiration in everyday activities and used in a wide variety of musical forms such as *coplas, tonadas, galerones, guasas, corridos, contrapuntos,* and *polos*. African influences are most apparent in the music of the northeast region of Barlovento, the heart of Venezuela's slave trade and culture. By far the most prevalent form of popular music in Venezuela is the *gaita*, and it originated in the western state of Zulia. It consists of improvised arrangements of rhyming vocals, accompanied by the *cuatro* (a four-string guitar) and *maracas*. The *gaita* has become Venezuela's ubiquitous Christmas music. Venezuela's national dance is the *joropo*, which originated in the *llanos* region. The musical accompaniment to the *joropo*, similar to the *gaita*, consists of improvised vocals accompanied by *cuatros* and *maracas*, with the added use of harps. However, the *merengue* of the Dominican Republic and the *salsa* of Puerto Rican origin, are the most popular dances in Venezuela.

Venezuela's long theatrical tradition dates back to the late eighteenth century, and reached a peak in popularity during the Guzmán Blanco era in the latter part of the nineteenth century. June 28 is celebrated in Venezuela as National Theater Day, for on that day, in 1600, the first known license was issued to allow the staging of a *comedia* (full-length play) to celebrate the feast day of Saint James the Apostle. Prior to that time, colonial drama primarily took the form of religious *autos*, or mystery plays. In 1784, the captain-general of Venezuela inaugurated Venezuela's first performing arts coliseum in Caracas, which was to exert a dramatic influence on the rest of the country, leading to the creation of similar institutions in other important Venezuelan cities. Along with the growth in popularity of the operatic genre, the popularity of stage plays led to their being performed routinely during major holidays and festivities during the colonial era—much to the chagrin of Church officials who viewed such theatrical displays as obscene. Despite Church opposition, Venezuela's theatrical affinity grew and theaters proliferated throughout the country in the nineteenth century. In 1904 Venezuela's *Teatro Nacional* (National Theater) was founded.

Venezuela's folk and popular culture is extremely rich. Every region has its own well-known popular icon, which embodies its character and personality and reflects the region's unique cultural heritage. Among these icons are the *caraqueño*, the fast-paced cosmopolitan workaholic; the *andino*, the hardy, introverted mountain man; the *guayanés*, the tough frontiersman; the *llanero*, the rugged plains cowboy; and the *maracucho*, the energetic, extroverted go-getter from the oil-wealthy Maracaibo region. The popular Juan Bimba cartoon character emerged in 1936. Juan Bimba represented everything that was typical about Venezuela's peasants, including their humble attire of *alpargatas* (rope-soled sandals) and straw hat. His popularity was such that, at one point, he became the symbol of the emerging *Acción Democrática* political party as it attempted to appeal to the rural peasantry.

Religion has played a significant role in shaping Venezuelan culture. A predominantly (96%) Roman Catholic nation, Venezuela's cultural identity has always been tied to the religious ideal of a close-knit family and community. This strong sense of community, as safeguarded by the religious principles of marriage and family, has helped to establish in Venezuelan society a strong sense of *machismo* (belief in male superiority), in which the male head of the family and predominant breadwinner has traditionally been valued as the highest aspiration of society's strength.

Coupled with this intensely *machista* mindset, Venezuelan culture has a very rich and intensely superstitious folklore, entrenched in both Christian and non-Christian cult worship, known as *santería*. This superstitious undercurrent is particularly powerful among Venezuela's black minority. Certain religious as well as secular figures have also become the focus of widespread popular devotion (especially among the poor) due to their reputedly miraculous powers. While the popular cults of San Benito (St. Benedict the Black) and of the Venerable José Gregorio Hernández (a very devout Venezuelan physician, scientist, and philanthropist) are fairly well rooted in Venezuelan lore, there is also a very unique cult surrounding the figure of earth goddess María Lionza, a powerful figure in Venezuelan myth. Rumored to be the daughter of an Indian princess and a Spanish conquistador, María Lionza was later imbued with the Catholic mystique equivalent to that of the Virgin Mary among the devout. Among the most significant mainstream or traditionally Roman Catholic devotional figures for which Venezuelans hold special affection are the *Virgen del Valle* (Our Lady of the Valley), the oldest of the venerated manifestations of the Virgin Mary in Venezuelan devotion; the *Virgen de Coromoto* (Virgin of Coromoto), Patroness of Venezuela; *Nuestra Señora de la Chiquinquirá* (Our Lady of Chiquinquirá); and *La Divina Pastora* (The Divine Shepherdess). Of particular interest, from a popular culture standpoint, is the belief in the benevolent image of the child Jesus, or *Niño Jesús*, as the proverbial bearer of gifts to young children on Christmas Eve.

Venezuela's strongest sporting tradition is the practice of baseball, or *béisbol*, which is believed to have been introduced into Venezuela by a group of Venezuelan students returning from the United States. Initially viewed with humorous skepticism, the game soon caught the populace's fancy and to this day thrives as the nation's most impassioned pastime.

In recent years, a strong interest in the game of soccer, or *fútbol,* has emerged, but baseball's passion among Venezuelans is so deeply entrenched, it seems it will never be eclipsed. Several major league baseball players have come to the United States from Venezuela, including such notable players as Luis Aparicio (1934–) and David Concepción (1948–). The American League Rookie of the Year in 1956, Aparicio holds the all-time record for most games played at shortstop (2,581) and the American League records for assists (8,016), chances (12,564), and putouts (4,548). He was inducted into the National Baseball Hall of Fame in 1984.

SYMBOLS

The Venezuelan flag's design is the inspiration of the precursor of South American independence, General Francisco de Miranda (1750–1816). Miranda first hoisted his tricolor flag on March 12, 1806, and, thus, Venezuela's Flag Day is celebrated on March 12. Miranda's flag first reached Venezuela during his second revolutionary expedition, landing at La Vela de Coro on August 3, 1806, marking the first time the flag was hoisted on Venezuelan soil. Venezuela's flag is made up of three horizontal bands, yellow at the top, blue in the center, and red at the bottom, with an arc of seven white five-pointed stars centered within the blue band. The seven stars were added in 1836 and represent the seven provinces (Caracas, Cumaná, Barinas, Barcelona, Margarita, Mérida and Trujillo) that signed the Act of Independence of July 5, 1811. The yellow band signifies the gold and riches of the New World; the blue signifies the blue ocean that separates Venezuela from Spain; and the red signifies the blood shed by Venezuela's heroes in their struggle to gain the country's independence. The same flag design was adopted, with slight variations, by the Republics of Ecuador, Colombia, and Venezuela—the three nations that formerly comprised Gran Colombia. The current Venezuelan flag was officially adopted on February 19, 1954.

The Venezuelan coat of arms displays on its three fields, or cantons, the colors of the national flag. The upper left canton is red and shows a bundle of wheat, symbolizing the union of the republic's states and the wealth of the nation. The upper right canton is yellow and, as a triumphant emblem, bears five symbolic weapons (three spears and two swords) as well as two national flags, tightly held by laurels. The third and lower canton is blue with a green field, and it holds the figure of an untamed white horse, with its head turned back, as a defiant emblem of independence and liberty, and commonly held to symbolize Simón Bolívar's white charger. The coat of arms has as its crown two cornucopias intercrossed at the middle, both filled with abundant tropical fruits, signifying the riches of the land. The coat of arms bears on its left side an olive branch and on its right side a palm branch, both tied at the bottom of the coat of arms by a tricolor ribbon (yellow, blue, and red). The blue ribbon contains the following captions: on the left, "19 DE ABRIL DE 1810" and "INDEPENDENCIA"; on the right, "20 DE FEBRERO DE 1859" and "FEDERACION"; and in the center, "REPUBLICA DE VENEZUELA."

ECONOMY

The Venezuelan economy is dominated by the petroleum industry, which provides about half of the government's revenue. Although projections are that the country will show growth in its 2004 gross domestic product (GDP), the 2003 GDP of U.S.$117.9 billion was a 7.7 percent decrease from the year before. In fact, each year since 1998 has witnessed a decline in the nation's GDP. The effects of the economic decline have been felt most severely in the employment sector. In 1998, when the current administration of President Hugo Chávez Frías (1954–) assumed power, the unemployment rate in Venezuela was 11 percent. At the end of 2003, the unemployment rate had increased to 14.6 percent. Reports vary, but current estimates place the number of Venezuelans living in poverty at approximately 80 percent of the population.

Petroleum

Since 1918, the exploitation of Venezuela's petroleum reserves has provided the government with revenues to an extent unknown in other South American countries. Although the enormous national revenue has allowed various administrations to undertake massive public works programs, the revenue has also allowed government leaders to grant infinite incentives to the petroleum exploration enterprise and line the pockets of a small circle of political friends. Contrary to the notion that the petroleum industry would drive the creation and emergence of an urban middle class in Venezuela, the petroleum era has not brought with it a true improvement in most Venezuelans' standard of living. Instead, at various times, the oil boom brought about a decline in domestic agriculture, an increase in imports, and inflation. In addition, several administrations have used the petroleum revenue to keep the military removed from politics, by spending considerable amounts of money on defense.

Long before the arrival of Europeans in Venezuela, the native inhabitants knew that the land contained petroleum deposits. Natural seepages of crude petroleum had been occurring around Lake Maracaibo for centuries. In fact, the early Spanish explorers noted that the natives used the black crude to caulk and repair their canoes. In 1879, the *Compañía Petrolera del Táchira* (Táchira Petroleum Company) began production in the Venezuelan Andes. As noted by historian Stephen Rabe (1977), such operations were limited, isolated, and primitive. Rabe noted that the company produced only 40 gallons of petroleum a day, and this was achieved by manually digging pits and scooping the petroleum out with buckets. The reality was that Venezuela lacked the capital and technology to exploit its petroleum deposits.

Once the United States began to use petroleum on a larger scale (in the 1860s), some Venezuelans recognized the commercial possibilities of petroleum production and export. However, the first commercial oil well in Venezuela was not drilled until February 1914, and by 1917 (the first year that Venezuela exported petroleum) the industry was producing only about 125,000 barrels a year. By the end of the First World War, Venezuela still had not become a major supplier of petroleum. This would all change during the 1920s. By 1928, Venezuela was producing slightly more than 100 million barrels a year, more than any other country in the world. Today, Venezuela produces approximately 3 million barrels per day.

Although the Second World War greatly benefited the Venezuelan petroleum industry, it would be the 1960 creation of the Organization of Petroleum Exporting Countries that allowed Venezuela to take a new stance in the hemisphere. For the most part, prices for Venezuelan oil hovered around $10 or $11[2] per barrel during the 1950s, 1960s, and early 1970s, but the 1973 Arab-Israeli War changed everything. With the subsequent Arab oil embargo against supporters of Israel, prices of crude oil skyrocketed. For Venezuelan Tía Juana Light crude (also referred to as Venezuelan Light Crude), the price jumped from $11.44 to $36.84 from 1973 to 1974. This 200 percent increase in the price of Venezuelan Light Crude in only one year provided the first administration (1974–1979) of President Carlos Andrés Pérez (1922–) with a bonanza of wealth.

Prices continued to increase throughout the 1970s and early 1980s. The price spiked in 1983, when the price of Venezuelan Tía Juana Light was $64.47 per barrel. The belief of many policymakers in the Venezuelan government was that the prices would continue to rise, and the government borrowed and spent accordingly. This optimistic outlook, however, turned out to be unrealistic.

In 1984, prices began to drop at a significant rate. By 1989, the price for Tía Juana Light was down to $19.33 per barrel. Aside from an increase in petroleum prices during the first Iraq War (1991), prices have remained relatively low. In fact, by 1999, the price of a barrel of Venezuelan Light Crude was down to pre-1973 levels, at $11.08. In 2000, crude prices rose again, with Tía Juana Light reaching $49.09 on July 15, 2005. In addition to price increases, export production, too, has increased dramatically. With the exception of a slump during the 1980s, the number of barrels of Tía Juana Light that the country exports has risen from 1.4 million per day in 1979 to 2 million per day (at $32.11 per barrel) in 2000. Although Venezuela experienced a major worker strike in the petroleum sector in 2003, the country is getting back on track in terms of petroleum exports. Venezuela continues to be a top provider of crude oil for the United States, accounting for 12.86 percent of U.S. petroleum imports in 2004. Currently, the petroleum industry accounts for more than 75 percent of the total value of Venezuela's exports. With approximately 78 billion barrels in proven oil reserves, it is clear that Venezuela has, and will continue to have for some time to come, a petroleum economy.

POLITICS

Venezuela is a federal republic with a multiparty system. Its current government is headed by the populist President Hugo Chávez Frías, who was elected in December 1998 and assumed power in early 1999. Enamored with the ideas of Simón Bolívar, the former paratrooper crafted the creation of the Bolivarian Republic of Venezuela. His policy efforts have been designed to win the support of the nation's poor, and in the process he has created a situation of increased hostility among many in the middle and upper classes.

The current Constitution, promulgated in 1999, was the brainchild of former insurgent Chávez, and it is modeled on his political and social ideas. The law mandates that the president be elected by a plurality vote with direct and universal suffrage. The term of office for the president is six years, with the possibility of one re-election in consecutive terms. The president appoints the vice president and a cabinet. The legislative branch, in which President Chávez' supporters have a majority, consists of a unicameral body, the National Assembly, with 165 seats. The Assembly consists entirely of the Chamber of Deputies, and its members serve five-year terms. Deputies may be re-elected for a maximum of three terms. Legislation can be initiated by the executive branch, the legislative branch, the judicial branch, the citizen branch, or by a public petition signed by at least 0.1 percent of the registered voters. Although the president can request that the National Assembly reconsider laws he finds objectionable, the National Assembly can override these objections with a simple majority vote. The judicial branch is headed by the Supreme Tribunal of Justice. This nation's highest court has six chambers, determined by areas of specialization. For example, the *Sala Electoral* (Electoral Chamber) hears cases involving elections and the electoral process. Supreme Court justices are appointed by the National Assembly and serve 12-year terms. The judicial branch also consists of lower courts, which include district and municipal courts.

As noted, the Venezuelan political and judicial systems include a citizen branch, which consists of a prosecutor general, an ombudsman, and a comptroller general. This branch has the authority to challenge actions that it believes are illegal or violate the Constitution. The members of the citizen branch are chosen by the National Assembly for seven-year terms.

NOTES

1. The demographic data in this chapter are from the 2004 version of *The World Factbook*, published by the United States Central Intelligence Agency.

2. All oil prices are expressed in 2005 U.S. dollars.

2

Venezuela to 1600

Most historians date the first appearance of the country's Amerindian groups somewhere between 20,000 and 15,000 years ago, when it is believed that the Beringial migratory groups reached South America. The indigenous population of Venezuela developed in three stages or eras: Paleo-Indian, Meso-Indian, and Neo-Indian. The Europeans arrived at the end of the Neo-Indian era. Christopher Columbus was the first European to explore the mainland of South America and the territory of present-day Venezuela. At the time of the Spanish arrival in Venezuela, the native population was estimated to have been between 350,000 and 500,000 persons.

PRE-HISPANIC VENEZUELA

Pre-Columbian history in Venezuela is largely based on archeological reconstruction and anthropological work among the existing indigenous tribes. As in the present day, the majority of the population lived in the northern part of the country, especially in the Andes, along the Caribbean coast, and in the Orinoco watershed.

Paleo-Indians

Paleo-Indian (20000–5000 B.C.E.) groups were hunter-gatherers. Archeological evidence places these groups primarily in the northwestern part of the country. They lived in small nomadic bands and developed a lithic (stone) culture of weapons and tools with which they hunted the large mammals of the last Ice Age. Skeletons from this period have been found with those of the mastodon and the megaterio, a clawed, furbearing herbivore the size of a horse. Paleo-Indians in Venezuela developed no agriculture or pottery, leaving little evidence of their lives except projectile points and tools. Around 5000 B.C.E. the world of the Paleo-Indians changed. They had hunted most of the large mammals into extinction and began moving south and east, looking for food. The end of the Ice Age brought warmer temperatures, warmer seas, and rising sea levels, which changed the coastal structure and submerged some previously inhabited areas.

Meso-Indians

These changes created the next age of the Pre-Columbian era, known as the Meso-Indian phase (5000 B.C.E.–1000 C.E.). The warm coast developed a rich ecology of flora and fauna that drew many groups eastward to exploit the marine environment. Especially precious was the shell of the large snail *Strombus jigs*, which was used for tools, weapons, and adornments. This era marks a dramatic shift away from lithic culture to one based primarily on the use of shell and bone. Stone was not completely deserted, but many of the stone tools and artifacts are highly polished to resemble shell and many are decorative. Exploration and settlement of the coast drew people toward the open seas. Many groups built boats and became excellent navigators. As they fished in open seas they discovered the many islands of the Lesser Antilles, which they gradually settled. Others found the islands a safe haven from aggressive neighbors. The Meso-Indians also exploited newly discovered lands by harvesting wild plants. The rich variety of vegetation increased food gathering, and many plants were utilized for medicinal purposes. Gathering led to horticultural activities, such as weeding out undesirable plants. The knowledge of plant life, in turn, led Venezuela's natives to early forms of agriculture. Agriculture developed mostly in the Andean highlands and along the shores of Venezuela's lakes and river systems.

Neo-Indians

The transition to agriculture marked the beginning of the Neo-Indian period (1000–1500 C.E.), during which the native population cultivated edible species based on environmental and cultural needs. The earliest form of agriculture is evident in finds along the Orinoco River, where the materials used in the production of bitter yucca or cassava were located. The appearance of the *mano y metate* (an indigenous stone tool used to grind corn) used in maize culture appeared in later strata in the Andes. These two types of evidence of agriculture shed light on two different and parallel cultures in Venezuela's history. The differences between eastern and western cultures also can be seen in the ceramics and funerary customs of this period. Cassava cultures created a simpler ceramic style of vessels (open bowls) with black painted lines and red handles, which they buried with their dead for use in the afterlife. Maize cultures developed a distinctly different ceramic style marked by vases with complex incisions and polychrome colors, often with numerous legs. Burials also tended to be more complex.

Venezuela's native population gradually settled into semi-sedentary and sedentary tribes, although none reached the grandeur of the Incas or Aztecs. Most people gathered into familial tribal groups based primarily on language. Anthropologists identify three main languages as Arawak, Carib, and Chibcha, with smaller miscellaneous language groups such as that of the Yanomami near the Amazon. It is more useful, however, to describe these pre-Hispanic peoples in terms of their cultures.

Indigenous Cultures in 1500

At the time of Spanish conquest, there were nine clearly different cultural areas in Venezuela. Near Lake Maracaibo were hunter-gatherers and fishermen whose most important tribe was the Guajiro. This Arawakan language group has retained the semi-nomadic culture of its ancestors. Their survival is primarily based on the successful integration of their culture with that of the Spanish, and today many continue their traditional pastoral ways, raising cattle, goats, and pigs. Southwest of the lake, the Western Caribs formed a second group, which included the Onoto, Motilón, and Pemón tribes. These tribes were extremely bellicose and repeatedly resisted incursions by the Spanish. They engaged in agriculture and used *kirora* (dams of stone and palm leaves) to increase the size of their catch of fish. Today only the Motilón remain in the Andes. The Onoto disappeared, and the Pemón moved to more remote regions of the interior with the invasion of the Spaniards.

A third group of peoples inhabited the Southern Andean Region of the *Cordillera de Mérida* and included such tribes as the Timoto-Cuicas (once separate tribes), by far the most advanced of the native inhabitants of modern-day Venezuela. Their highly developed agriculture used terracing to produce maize and *canuco* agriculture (a local version of the slash-and-burn technique) for tuberous root crops. They varied their diet by domesticating birds and constructed fishing dams like the *kirora* of the Motilón tribe. They also planted *chimó*, a tobacco used in smokeless form, which was often used ceremonially in liquid or powdered form. The Timotocuicas also spun vegetal fibers, which were used to produce woven textiles and mats for housing.

The Western Arawak groups stretch from the Paraguaná Peninsula through the Segovia Highlands and down into the western *llanos* region south of the *Cordillera de Mérida*. Among the various tribes were the Caquetíos and Cuibas. Of all of these western Arawak tribes, the Caquetíos were the most numerous and culturally dominant. Located in villages near Coro, they lived in cabins of wooden stakes tied with *lianas* (vines) and covered with palm branches or straw. Some homes had walls; others had no walls to allow for circulation. A few of these homes can still be observed in rural Venezuela.

The Caquetíos began as hunter-gatherers exploiting the coastal environment. They raised moderate amounts of maize, which they ate and also fermented into an alcoholic drink called *chicha*. In addition, they used mud dams to trap more fish to enhance their diet. The Caquetíos used shell and bone for tools, weapons, and adornment. They developed ceramics for both domestic (eating and drinking) and burial needs. Coro ceramics have a distinctive rich brown color with red and black designs on a white background.

Perhaps the most striking accomplishment of the Caquetíos is their rich legacy of petroglyphs and cave paintings. The stones bear images of figures and decorative drawings, painted in black, white, and ocher. Some stones mark the property of various families, while others marked cultivated fields. Even today, some stones remain undeciphered. The Caquetíos, at one time, were the largest of the Arawak groups in the region, but they migrated from the area for various reasons. Some were attacked by the Jirajara living to the south in the mountains of the modern state of Lara, while others became part of the general Arawakan migration into the Antilles. The pace of this migration was quickened by attacks from the coastal Caribs and from the Spanish.

In the Andes south of the Western Arawaks, the tribes of Ayamanes, Ajaguas, and Jirajaras were a marked contrast to their more peaceful neighbors. During the pre-Hispanic period, the Jirajaras and Ayamanes formed a unified tribe and conquered a portion of the Caquetíos to the north. These more southern Arawak tribes used intensive agriculture in irrigated fields to grow maize, sweet potatoes, and manioc. Their thatched houses were built in groups of two to four houses, and their weaving was less advanced than that of the Timotocuicas because they wore little clothing other than genital covering.

In general, the sociopolitical structure of the Arawak tribes was a chiefdom that sometimes included subchiefs. Their social hierarchy included a nobility who practiced polygamy and who were the chief artisans. A second social class was comprised of the farmers, fishers, and laborers. The Arawak tribes generally worshipped nature gods, including the Sun and the Moon. Each tribe had a special, representative god called *Zemis*, and every family worshipped individual household idols.

At the end of the Pre-Columbian period, the Carib immigrants dominated the northern Caribbean coast. Their tribes included the Caracas, Mariches, Teques, Palenques, and Tamanacos. The Caribs moved northward from the Amazon, inhabiting the Orinoco River valley and continuing into the mountains of the *Cordillera Central* and finally settling along the coast. As they moved, they developed individual agricultures for each area, progressing from swidden (slash-and-burn) agriculture in the rainforests, to mixed cropping along the riverbanks and beaches, to drained fields in river bottoms and floodplains, and to house gardens on the *mesas* of the savannah. As with other early tribes, the Caribs supplemented their agriculture with fishing and hunting.

Carib villages varied depending on their location. Some villages had only 30 houses; in areas where game was plentiful and arable land was available, villages might be as large as 500–600 persons. Houses were built of local materials and were of two types: the *sura* and the *tabouii*. The *sura* was a family house, and the *tabouii* was male housing and was often the focal point of the village architecture. Carib men married outside the family and often kidnapped wives from other groups. Like the Arawaks, they also practiced polygamy.

The Caribs practiced astronomy; as agriculturalists, they developed a planting calendar and related variations in climate and natural phenomena to the changing of the seasons. Like the Arawaks, their two main deities were associated with the Sun and the Moon. Venus also played a major role in astronomy and agriculture because it could be seen with the naked eye and ascended and descended each night.

Carib tribes had dual leadership under a formal chief and a war chief. War was a natural part of state-building, and Caribs often gathered in large groups to create excuses for conquest. Reasons for attacking another tribe included some slight in the past, not being received in proper fashion, or merely to obtain women for wives or collect slaves. To enhance their "reasoning," they often consumed *ouicou*, a cassava beer with a high alcohol content. Warfare included the maiming of opponents, and sometimes portions of the enemy were eaten. The word cannibal (Spanish *caríbal* or *caníbal*) comes to us from Christopher Columbus's description of the Carib Indians and their strange eating habits.

Trade often followed conquest, and the extensive areas of Carib settlement became a significant trading system. The Caribs moved goods from the Guayana Highlands, through the Orinoco River basins, and into the mountains. From here goods such as jade, gold, and trinkets were traded to coastal areas and into the Caribbean. Some Carib trade expeditions covered hundreds of miles. As the Caribs migrated, they encountered numerous tribes in the central *llanos* and Orinoco River valley. Most of these tribes were nomadic or semi-nomadic hunter-gatherers and fishers and included tribes such as the Yaruros and Otomoacos. The latter, near the Apure River, fiercely resisted Carib incursions. The Carib tribes in the Central Cordillera dominated the region until the Spanish defeated them in the 1560s, enslaving the survivors and dividing their lands among the troops.

Traveling down the Orinoco River, the river basin gives way to a rich deltaic region inhabited by a number of pre-Hispanic tribes. Here lived the Waraos (Guaraúnos), Píritus, and Cumanagotos. The Warao dominated the area along the Orinoco and built huts on stilts over the water. The huts had thatched roofs with no walls, and the inhabitants slept in hammocks around a central fire pit. The Warao spent much of their time in boats along the waterways, and the children learned at an early age to paddle a boat, often before they could walk. A peaceful people, the Warao remained in their marshy homes throughout the conquest and colonial period. They survive today much the same way their pre-Columbian ancestors did along the rivers, catching fish and weaving baskets.

To the south of the Orinoco stretches the vast length of the Guayana Highlands and the northerly reaches of the Amazon basin. Most of the tribes native to this region remain isolated hunter-gatherers to this day. Carib groups like the Pemóns and Guahibos (Hiwi) dotted the highlands, and the Yanomami of the Amazon settled the southern sections. The Yanomami lived in large communities of up to 400 persons. Their homes or *yanos* are circular and, similar to those in the Orinoco delta, are built with thatched roofs and open walls. Largely hunter-gatherers, the Yanomami lived in virtual isolation until their rediscovery in the 1900s.

During the conquest and into the colonial period, Venezuela's native population suffered increasing depredations from war and slavery. The Spanish differentiated peaceful tribes from nonpeaceful tribes according to whether they were Carib. Non-Carib tribes were perceived as peaceful and as suitable trade partners. Carib tribes were seen as enemies and, therefore, available for slaving. It is ironic that when the pearl beds on the Orinoco were depleted, the once non-Carib Indians quickly found their status changed to Carib and their families sold into slave labor. The Spaniards were followed by the French and the Dutch, who first traded with and then attacked the Indians. As the colony progressed, many tribes simply left the area to avoid death by disease or abuse. Many of their relatives still live in isolation today. For example, the Orinoco River delta is still home to the Waraos, among others; the Amazon Rain Forest is still home to the Guahibos, Piapocos, and Yanomami, among several other tribes. As of April 2005, Venezuela is home to 28 ethnic indigenous groups, speaking 37 languages.

EUROPEAN ARRIVAL

Upon his return to Spain from his second voyage (1496), Christopher Columbus (1451–1506) found little enthusiasm for his accomplishments. A seemingly ungrateful Spanish Crown revoked his monopoly and began to license other expeditions to the New World. Undaunted, Columbus managed to raise enough men and ships for a third voyage in 1498. When the fleet reached the Canary Islands, it divided in two, each with a different goal. The main fleet sailed toward Española (Hispaniola), while the secondary fleet under Columbus and his son, Fernando, turned south. Contemporary beliefs held that the Western Hemisphere contained another large land mass.

The voyage was long and difficult. Their southerly route led the fleet into the doldrums (region of the ocean near the equator that is characterized by calm or light winds), where it drifted for days in the equatorial heat. According to Columbus's diary, the food rotted and many of the water barrels burst, leaving the men and their captain desperate. On July 31, 1498, the ship finally sighted the hills of the island that would come to be known as Trinidad. After landing to collect water, he rounded the coast and continued westward. On August 5, 1498, Columbus and his three ships discovered the Gulf of Paria. On Sunday, August 7, he chose to stop for the day, anchoring just offshore. He sent several rowboats to search for food and supplies. Thus, Columbus became the first European to explore the mainland of South America and the territory of present-day Venezuela.

After resting overnight, the crew continued along the coast toward the Araya peninsula, where their boat encountered the massive outflow of fresh water from the Orinoco River. The intensity of the current so impressed Columbus that he believed he had encountered one of the four rivers flowing out of the fabled Terrestrial Paradise. Here Columbus and his men bartered with the natives for their pearl bracelets in exchange for needles, buttons, scissors, and pieces of broken pottery. Upon being asked the origin of their pearls, the natives pointed north and west. Columbus subsequently sailed toward the Islands of Cubagua and Margarita. It would be on the Island of Cubagua that Nueva Cádiz, the first European settlement in South America, was founded. The island of Margarita (named after the Austrian princess Margarita [1480–1530], who was the recent widow of the Prince Don Juan [1478–1497], only son of King Fernando V and Queen Isabel I of Castile and León) possessed one of the richest pearl beds of the Americas. As Columbus explored, he also captured 12 natives, whom he brought back to Santo Domingo as slaves, to prove the possibility of an *in situ* labor source.

Columbus's third voyage ended in misery. His neglect of Española led to revolt, and he stayed on the island to try to mediate the problems. He sent two ships to Spain to tell of his discoveries; the sailors said nothing of pearls but quickly sold them, a fact that soon reached the ears of the Spanish monarchs. This failure to report treasure compounded other rumors about Columbus's mismanagement of the colony and his reported cruelty to the natives and his sailors; in 1500, Columbus returned to Spain in chains.

Columbus sailed one last time in 1502, reaching the coast of Central America, but returned again without report of treasure and pearls. He was dismissed from court and summarily imprisoned under house arrest in Valladolid, where he died in 1507. The discovery of Venezuela did little for Columbus, but it led to a flurry of new explorations. Between 1499 and 1501, the Spanish Crown licensed a number of expeditions under Alonso de Hojeda (also spelled Ojeda) (1466–1516), Pedro Alonso Niño, and the brothers Cristóbal Guerra (d. 1509) and Luis Guerra (d. 1509). These expeditions confirmed the existence of pearls on the Venezuelan coast. *Niño,* formerly a part of the voyage of 1498, returned in 1500 with 96 pounds of large pearls. Exploration in 1512 discovered huge pearl beds, and Spanish merchants soon followed and developed a regular trade in pearls with the local natives.

The pearl trade ultimately led to the slave trade. Both Hojeda and the Guerra brothers obtained royal licenses to transport Venezuelan natives as slaves to Española. As noted previously, Spain designated Indian populations in Venezuela as either Carib or non-Carib, and only the former were seen as being available for slavery. The slave traders soon established bases at Coro and El Tucuyo in western Venezuela. The discovery of gold in

Trinidad exacerbated the problem of slavery. By 1520, the pearl beds were depleted, and the Spanish concentrated on slave raids to supply native labor for colonists in Central America and the Antilles. The natives of the pearl coast were now seen as part of the Carib population (i.e., available for slavery), and raids provoked hatred, resentment, and resistance for over a century. Interference from the clergy added to the resistance.

During the 1520s, the Spanish refortified Cubagua, renamed the site Nueva Cádiz, and built a fort against further native incursions. The fort and its soldiers did not end the warfare, in large part because the discovery of new pearl beds near Coche Island brought more merchants and slave traders to the islands. This constant conflict continually hindered the initial conquest of Venezuela.

At the end of the 1520s, the Spanish monarchy found itself deeply in debt. King Carlos I (1516–1556) [also reigned as Holy Roman Emperor Carlos V (1519–1558)] gave a consortium of German bankers, under the House of Welser, the right to exploit the resources of the Venezuelan coast as a form of debt reduction. A series of German governors occupied western Venezuela for the next 20 years. Their practice of slavery was considered harsher than the legendary cruelty of their Spanish predecessors. Indeed, the German governors spared little in the way of resources and lives in search of the fabled treasure of *El Dorado*, until their dismissal in 1556.

In the meantime, Spain concentrated its efforts on colonization and the endless search for treasure. By 1534, Antonio de Sedeño had conquered Trinidad and established a Spanish colony there. This conquest was followed by a two-pronged attack on the mainland, moving up the Orinoco River and the Magdalena River (in present-day Colombia). The Spanish conquered the northern coast of Colombia in 1530 and explored the waters of the Magdalena River, where Conquistador Gonzalo Jiménez (or Ximenes) de Quesada, subdued the Chibcha Indians in 1536 and established Santa Fe de Bogotá in 1538.

As Quesada explored the Magdalena River, Diego de Ardás penetrated the Orinoco River looking for treasure in "the province of Meta," which he assumed to be the location of the treasures of *El Dorado*. Turned back by angry natives, he died on the return journey. A subsequent series of expeditions also failed. In the meantime, conquistadors entering from the north established many of Venezuela's colonial cities. In 1555, Spanish explorers pushed eastward from El Tocuyo and founded Valencia. This was followed in 1567 by the establishment of Santiago de León de Caracas and the establishment of Trujillo in 1558. Moving quickly through the Andean region, the Spanish established Santiago de Los Caballeros (now Mérida) in 1558 and San Cristóbal in 1561.

The activity in western Venezuela attracted the attention of Antonio de Berrio (1527–1597) who set out from Bogotá in 1583 to find the fabled treasure of *El Dorado*. He reached the Orinoco River just as the rainy season began, encountering both heavy rains and native resistance. From natives he heard another legend—the legend of *más allá* (further down). The natives informed Berrio that there were many people with gold and precious stones to the south, on the other side of the highlands. The inhabitants of each village assured the Spaniards that *más allá* was an Indian site larger than any on the *llanos*.

When the rains ended, Berrio headed south, but illness and fatigue brought an end to his first expedition. After 17 months of fruitless searching, he returned to Bogotá. In 1584, Berrio received word that several of the *caciques* (Indian chieftains) in the Orinoco delta had told the Spaniards of a tribe on the Caroní River who traded in gold. He mounted a second and unsuccessful expedition, but a third expedition in 1589 actually located the Caroní River. Eventually, the conquistador made his way downriver to the Orinoco delta, where he sailed for Trinidad.

Between 1591 and 1593, Berrio recruited troops for yet another expedition to penetrate the highlands. Unfortunately, the governor of the island of Margarita allowed slave traders to attack the *caciques* allied with Berrio and forbade him to enter the Orinoco. In return, the conquistador secretly sent his son up the river with a small force of Spaniards and sent a friend to the Spanish court to argue his case. While Berrio struggled with Spanish administrators, Sir Walter Raleigh (1552–1618) arrived in Trinidad seeking the fabled *El Dorado*. Raleigh and his men captured the main port, and Berrio with it. He questioned both the Spaniards and the natives about possible locations of the legendary City of Gold. He also sent his captain, Laurence Keymis, to incite the Indians against the Spanish, a ploy that proved successful, especially among the Caribs. Leaving two men among the natives in exchange for two sons of the local *caciques*, Raleigh released Berrio and returned to England in 1595, where he later published *The Discoverie of the Large, Rich, an Bewtiful Empyre of Guiana*.

That same year, Berrio joined his son on the Orinoco and founded the city of Santo Tomé de Guayana at Morequito on an island near the mouth of the river. His attempts at colonization failed because of starvation and native attacks. Deserted by his captains and many of his men, Berrio tried one last time in 1596 to discover *El Dorado*. This time disaster took the form of mutiny among the men, who argued over leadership, which in turn angered the local Indians, who killed many of the Spaniards. Berrio returned to Trinidad, where he died in 1597. His title as Governor of Trinidad and the Orinoco passed on to his son, who tried valiantly to protect the threatened outpost of Santo Tomé.

SUMMARY

The territory of modern-day Venezuela had a thriving, yet moderately developed, native population when the first Spaniards arrived in the area. Although many of the tribes are still found in Venezuela today, most have disappeared as unique and identifiable cultural entities. Unlike so many of the other areas of European discovery, Venezuela was not an area of high priority for early conquest and colonization. After the discovery of the Pearl Coast by non-Spanish explorers and pirates, the need for more-permanent defenses of the area became intensified. As the next chapter details, *Tierra Firme* thus became an area of greater concern for Spain, even though it initially granted the handling of that concern to a German banking house.

3

The Colonial Era (to 1810)

As the years passed, Venezuela's society became more and more racially mixed. This process of *mestizaje* would bring with it a unique system of social stratification that would become a crucial element of the territory's mature colonial identity. With the rapid growth of colonial society, it became imperative for the mother country to establish institutions that would meet the challenges of the emerging New World societies. Imperial Spain had chosen to initially impose its own institutions of government on its American colonies, which led to a seemingly never-ending series of orders and amended counter-orders. This cycle illustrates the slow and tentative trial-and-error process of adaptation undergone by peninsular institutions as they attempted to reflect the unique realities of the New World.

As noted in the previous chapter, Spanish weakness on the eastern coast of Venezuela became general knowledge in the courts of Europe by 1599. Translations of Raleigh's book informed other Europeans of the gold on the Caroní River and the possible existence of *El Dorado* in the highlands. By 1604, the Dutch began to survey the Orinoco River, followed by the Swedes in 1605. Initially the Spaniards stopped incursions by other European powers, but constant war with the Caribs turned their attention away from the Pearl Islands whose slaves were soon captured by English pirates and transported to St. Vincent. The Governor of Santa Fe de Bogotá was dismayed at the seeming ease with which foreign powers attacked Venezuela's possessions (at that time, Venezuela fell under the leadership of the *Audiencia* established in Bogotá). News of another offense soon reached the governor's ears. In 1611, he accused Fernando de Berrio of illegal trade with the Dutch. Berrio claimed his tobacco had been seized by Dutch troops, but after questioning planters in Trinidad, Spanish officials learned that Berrio had indeed traded tobacco for slaves. Berrio was fined and removed from office.

The Spanish tried to ensure order along the coast. They banned the planting of tobacco on Trinidad and patrolled the coast. In return, the Dutch and English allied with the Caribs against the Spanish and the Arawaks. In 1614, the Dutch built a fort at Essequibo (present-day Suriname) from which they began to arm the Caribs. A new settlement by the English appeared on the coast near Margarita. Spain sent troops to evict the invaders, but their attempts were only partially successful. Three years later, Raleigh and his son returned to Trinidad and were warned not to molest Spanish possessions or ships upon pain of death. In December 1617, Raleigh and his son took the Spanish fort at Santo Tomé. The attack cost the lives of the Spanish governor of Guayana and Raleigh's son. Both the English and Spanish drew allies from among the natives to use in the war along the Orinoco. Eventually, the English left but not before they burned a Carib village and blamed it on the Spanish, ending any possibility of a Spanish-Carib alliance. Raleigh's last expedition failed miserably. The English Crown ordered his return. Infuriated over his insubordination, England's King James I accused Raleigh of treason, imprisoned him in the Tower of London, and executed him in 1618.

Raleigh's loss proved to be Fernando de Berrio's gain. Spain reinstated Berrio's title as Governor of Trinidad, Guayana, and *El Dorado*. Once in power, Berrio began a concerted effort to subdue the Caribs. He rebuilt the fort at Santo Tomé and ordered troops to attack and enslave the Caribs in an effort to end their cannibalism. He also opened free trade with the Dutch. This last ploy worked to suppress the Caribs, but Santo Tomé and the Orinoco remained isolated for the next 10 years, under constant attack by English pirates, and with little help from the Spanish in Trinidad. The Dutch became Berrio's only lifeline.

Berrio's trade with the Dutch insured their return to Essequibo in 1624, and his death in 1629 prompted the Dutch to burn the fort at Santo Tomé and settle among the native population. During the 1630s, the Spanish retook Santo Tomé and rebuilt the fort, but their hold on the Orinoco was tenuous. Toward the end of the decade, the Dutch attacked with a large contingent of Caribs from Caroní and Essequibo, destroying the fort. By December, they had driven the Spanish from Guayana and burned the fort in Trinidad. The Spanish reacted by trying to create alliances among the Caribs on the Orinoco. They allied with tribes, not against the Dutch but against other tribes who were Dutch allies. The diplomacy worked, and the alliance held for 15 years. The Spanish in Cumaná continued to enslave the natives of the Venezuelan coast, which hardened native resistance to Spanish rule and eventually sent them into the arms of the French in the Lesser Antilles. In 1649, Spain accepted the legitimacy of Dutch colonies in Guayana under the conditions of the Peace of Westphalia.

Despite the creation of several permanent settlements in the highlands and forts along the Carib coast, the majority of Venezuela remained untouched by Spanish conquistadors. The first missionaries undertook evangelization of Venezuela's natives on their own initiative, acting with the blessing, but not under the orders, of the Crown. Both the Franciscans and Dominicans built their missions on the eastern coast of Venezuela and fell at the hands of the Caribs. The missionaries who established themselves at Santo Tomé under Antonio de Berrio were also forced to abandon the Orinoco. Not until 1652 did Spain decree an end to the armed conquest in Venezuela. At that time, King Felipe II (1556–1598) ordered the beginning of a mission system to "civilize" the Amerindian population. Despite royal support, constant conflict and competition among the various religious orders limited missionary work until the eighteenth century.

By 1595, there were 18 notable cities in the territories that comprise present-day Venezuela. Among them was the city of Santiago de León de Caracas, which eventually emerged as the major governmental and commercial center of colonial Venezuela. Colonial society also experienced its seminal stage of development during the seventeenth century and first two decades of the eighteenth century. However, a more mature colonial society, such as that already found in New Spain and Perú, would not become firmly established in Venezuela until the first decade of the nineteenth century.

Due to the fact that the sixteenth century was primarily characterized by efforts to tame the Venezuelan wilderness and build settlements and towns more in keeping with the practical needs of self-protection and survival, artistic endeavors remained mostly utilitarian in nature, and architectural embellishment was limited only to the most important cities. However, the seventeenth century's economic growth would bring with it an increase in the number and scope of both civil and religious construction. Aesthetic considerations with regard to architectural styles and choice of building materials and techniques would become increasingly important in conveying the prosperity and power gained by the new *criollo* (Creole) elite, although, as a whole, the Venezuelan provinces would never rise to the creative heights achieved in older, more sophisticated centers of New World Spanish colonization, such as Mexico, Perú, and Ecuador. In the eighteenth century, military construction reached its zenith, while civil and religious architecture continued to reflect *criollo* economic prosperity. It was also in the eighteenth century that academic intellectualism became a prominent pursuit. This intellectual curiosity was also experienced in the pursuit of the visual arts, which were predominantly expressed in the form of religious iconography, reflecting the power of the Catholic Church in colonial life.

COLONIAL ADMINISTRATION

Spain's policies of New World administration were established in the period between 1492 and 1550. By the later date, the Crown had put in place a rigid and centralized system of offices, regulations, and relationships. The *audiencia*, made up of *oidores* (judges), was the first centralized institution devoted to overseeing the colonial territories. Eventually, the Spanish New World would be divided into four large administrative units, called *virreinatos* (viceroyalties), which were each governed by a *virrey* (viceroy). Smaller territorial units were headed by *capitán generales* (captains-general). For most of the colonial period, the *virrey*, *capitán generales*, and an *audiencia's oidores* were the royal officials most closely associated with the Spanish monarchy. However, the *virrey* was the chief official in the New World.

During the entire colonial period, there were 13 *audiencias* established throughout Spanish America. The first one was established at Santo Domingo (1511); the last one was Cuzco (1787). When the Province of Venezuela was created (1528), it was under the jurisdiction of the *Audiencia* of Santo Domingo. Some provinces, such as Maracaibo and Guayana, were temporarily associated with the viceroyalty of Nueva Granada, established in 1717. Other administrative levels were the *gobernaciones* (provincial territorial divisions) presided over by a *gobernador* (governor), and *presidencias* (presidencies), which were governed by *audiencias*. In a *presidencia*, the president of the governing *audiencia* served as the chief executive.

The *gobernación* of Margarita was established in 1525 and awarded to the conquistador Marcelo de Villalobos. The province initially comprised the islands of Margarita, Coche, Cubagua, and Trinidad and was under the jurisdiction of the *audiencia* of Santo Domingo until 1739, when it was briefly transferred to the jurisdiction of the viceroyalty of Nueva Granada. The seat of the *gobernación* of Margarita was the City of Asunción, founded in 1567.

Three years after the establishment of the Margarita provincial territory, the *gobernación* of Venezuela was created and entrusted to the German Welsers, under the stewardship of Ambrosio de Alfinger. Venezuela also fell within the jurisdiction of the *audiencia* of Santo Domingo, except from 1717 to 1742, when it came under the jurisdiction of the viceroyalty of Nueva Granada. Although a governor was named in 1521 to Trinidad, its actual establishment didn't take place until 1532, when it was granted to Antonio de Sedeño. The first capital was San José Oruña, founded in 1592. In 1596, Trinidad was annexed to the province of Guayana. However, Spain would lose Trinidad to Great Britain in 1797.

The *gobernación* of Cumaná or *gobernación* of Nueva Andalucía was created in 1568, under the leadership of conquistador Diego Fernández de Serpa (d. 1570), on the site of the former city of Nueva Córdoba. Guayana was established in 1565 and granted to Gonzalo Jiménez de Quesada. It was originally under the jurisdiction of the *audiencia* of Santa Fe de Bogotá. In 1729, the province of Guayana was annexed to Nueva Andalucía until 1762, when it regained its autonomy. From 1766 to 1771, it became a military dependency of the *gobernación* of Caracas. The *gobernación* of Maracaibo was established in 1676 and became an autonomous province in 1768. The *gobernación* of Cumaná was under the jurisdiction of the *audiencia* of Santo Domingo, with the exception of the brief period between 1739 and 1742.

By the seventeenth century, colonial *cabildos* (town councils) had become the fundamental organ of city administration in Latin America. Such was the pressure exerted by colonial *cabildos* on the Spanish Crown that, for a brief time, the latter eventually granted the former the right to occasionally assume the role of governing in the absence of a governor. For example, by 1676, a royal decree had confirmed the right of the Caracas town council to assume its provincial government in the absence of a governor. *Cabildos* were at first very democratic, closely reflecting the popular and direct election of their members, as well as the considerable autonomy they enjoyed from Spanish intervention. In the seventeenth century, however, *cabildos* took on a more oligarchic nature, due to the common occurrence of selling government offices, which led the government to fall under the control of a select few landowning *criollos*. At the same time, the control exercised by the Spanish Crown over the *cabildos* became more strictly regimented.

With the death of King Carlos II (1665–1700) in November 1700, the
Hapsburg line of rule came to an end in Spain. On his death bed, Carlos II
named his grandnephew, Philippe d'Anjou, as his rightful heir. Philippe
was also the grandson of King Louis XIV of France, and the ascension of
Philippe as King Felipe V of Spain triggered a war among the European
powers, most of whom did not want a French Bourbon (in Spanish,
Borbón) on the Spanish throne. This conflict, known as the War of Spanish
Succession (1701–1713) ended with the recognition of Felipe as Spain's
rightful king. Felipe (reigned 1700–1746 with a brief interruption in 1724)
began a program of reform and renewal, which became known as the
Bourbon Reforms. The *intendencia* system, already in place in France at
that time, was among the institutional changes that the Bourbons introduced in the New World.

The *intendencias* were territorial subdivisions of the viceroyalties. Each
intendencia was presided over by an *intendiente* (intendent), whose primary
role was the more-efficient collection of royal taxes on behalf of the Crown.
In addition, the *intendiente* was also responsible for the centralization of
the fiscal resources of the provinces, the establishment of expenditure
budgets for troop salaries, the establishment of military outposts, and the
fostering of economic growth in the provinces. The *Intendencia de Ejército y
Real Hacienda de Caracas* or *Real Intendencia de Caracas* (Royal Military and
Fiscal Intendancy of Caracas) was established on December 8, 1776, by
royal decree of King Carlos III (1759–1788), in order to oversee the military,
fiscal, and economic affairs of colonial Venezuela. Of even greater fundamental importance for the emerging nation was that the creation of the
intendencia constituted one of the seminal steps toward the achievement
of the political and territorial unification of the group of provinces and
colonies that would eventually become present-day Venezuela.

Another important step toward provincial unification was the estab-
lishment of the *Gran Capitanía General de Venezuela* or *Gran Capitanía
General de las Provincias Unidas de Venezuela* (Captaincy-General of
Venezuela or Captaincy-General of the United Provinces of Venezuela).
At the start of the eighteenth century, the territory of what would later
become Venezuela was a collection of autonomous provinces: Maracaibo,
Coro, Guayana, Trinidad, Cumaná, Puerto Cabello, Margarita, and
Caracas. These autonomous provinces had once belonged to the judicial
jurisdictions of the *audiencias* of Santo Domingo and Santa Fe de Bogotá
until King Carlos III established the *Capitanía General de Venezuela* on
September 8, 1777.

From that point on, these provinces collectively came under the military
control and jurisdiction of the *capitanía general* of Venezuela. Thus, a new

era of official administrative unification began, leading to definition of the geographic boundaries of the territories that later became known collectively as the United Provinces of Venezuela, comprising the territory corresponding to present-day Venezuela. The establishment of the *capitanía general* also represented the official beginning of the social process of creating a national identity. Thus, the former collection of provinces now began to gain and assert their own sense of a collective national identity. This sense of a collective identity would later be reinforced during the struggles for national independence in the nineteenth century.

Among the *capitán general*'s chief functions was the enforcement of the king's supreme command over the provincial governors. In addition, he acted as the Crown's representative in all governmental affairs within the United Provinces of Venezuela, exercised supreme command over the military, and presided over the *audiencia* and *cabildo* in Caracas.

The *Real Audiencia de Caracas* was created in July 1786, with the purpose of overseeing the legal and judicial affairs of the Venezuelan provinces. Among the chief functions of the *audiencia* were to act as the supreme judicial tribunal, as well as to oversee and control the role of Spanish colonial officials. The *audiencia* was comprised of the captain-general, who presided over the tribunal, as well as of a regent, three *oidores*, and a fiscal officer.

The *Real Consulado de Caracas* was created in June 1793, with the goal of fostering and regulating commerce between the United Provinces and Spain and between the United Provinces and other Spanish colonies. Among the functions of the *consulado* were to act as the supreme tribunal for mercantile affairs, to foster and provide incentives for the cultivation and trade in export products, and to exercise control over and safeguard commercial affairs, especially in light of the booming cacao trade of the eighteenth century between the United Provinces of Venezuela and Spain and between the United Provinces and Mexico. The *consulado* of Caracas had representatives in the provinces of Maracaibo, Coro, Puerto Cabello, Margarita, and Guayana.

COLONIAL CHURCH

The establishment of the Catholic Church as an institution in colonial Venezuela began in 1531, when Rodrigo de Bastidas (d. 1527) was named Bishop of Coro. Although the Spanish Crown expected the colonial church and state to establish distinct divisions, Venezuela's bishopric was transferred from Coro to Caracas in 1656. In 1777, the bishopric of Mérida was established, encompassing the provinces of Mérida, Maracaibo, and Trujillo. Thirteen years later, the diocese of Guayana was established. Due to the loss of Santo Domingo to the French at the end of the eighteenth century, the archdiocese of Caracas was established in 1803. Under the jurisdiction of the archdiocese were the dioceses of Mérida and Guayana. Prior to the establishment of local dioceses, clergy from the various religious orders had arrived in Venezuela through Santo Domingo. The Franciscans began to arrive on the eastern coast of what is now Venezuela in the year 1512, and by 1514, Dominican missionaries had already established a foothold in the Paria peninsula in the eastern part of present-day Venezuela. By 1652, the colonial mission system had been officially put in place by royal decree of King Felipe IV, and, by 1656, the Franciscans had become firmly established in Píritu, in the eastern coast of present-day Venezuela. The Capuchins, a branch of the Franciscan Order, also established a mission in the Province of Venezuela in 1658. The Jesuits failed at establishing a presence in colonial Venezuela in the latter part of the late sixteenth century. It wasn't until 1628 that the first viable Jesuit foundation was established in Venezuela, in the College of San Francisco Javier in Mérida. The Jesuits would be expelled by royal decree from Spain's colonies in 1767.

COLONIAL EDUCATION AND LEARNING

The origin and evolution of education in Venezuela closely follow the establishment and evolution of colonial administrative institutions. As the process of colonization became complete in the second half of the sixteenth century, an educational infrastructure began to develop. As early as 1515, Franciscan missionaries started to Christianize and educate the Indians in the Cumaná region. The first Latin grammar school in colonial Venezuela was established in Coro in 1534. In 1576, Franciscan and Dominican missionaries made their appearance in the Province of Venezuela, setting in motion a civilizing enterprise that laid the religious foundations necessary for the establishment of Spain's social, administrative, and political institutions on *Tierra Firme*. The local *cabildos* were in charge of establishing public schools in their respective jurisdictions. In short, the establishment of a colonial cultural tradition became dependent on the collaboration among *cabildos*, the Church hierarchy, and the religious orders, for it was this triumvirate that controlled the creation of the municipal and religious schools that would spread Spanish and Latin grammar, the arts, as well as the Catholic faith among the illiterate masses. The first public school in colonial Venezuela was established in Caracas in 1591.

The Seminary of Santa Rosa in Caracas, the first center of higher education of colonial Venezuela, and which had been founded in 1641, became in 1722 the Real y Pontificia Universidad de Caracas (Royal and Pontifical University of Caracas). This constituted the first university founded in the provinces of present-day Venezuela, and eventually included schools of Latin, philosophy, law, rhetoric, ethics, music, and medicine. The University of Caracas and its seminary were available only to white Spaniards and *criollos*. The second colonial seminary in the United Provinces was founded in Mérida in 1785, and other seminaries that would later become universities followed in the major urban centers.

In 1808, printers Matthew Gallagher and James Lamb brought the first printing press to colonial Venezuela from the nearby British colony of Trinidad. In October of the same year, the colony's first periodical publication, the *Gaceta de Caracas*, made its debut.

COLONIAL COMMERCE

The foundations of colonial Venezuela's economic development had originated in the sixteenth century under the governorship of the German Welsers, who had established Venezuela's first fiscal system, the *Real Hacienda*. In 1545, the initial exploration of colonial Venezuela's interior began. Although Coro was the original seat of the *Real Hacienda*, the seat was transferred to Caracas in 1578. The first of colonial Venezuela's fiscal gains came as a result of the slave trade boom of the last years of the sixteenth century.

In the sixteenth and early seventeenth centuries, wheat flour constituted the primary export product in the Venezuelan colonies. Later in the seventeenth and well into the eighteenth centuries, cowhides, cacao, and tobacco dominated export trade, along with indigo dye and sugarcane. In the mid 1600s, cacao and cowhides constituted nearly 97 percent of colonial Venezuela's exports. Tobacco was another important colonial crop introduced into the Venezuelan provinces in the eighteenth century that, along with cotton, contributed to the colonial economy's growth. In the eighteenth century, livestock, pack animals, and horses also became important colonial exports. Wheat was primarily cultivated in the Andean region of Mérida. Cacao was primarily cultivated in the Andean and in the central and coastal valleys. Livestock for the cowhide industry was primarily raised in the eastern part of the country. Tobacco was grown principally in the Andean region around San Cristóbal and in the Barinas highlands. Cotton was grown predominantly in the Andean region.

At the start of the seventeenth century, the economy was still a largely precarious enterprise due to the sparse population, the lack of urban centers, the resulting inability of the Venezuelan provinces to meet the demands of foreign markets, and the lack of a viable currency that could be used in foreign exchange. This uncertain currency situation stemmed from Spain's often capricious involvement in European military conflicts and the resulting sporadic interruptions of trade routes. These circumstances often led to low supplies and periods of scarcity of luxury imports to colonial Venezuela. These were the chief reasons that ultimately forced the Venezuelan colonial economy to subsist on a bartering system, along with the use of a variety of alternative currencies not based on the gold or silver standards.

Colonial commerce at the start of the seventeenth century was primarily based on the cultivation and export of wheat (wheat flour), grown principally in the fertile valleys of Caracas and Aragua, and representing approximately 60 percent of the overall agricultural output of the region. Tobacco was another important crop, comprising roughly 15 percent of exports. It was primarily harvested in the coastal and Andean regions, although it was also cultivated in the *llanos* region. Cowhides comprised the third largest export crop, comprising about 7 percent of exports. Halfway through the seventeenth century, cacao had become the predominant export crop. Cacao cultivation in the Barlovento region east of Caracas resulted in this region becoming the focal point of slave culture in colonial Venezuela. The slave labor force increased yields of cacao, which fueled the productivity of the colonial *haciendas*. This lucrative productivity, in turn, gave a remarkable impetus to the provincial economy.

Coffee was introduced into present-day Venezuela by Spanish missionaries in the eighteenth century, and was originally cultivated in the Andes, in the coastal areas, and in Guayana. The cultivation of sugarcane was introduced into present-day Venezuela from the Caribbean islands in the late sixteenth century, and it thrived in the fertile valleys of Caracas, Valencia, El Tocuyo, Guanare, Barquisimeto, and Carora. Among other lesser crops that also played a role in colonial commerce were cotton, indigo (used in textile production), corn, potato, yucca, plantain, and a variety of *frijoles* (beans). A favorable and profitable trade in native fruits such as guava (*guayaba*) and custard apple (*guanábana* or *chirimoya*) also flourished. The true origins of a viable colonial economy were not in evidence until it was found that the valleys in the vicinity of the city of Caracas could sustain the profitable cultivation of wheat and cacao.

The eighteenth century brought war and crisis to the Spanish peninsula in the form of the War of the Spanish Succession, which pitted the interests of Spain against those of England and Austria. As a result of this conflict, the Spanish colonies in the New World suffered prolonged periods of scarcity of all manner of import products vital to the colonial economy. In 1728, a deal was struck between the *criollos* and the *Compañía Guipuzcoana* or *Compañía de Caracas* (Caracas Company) whereby the latter would guarantee the export of colonial cacao from the provinces of present-day Venezuela into Spain, as well as safeguard the integrity of foreign commerce in general. In 1748, open protests were waged by the dissatisfied *criollos* against the *Compañía de Caracas*, and between 1749 and 1751 open armed conflict against it broke out, most notably the organized rebellions led by Juan Francisco de León. Such adverse reaction against the *Compañía*'s practices led to its eventual demise. The resulting pressure levied against the Crown by the powerful *criollo* commercial elite led the king to eventually allow the *criollos* to openly and freely engage in commerce with Spain. It was around this time that the colonial merchants of modern-day Venezuela initiated relations with the North American colonies. The colonial society of the soon-to-be-unified provinces of Venezuela was on the verge of reaching full maturity.

COLONIAL FORTIFICATIONS

In the seventeenth century, colonial Venezuela's coastline, long the target of pirates and buccaneers, saw the construction of several military *fuertes* (forts) and *castillos* (castles) in locations of strategic commercial importance or in areas that historically had been particularly vulnerable to piracy. Among the chief fortifications constructed were Fort Santiago de Araya, built on the Araya Peninsula between 1622 and 1642; Fort San Carlos Borromeo, built in Pampatar (on the eastern coast of the Island of Margarita) between 1664 and 1684; the Castle of San Francisco, built in Guayana between 1678 and 1681; and Fort San Carlos of Maracaibo, whose construction started in 1679. The fortifications of such strategic commercial ports as Puerto Cabello and La Guaira date back to 1730. La Guaira alone had five different fortifications. By far, however, the most important of the fortifications of colonial Venezuela was that of Fort San Felipe in Puerto Cabello. The port's name alludes to the fact that ships seeking to dock in its shores could be moored by using a single strand of hair (*cabello*, in Spanish), since the port's water currents were so benign.

In addition to their primary purpose of safeguarding the colony's military integrity from the frequent incursions of marauding pirates and buccaneers, these fortifications also protected the commercial monopolies of the Spanish Crown. The *Compañía Guipuzcoana* was naturally one of the primary forces behind this effort to fortify such strategic ports as La Guaira and Puerto Cabello. The *Compañía* also engaged in the zealous persecution of the illegal yet ubiquitous contraband traffic between pirates and *criollo* merchants in order to protect its own commercial interests.

COMPAÑÍA GUIPUZCOANA DE CARACAS

The economic reforms instituted by King Felipe V ushered in a new era of colonial commerce. The monopolies previously enjoyed by the Spanish port cities of Seville and Cádiz were abolished in favor of opening up such peninsular ports as Málaga, Almería, Cartagena, Alicante, and Vigo, among others, to the New World trade. Colonial Venezuela's provinces thrived under the new policies, with the port cities of la Guaira and Puerto Cabello enjoying the lion's share of the trade monopolies.

Several trading companies were authorized to conduct trade with Spain's New World colonies. Among these were the *Real Compañía de Guinea* (Royal Guinea Company) and the *Real Compañía Inglesa de los Mares del Sur* (Royal English South Seas Company), both of which controlled the monopoly to supply African slaves to colonial Venezuela's markets. Of particular importance was the *Compañía Guipuzcoana* or *Compañía de Caracas* (Caracas Company), which, as previously mentioned, was established in 1728 to guarantee, protect, and expand the export monopoly of colonial Venezuela's ports with Spain, especially the lucrative cacao trade. Although the *Compañía Guipuzcoana* was established in 1728, it did not begin its New World operations until 1730. The *Compañía* operated chiefly out of the ports of La Guaira and Puerto Cabello, but also exercised control over export trade in the Venezuelan provinces of Cumaná, Margarita, and Trinidad.

In fact, the demand for cacao from the Venezuelan provinces was so great that the merchants of the most lucrative colonial market of the time—Mexico—decided to deal directly with their Venezuelan counterparts. In 1674, King Carlos II awarded the Venezuelan provinces the exclusive monopoly to supply cacao to the merchants of Veracruz, with the port of La Guaira as the chief Venezuelan export outlet. In fact, the La Guaira–Veracruz cacao trade route was the most important colonial enterprise in the seventeenth and well into the eighteenth century. The La Guaira-Veracruz commercial supremacy came to an end with the beginning of operations of the *Compañía de Caracas* in 1730, and the subsequent establishment of Spain as the primary export destination of Venezuelan crops, including cacao.

The *Compañía de Caracas* succeeded in expanding trade in colonial Venezuela's still predominantly agricultural economy. The *Compañía* was also successful in regulating the colonial export trade. However, these overzealous controls and regulations inevitably stifled the prosperity of the colonial merchant classes, who, in turn, became increasingly hostile to the *Compañía's* practices, especially its fixing of prices highly unfavorable to local merchants and growers. So detrimental was the *Compañía's* stranglehold on the interests of local merchants and growers that its policies led to the unintended consequence of making contraband trade even more ubiquitous than ever among local merchants.

As seemed inevitable, there came a time when local colonial merchants could no longer tolerate the *Compañía's* practices; widespread revolts and armed opposition ensued and ultimately led to the *Compañía's* demise in the New World. In 1778, King Carlos III, staying true to the spirit of Bourbon reform, decreed the free trade between Spain's New World colonies and the English-speaking North American colonies. This royal decree was finally put into practice in the Venezuelan provinces in 1785, the very year in which the *Compañía de Caracas* ceased to operate.

COLONIAL SOCIETY

The sixteenth century saw the introduction of African slaves (predominantly Congos, Dahomeyans, Fanti-Ahsantis, and Madingas) into the provinces of present-day Venezuela, predominantly along the eastern and central coasts. The majority of this slave work force was used on plantations for crop cultivation and processing, further fueling economic prosperity. With the growth of colonial towns and urban centers, the black slave force adapted to urban environments and were used as personal servants. The ownership of slave servants became a symbol of great prestige in colonial society.

The second half of the seventeenth century saw an increase in the local population due to an influx of Spanish and Portuguese immigrants. The resulting demographic transformation meant that, from the initial five predominant urban areas of the sixteenth century, the Venezuelan provinces had now grown to include 17 towns, each with a population of more than 800 inhabitants. The intermarriage of whites and Indians further fueled the population growth.

Racial mixing initially occurred between white men and Indian women, creating the prototypical "mixed race" or *mestizo* ethnic group. With the introduction of African slaves into the New World, racial mixing also occurred between white men and black women, creating the *mulato* or *pardo* ethnic group; and between Indian men and black women, creating the *zambo*, or *sambo*, ethnic group. With such a high degree of racial mixing, colonial Venezuela's society grew to be extremely stratified according to skin color. Colonial Venezuela's society was also static, in the sense that it only allowed a limited degree of social mobility, and not without resistance. This created an antagonistic social environment, due to the constant struggle of the inferior classes in attaining social acceptance and equality with the white *criollos*, who resisted any change to their superior status quo.

In the eighteenth century, the majority of the population in the Venezuelan provinces belonged to the *pardo* ethnic group. *Pardos* controlled the majority of commercial interests, creative activities, and manufacturing. Thus, to the degree that they were able to acquire a certain economic mobility that would allow them to improve their standard of living, and also due to their sheer numbers, the *pardos* began to demand social equality with white *criollos*. By the end of the eighteenth century, *pardos* had gained access to an education, the army, and to purchase titles of nobility, all of which contributed to their steady rise in the social hierarchy.

The social hierarchy and roles of each of colonial Venezuela's social classes can be summarized as follows: *Peninsulares*, or whites born in the Iberian Peninsula, constituting a very small elite, were the only ones allowed to exercise high administrative and ecclesiastical posts. They were the most educated and cultured segment of colonial society. *Criollos*, or Iberian whites born in the New World, were predominantly landowners and constituted the most powerful economic group in colonial society. They, however, lacked the right to exercise high administrative offices, although they were able to buy public offices. They were the first and largest group to have access to an education, to a military career, to join the religious orders, and to the purchase of nobility titles.

During the height of the cacao trade after the mid-seventeenth century, *criollos* made up the powerful "cacao aristocracy" and were often referred to as *gran cacaos*. *Canarios*, or white Spaniards from the Canary Islands, were a less-educated group who mostly worked as craftsmen or as overseers for *criollo* bosses in their large *hacienda* plantations. *Pardos* constituted the largest ethnic group in colonial society. Despite their limited access to education, they controlled the majority of commercial, agricultural, and manufacturing industries. Indians, although theoretically enjoying personal freedom, were often marginalized and relegated to remote missions and towns to work for and pay tribute to *encomenderos* (holder of a trusteeship over the native population).

Initially used as slave labor, Indians were ultimately protected from slavery by the *Nuevas Leyes de Indias* of 1542. The Venezuelan Indians' marginalized status has remained relatively unchanged to this day. Blacks constituted the least powerful social class in colonial times and provided the labor force in the *haciendas* for the cultivation of agricultural crops. Black slaves were not allowed to handle currency or to circulate freely. Blacks who had gained their freedom were referred to as *manumisos*, and blacks who had fled into wilderness areas to avoid slavery were referred to as *cimarrones*. Blacks lacked any social rights or possibilities for social mobility or advancement.

The remarkable economic growth of the eighteenth century in the territories of modern-day Venezuela, due in large measure to the booming cacao trade with Spain and Mexico, fueled the desire of many *criollos* to demand and be granted a greater participation in provincial affairs. This desire among *criollos* to have their colonial roles expanded met with favorable support from the newly established Bourbon dynasty of Spain, which took great interest in actively controlling the increasingly lucrative economic prospects of the Venezuelan territories. The *criollos'* aspirations thus were rewarded by the introduction and establishment of the administrative institutions that already existed in other Spanish colonies of the New World.

MOVEMENT TOWARD INDEPENDENCE

In 1781, the rebellion of the *comuneros del Socorro* in the viceroyalty of Nueva Granada (in present-day Colombia) spread to the province of Mérida and, from there, to the other Venezuelan provinces. The *comuneros* protested the oppressive taxes imposed by the Spanish colonial administration, which, in 1779, were further increased in order to help finance Spain's war with Great Britain. In the Venezuelan provinces, the Caracas *cabildo* sympathized with and was favorably disposed toward the *comuneros'* plight.

Agitation grew between autonomists and those who sought independence. Among those calling for independence was a young aristocrat by the name of Simón Bolívar who became Venezuela's Great *Libertador* (Liberator). Born Simón José Antonio de la Santísima Trinidad Bolívar y Palacios as the second son of a Venezuelan *mantuano* cacao planter on July 24, 1783, Bolívar was a wealthy *criollo* with a bright future. Orphaned by age nine, he and his siblings spent their childhood among several close relatives. He was stubborn and often insubordinate as a child, traits not appreciated by his intolerant paternal uncle and guardian, who eventually placed him in a military academy. In addition to his military training, Bolívar received private tutoring. He studied the classics and French, but his real interests lay in the writings of the French philosophers. One of his tutors, Simón Rodríguez (1769–1854), was an adamant republican who followed the teachings of Rousseau. He greatly influenced the young Venezuelan's ideas on government, equality, and liberty. Accused of involvement in a conspiracy against the government, Rodríguez fled to Europe by way of Jamaica and the United States.

In 1799 Bolívar used his inheritance to travel to Madrid. He enjoyed the company of other young men who spoke of revolutionary ideas and of the possibility of travel and adventure. He met and married María Teresa Rodríguez del Toro (1781–1803) in 1802, and the couple returned to Venezuela to begin married life. María died of fever (probably yellow fever or malaria) eight months later. Grieving and alone, Bolívar returned to Europe and lived in Spain and then in Paris, where he was reunited with his old friend Simón Rodríguez. The two friends traveled to Rome to visit the ruins of the classical world and enjoy the mountains. Gazing at the beauty of the world atop Monte Sacro, in August 1805, Bolívar made a solemn promise to liberate the Americas. The two men returned to Paris, where the plans of Francisco de Miranda to free Venezuela had become the latest gossip.

Having spent the better part of 40 years participating in various revolutionary plots, Francisco de Miranda (1750–1816), a *criollo* soldier, republican, and precursor of Venezuela's independence movement, put forth (in 1790) his plan for the liberation of the Spanish American colonies. Seeking financial backing from the British government, Miranda's initial proposal called for the liberated Spanish American colonies to be henceforth called "Colombia," in honor of South America's discoverer, Christopher Columbus. Miranda also proposed a monarchical government headed by an emperor known as "Inca," and a Congress comprised of senators and commons, with the stipulation that all administrative posts be held for life.

There were also several other notable revolts at the end of the eighteenth century. In 1795, in Coro, José Leonardo Chirino (d. 1796), a *zambo*, led a major uprising inspired by Haiti's slave movement. Although the Coro rebellion was joined by the majority of Venezuela's *mestizo* population, the rebels were eventually subdued and their leaders executed. In 1797, in the port city of La Guaira, a group of white *criollos* led by Manuel Gual (1759–1800), José María España (1761–1799), and Juan Bautista Picornell (1759–1825), rebelled against the Spanish Crown, seeking to overthrow and oust Spanish colonial authority from Venezuelan soil. They would then institute free commerce and economic production; create a republic; declare the rights to freedom, social equality, property, and security; and abolish the practices of slavery and of Indian tributes. This uprising was also subdued and its rebels swiftly prosecuted. In 1799, a conspiracy plot was discovered in the city of Maracaibo. Inspired by the rebellion in La Guaira, the Maracaibo plot was also thwarted.

These plots and uprisings, although failures, made it clear that the ideals of liberty and equality that had spread throughout the Americas as a result of the American and the Haitian Revolutions, had irrevocably sparked the fire of Spanish American independence.

In 1805, Francisco de Miranda traveled to the United States and gathered resources for a revolutionary expedition to Venezuelan shores. In 1806, Miranda sailed from the United States to Haiti, where Miranda first hoisted the tricolor flag of his own design, the prototype for the future Venezuelan flag. From Haiti, Miranda's expeditionary force set sail for the Venezuelan city of Puerto Cabello. However, this first landing attempt met with failure, as Spanish forces captured Miranda's ships, forcing Miranda and his companions to flee to neighboring Trinidad. In August of the same year, Miranda set sail from Trinidad on his second revolutionary expedition to Venezuela, with the aid of British authorities. This time, Miranda was able to land at the port of La Vela, near Coro. However, Miranda found the city completely deserted, due to a clever Spanish ploy that had spread accusations among the local population, labeling Miranda a secret agent for the British Crown. The residents did not trust a Spaniard who had given his word to the French, been imprisoned twice, and had possibly been tainted by the British. After the failure of his second expedition, Miranda once again fled to Trinidad and, later, in 1807, to Britain.

That same year, Bolívar left for his homeland, stopping in the United States and returning in 1807. As he settled into his estate, he was eager to join the discussions about the necessity of independence or autonomy. He did not, however, join the *mantuano* conspiracy of 1808, which petitioned for a *junta* in Caracas.

A number of longstanding issues caused the *criollo* overthrow of Venezuela's captain-general. As in other colonies, the failures of the Bourbon reforms had exacerbated already-existing colonial complaints. The Crown's favoritism for *peninsulares* was irritating but not as threatening as its preferential treatment of *pardos*. This partiality became especially galling in 1795, with the issuance of the *Real Cédula de Gracias al Sacar*, which decreed that *pardos* might buy their way into equality with the *criollos*. However, the *criollo* elite, which controlled the Caracas *cabildo*, successfully opposed the enactment of the *cédula*. The colony had a large Afro-Latin population, both free and enslaved. Many colonists feared the political power of freedmen and the very real possibility of a slave revolt. There was, of course, the continued refusal to grant free trade and, finally, the inability of Spain to stop incursions by both the British and the

United States into Spanish colonies in Central America and the Caribbean, particularly the British occupation of Trinidad in 1797. By the turn of the century, Venezuela's *criollo* elite grew restive. Some argued for autonomy and others conspired for independence.

In 1808, events in Spain brought Venezuelan arguments to a head. Napoleon Bonaparte (1769–1821) of France forced the Spanish King Carlos IV (1788–1808) to abdicate in favor of his son, Fernando VII (1808, 1814–1833). Napoleon then put them both under house arrest and immediately placed his own brother, Joseph, on the Spanish throne. Angered by Napoleon's imposition, many Spaniards established *juntas* in the name of Fernando VII, their captive king. Following suit, Juan de Casas (b. 1740), interim governor and captain-general of the United Provinces of Venezuela, had chosen to openly support Fernando VII but refused the colonists' request to install a *junta* in Caracas.

By 1810 the need for action was again dictated by European events. While most Venezuelans probably wished to remain loyal to Fernando VII, they also wanted a larger part in their own government, a part which the council at Cádiz had discussed but had not implemented. The *junta* replaced Captain-General Juan de Casas and quickly pledged its fidelity to Fernando VII, but it clearly intended some form of self-government.

SUMMARY

The years from 1600 to 1800 witnessed the transformation of the land initially called *Tierra Firme* from a great wilderness to a thriving colonial region. In the course of these two centuries, a new American culture emerged, through the racial and cultural mixing process of *mestizaje*. In addition, the territory changed administrative hands a number of times, and its economic and military importance waned and waxed with these political changes. The ascension of the *Borbón* line to the Spanish throne also brought greater significance to Venezuela. By 1810, the political events in Europe and discontent in the Americas brought even greater change to Venezuela, as many began to openly speak of independence. In the next chapter, we describe how the words of these leaders turned into actions and the colony achieved its sovereignty.

4

Movements toward Independence (1810–1830)

On April 19, 1810, Venezuela's *criollo* population organized a peaceful demonstration in the streets of Caracas against the government. They claimed that the present government officials were representatives of a French usurper, José I, and forced Captain-General Juan de Casas to resign. The newly formed *junta* legitimized its rule in Venezuela as representative of Spain's King, Fernando VII (1808, 1814–1833). The bloodless *golpe* of 1810 began the events that ultimately led to Venezuela's independence in 1824.

As noted in the previous chapter, there were a number of long-term causes for the overthrow of colonial Venezuela's captain-general. While Venezuelans wished to remain loyal to Fernando VII, their even greater desire for a larger role in their own government—a desire that the council at Cádiz had been unwilling to satisfy—proved too powerful. Although the *junta* that replaced Captain-General Juan de Casas had quickly pledged its fidelity to Fernando VII, it clearly intended to gain some measure of self-government. Its leadership remained divided between autonomy and independence, with Simón Bolívar calling loudly for independence. Loyalists and Spanish troops quickly organized in opposition to the *junta*, whose leadership decided the wisest course of action was to remove Bolívar as quickly as possible.

The *junta* gave Bolívar a commission to go to London to seek aid, along with the delegation's secretary, Andrés Bello. Parliament was sympathetic, but Spain was England's ally against France, and the island nation could offer little material help without seeming disloyal. While in London, Bolívar finally met Francisco de Miranda and convinced him to return to Venezuela and take command of a patriot army. The two men landed at the port of La Guaira (near Caracas) on December 5, 1810, and proceeded to Caracas. The *junta* had already opened Venezuela's ports to free trade and shut down the slave trade to please Britain. However, if Venezuelans seemed happy with the idea of free trade, they were clearly unhappy with what many deemed authoritarian actions in Caracas. The *junta* faced fierce opposition from segments of the Venezuela population who decried such authority. Fractious groups quickly split between those who favored the *junta* and those who remained loyal to some semblance of Spanish royal authority. A failed attempt to coerce obedience by sending troops to Coro only deepened the distrust.

Bolívar became convinced that revolution was the only answer. In March, a new Venezuelan Congress met. After several months of deliberation, they announced Venezuelan independence and the establishment of the first Venezuelan Republic on July 5, 1811. The new constitution established a republican government under a triumvirate leadership. It eliminated feudal traditions, like the Indian tribute and the *fueros* of the military and the church, but retained Catholicism as the state religion. It also abolished African slavery but limited the rights of full citizenship to property owners, which thus excluded many free blacks and *pardos*. Lastly, it required the *llaneros* to carry documents showing their full-time employment at *haciendas* and enacted vagrancy laws to allow for the arrest of unemployed *llaneros*. The arbitrariness of the 1811 constitution aggravated the conflict that was already simmering under the surface. The ranks of the loyalists swelled with the addition of fresh troops from Puerto Rico and of frustrated *pardos* and *llaneros*. At the same time, many black slaves took advantage of the war to mount revolts against plantation owners.

It was clearly time for patriot action, but Miranda hesitated. Many of the young officers, especially Bolívar, became frustrated with Miranda's indecision. Fate intervened in the form of an earthquake that shook Caracas on March 26, 1812, and destroyed large parts of the city and other territories held by the patriots. Between 15,000 and 20,000 people died in the aftermath. Ironically, it spared the regions under loyalist control. The Spanish clergy proclaimed that god had punished the wicked patriots and spared the righteous; however, Bolívar refused to bow to nature. Sword drawn, he entered the ruined areas of the city to stop banditry and begin the clean-up. He organized the burning of damaged buildings and the clearing of streets.

The *junta* invested Francisco de Miranda with supreme command of its forces, but Miranda continued to delay drilling his troops and organizing more recruits. Bolívar worked alongside Miranda and other members of a pro-independence group called the *Sociedad Patriótica* (Patriotic Society), to further revolutionary ideals. Bolívar offered his services to the republican cause and was given a small command. Finally, Miranda moved into battle but suffered a series of defeats. As his forces disintegrated, Miranda tried in vain to negotiate with the Spanish, leading to his surrender and his failed attempt to flee the country. While the treaty for surrender was being signed, Miranda prepared a ship at La Guaira loaded with his papers and most of the republican treasury. The following morning, Bolívar and other republican troops seized Miranda, whom they deemed a traitor, and turned him over to the Spanish. Sadly, Francisco de Miranda, the precursor of Venezuelan independence, died in a Spanish prison four years later (1816). Bolívar escaped to Caracas, where he took refuge in the house of the Marquis de Casa León (1750?–1826). And so, the First Republic died a short year after its birth.

Bolívar left Venezuela and traveled to Nueva Granada, where republican forces had also declared independence. The *criollos* in Cartagena were squabbling over the form that their new government should take. The young Venezuelan entered the fray on the republican side. However, before he entered the battle, he issued his *Manifiesto de Cartagena* (Cartagena Manifesto), calling for the unity of Colombia's forces and condemning the impracticality of the federal system. He also identified Venezuela's cause with that of Colombia's, urging the liberation of Venezuela to protect Colombia from Spanish invasion.

The leadership in Gran Colombia gave Bolívar a commission in the army. With a small detachment of men, he cleared the Magdalena River of royalist troops and advanced westward. He then moved across the mountains to seize Ocaña and Cúcuta. Victory brought Bolívar the reward of a generalship in the Colombian army and Colombian support for the liberation of his homeland. From Cúcuta, Bolívar led his forces north through the Venezuelan Andes, capturing the cities of La Grita and Mérida. Angered by Bolívar's actions, Spanish troops began a campaign of terror against suspected Venezuelan patriots, by confiscating land, imprisoning suspects, and burning houses. Bolívar, however, continued northward toward Caracas. Capturing Trujillo, he declared a counter-insurgency campaign against the Spanish. With Bolívar advancing from the west and patriot forces invading from Trinidad in the east, the Spanish realized they could not hold Caracas and, thus, withdrew. It was his *Proclama de Guerra a Muerte* (Proclamation of War of the Death) at the outset of this 1813 *Campaña Admirable* (Admirable Campaign) to invade and seize control of Venezuela that became the turning point of Venezuela's independence. The patriot army entered Caracas in triumph. Bolívar received the title of *Libertador* from the city council, and the Venezuelan Congress declared him supreme dictator of the Second Venezuelan Republic.

This patriot victory was also short-lived. Once again, European affairs dictated events in Venezuela. With the fall of Napoleon (1814), Fernando VII returned to the Spanish throne. The king sent reinforcements to support the loyalists in Venezuela. In addition to the Spanish royalists, the republicans had other enemies. Many *criollo* planters refused to free their slaves, and breaking up the continued slave revolts thinned the patriot army. Furthermore, under the Spanish merchant and smuggler José Tomás Boves (1782–1814), many *llaneros* deserted the patriot cause in response to the continued enforcement of the *llanero* vagrancy laws.

The Spanish army continued to attack, its ranks swelled with fresh recruits. The *llaneros* swept across the highlands toward Caracas, where a weakened republican army frantically awaited reinforcements from Colombia and hoped that the British might change their mind and send help. Boves and Bolívar fought several battles against each other's forces. Bolívar won most of the battles but lost the war. The patriots retreated eastward, and Boves recaptured each city in their wake. Valencia surrendered, hoping to ease the trauma, but the *llaneros* rounded up all the patriot supporters and executed them, treating their families with great cruelty. Boves was notorious for this cruelty toward the enemy during the Venezuelan struggle for independence.

Like Miranda before him, Bolívar readied a ship at La Guaira with the treasury and the silver and jewels he had taken from various churches in Caracas, so that he could buy arms in the British Antilles. He retreated to Barcelona, in the state of Anzoátegui, where his forces were again defeated. The survivors pushed toward Cumaná, where Bolívar boarded his ship to stop the captain from leaving with the treasury. In September 1814, Bolívar sailed for Cartagena to regroup. The remainder of his forces retreated farther east and were continuously harassed by Boves. By December the patriots had been defeated in the east, although Boves lost his life in battle. By this time, only a handful of *guerrillas* remained in the west. The Second Republic was dead and Venezuela lay in ruins. War had reduced its population, while disease and malnutrition afflicted scores of others. Many Venezuelans fled to Nueva Granada and the Antilles, causing agricultural production to decline sharply in the wake of rampant banditry throughout the countryside. Cartagena gave Bolívar a hero's welcome. Although he'd hoped to tour the country to gather a new army to liberate Venezuela, he was sadly disappointed. While Nueva Granada's federation was glad to have the *Libertador* join its armed forces, they could not settle their own internal affairs, much less send an army to Venezuela. In the meantime, Spain sent a fleet under General Pablo Morillo (1778–1837) to suppress the remainder of the revolutionaries in Venezuela and retake Nueva Granada. Believing that the situation was hopeless, Bolívar sailed for Jamaica in 1815.

General Morillo subdued both Venezuela and Nueva Granada. La Plata remained the last Spanish holdout in South America. Historians point out that, if King Fernando VII had treated his supporters more liberally, the empire might have survived. Others argue that republican ideas were too ingrained in the populace and that independence was inevitable. Royal action tipped the scales in favor of independence. The siege at Caracas killed one third of its inhabitants. Afterward, royalist troops hunted down and executed patriot forces or forced them into exile. A fanatical reactionary toward liberal ideas, the king also failed to reward his supporters in Venezuela. No citizens of *mestizo* or *pardo* ethnicities were granted political equality. These acts eventually cost the king the support of many colonists.

In Jamaica, a penniless Bolívar accepted the help of Maxwell Hyslop (1783–1837), a British merchant who sympathized with the republican cause. Like many Englishmen, he realized that a liberated Venezuela would be ripe for trade. Bolívar spent his days begging for aid and dodging assassins. He insisted that the revolution was not over. He spoke to anyone and everyone who would listen about the necessity of freeing not only Venezuela, but all of South America, and he wrote tirelessly to friends and politicians. In one of his letters, he suggested that British military aid might be rewarded with possession of Panamá and Nicaragua. In September 1815, the *Libertador* penned his now-famous *Carta de Jamaica* (Jamaica Letter), which accused Spain of being an aged serpent who could not keep Spanish America subject any longer. Finding little aid in Jamaica, Bolívar sailed to Haiti. President Alexandre Pétion received the *Libertador*, sympathizing greatly with his cause. While he could send little in the way of troops, he did offer material support. All he asked in return was freedom for the slaves in any territory they liberated.

In March 1816, Bolívar and his small liberation army landed on the island of Margarita. However, his attempts to gain a foothold on the mainland were repulsed. Refusing to accept failure, he retreated to the Antilles and regrouped. He decided that taking the northern coast was too costly. A wiser course of action was to invade through the Orinoco River, away from Spanish strongholds. After rebuilding his army, he landed on the eastern shore of Venezuela and made his way up the Orinoco to Angostura (present-day Ciudad Bolívar). He began recruiting roving bands of patriots and *guerrillas* who were soon joined by the disillusioned *llaneros*. With the Napoleonic Wars over, a number of British soldiers also made their way up the Orinoco, where they formed the loyal and distinguished British Legion. With help from Hyslop and other merchants, the patriots also received money and loans to buy arms and supplies. The British had grown impatient with King Fernando VII's imperiousness.

In 1819, Bolívar created a new republican Congress, which in turn invested the *Libertador* with dictatorial powers. He ordered the new Congress to create a new constitution with the reforms none of the earlier republics had carried out. He reminded them of the necessity of agrarian reform and the need to abolish slavery. From previous experience, he advised that the new government have one leader rather than a triumvirate and that the president hold tremendous authority to maintain order. Congress agreed to the structure of government but was loath to implement all of his reforms.

As Congress deliberated, Spanish forces under Morillo moved south into the *llanos* to take the Orinoco. Bolívar and the *llaneros*, under General José Antonio Páez (1790–1873), adopted a strategy of swift hit-and-run attacks combined with a "scorched earth" policy. Morillo eventually retreated at the onset of the rainy season. Bolívar had planned to continue across the *llanos* into the highlands, but intelligence from his aide, Francisco de Paula Santander (1792–1840), changed his mind. Nueva Granada was ready to fall. Leaving Venezuela to the *llaneros*, Bolívar pushed westward into the Andes. At the Battle of Boyacá (near Tunja) he crushed the royalist army and quickly took a virtually defenseless Bogotá. Santander stayed behind to establish order and create a new government while the *Libertador* retraced his steps toward Angostura.

The return of Bolívar and the news of victory in Nueva Granada allowed the small Congress at Angostura to begin the creation of Gran Colombia along the lines of the old viceroyalty. Gran Colombia would combine the territories of Nueva Granada, a newly created Colombia and Venezuela, plus a third region near Quito. They naturally suggested Bolívar for the presidency, but he split the region into several vice-presidencies. The liberated portions of Nueva Granada fell under Santander, forming the basis for a new country under the Fundamental Law of the Republic of Colombia, with Francisco Antonio Zea (1766–1822) as its new vice president. The other parts of Gran Colombia would become present-day Venezuela and Ecuador.

The coast of Nueva Granada and Cartagena needed to be reconquered, and northern Venezuela was still in Spanish hands. Bolívar decided that Morillo was not yet a threat to the *llanos* and headed for the coast. In March 1820, he arrived at Ríohacha by sea. The campaign turned sour as some of his troops deserted and the loyalists strengthened their position. Things might have gotten worse except that fate intervened in the form of a revolt in Spain.

Fernando VII seemed oblivious to his country's desire for constitutional government and liberal reform. Revolution in the Americas was an affront to his absolutism, and, in December 1819, the king ordered Spanish troops to sail for South America. The attack never happened. On January 1, 1820, a regiment of young, liberal soldiers revolted against the Crown. Known as the Riego Revolt, the movement soon gained more followers, and they eventually forced Fernando VII to restore Spain's liberal constitution of 1812 and rule as a constitutionally limited monarch. The new government also refused to support his plans to send troops to the colonies. It believed that the restoration of liberalism in Spain would regain their loyalty. They were wrong.

The Riego Revolt caused much gloom among Venezuelan royalists, and many deserted to the patriot side. In Venezuela, Morillo requested negotiations for an armistice. At the same time, republican troops seized Cartagena, and Bolívar advanced into Western Venezuela, reaching Trujillo. He signed a six-month armistice with General Morillo, but this turned out to be only a brief hiatus in the fighting. By April, the war was in full swing. Morillo, however, had returned to Spain, leaving Marshal Miguel de la Torre (1786–1843) to face the patriot army set to strike Caracas.

Páez and the *llaneros* attacked from the north, and Bolívar advanced in a pincer movement from the south. After several battles, de la Torre surrendered at Carabobo near Valencia. As the battle raged on, the Congress at Angostura moved to create the union of Venezuela and Colombia on paper, by finalizing the creation of Gran Colombia. The Congress moved to Cúcuta, near the border between Venezuela and Nueva Granada. The combined Congress created a highly centralized government with a liberal constitution. They ignored Bolívar's suggestions for a power presidency and shared power between the executive and legislative branches. Bolívar continued in the presidency, and Santander became the new vice president.

By July 1821, Bolívar and Páez finished the military conquest of Venezuela with the exception of a few forts and coastal areas. Only Quito remained to cement the plan for Gran Colombia and, beyond it, the royalist stronghold of Perú. Leaving Páez in Venezuela, Bolívar turned south, stopping only at Cúcuta to take the oath of the presidential office before continuing his journey. He set up temporary headquarters in Calí to prepare for the campaign. Before him lay a royalist stronghold, with the exception of Guayaquil, which had rebelled against Spanish rule in October 1820. The Andes needed to be liberated in order to secure independence and, with it, the future of Venezuela.

Hearing of the insurrection in 1820, Bolívar commissioned General Antonio José de Sucre (1795–1830) to aid the rebels in Guayaquil. A year later, he marched to meet Sucre with the meager 3,000 troops Santander could raise. Their path lay along a tortuous land route in the Andes. He lost men to the weather, sickness, and finally in a long battle at Bomboná near the Guáitira River. At the end of the battle, even Bolívar was ill and had to be carried from the field on a stretcher.

Sucre moved to meet his general, leaving Guayaquil with reinforcements sent by the Argentine General José de San Martín (1778–1850), known as southern South America's *Libertador*. San Martín had successfully crossed the Andes to liberate Chile, and his troops occupied Lima by July 1821. From Lima, he ordered the sending of troops from Perú, Chile, and Argentina to aid in the liberation of Quito. By May 1822, Sucre's army camped just outside the city. After a brief battle, the city capitulated, and Quito became a *de facto* province of Gran Colombia. Bolívar entered Quito in June to the cheers of its citizens. He stayed briefly to put his affairs in order and continued southward. By July 26, both Bolívar and San Martín were in Guayaquil.

Bolívar, who had reached the city on July 11, greeted the southern *Libertador* as the "first friend of [his] heart." It was a jubilant moment for Bolívar but a disappointing one for San Martín, who had hoped to take Guayaquil himself. At their now-famous meeting, the two leaders discussed their different visions for the future of the continent. San Martín favored a constitutionally limited monarchy, while Bolívar remained profoundly republican. Regardless of their differences, they had to discuss the liberation of Perú. On the evening of July 27, San Martín quietly left Guayaquil for Lima. Little is known of the true nature of their negotiations. There were no witnesses to the discussions and neither spoke about it afterward. Historians take their interpretations from the report by Bolívar's secretary and the so-called *Carta de Lafond* (Lafond letter), reportedly written by San Martín on August 29, 1822. Venezuelan historians argue that San Martín was upset over his failed aspirations at Guayaquil, as well as the fact that Bolívar would not give him any troops for his Perú campaign. He ultimately left Lima for personal reasons. Argentines argue that San Martín felt rebuffed when the *Libertador* would not give him troops for his liberation of Perú and magnanimously left, allowing Bolívar to take all the glory. The truth remains unknown. San Martín did go to Lima and in September announced his resignation. He returned to Buenos Aires and found that his wife had died. In 1823, he sailed with his daughter for France, where he died in 1850. Bolívar returned to Quito to oversee the *de jure* ratification of Quito into Gran Colombia. The *quiteñas* (female residents of Quito) entertained their liberators at social gatherings and balls. A number of Venezuelans, among them Antonio José de Sucre and Bolívar, found permanent relationships with *quiteñas*. The *Libertador* began a long-term relationship with Manuela Sáenz (1797–1856), who became his companion until his death in 1830.

Bolívar waited to see what would happen in Lima. After San Martín's departure, the political situation in Perú began to disintegrate. The Peruvians urged the *Libertador* to come to Lima. They feared the strong retinue of royalist troops still in the highlands. In response to their request, he sent troops but did not come himself. Rival factions in the triumvirate government and among the Chilean-Argentine troops argued with each other and the Peruvians. Fearing the worst, Bolívar sent Sucre ahead to take control of the troops.

Sucre reached Lima just as the royalist army attacked. Lima repulsed the royalists, but the battle convinced Bolívar that he must leave Guayaquil. On September 1, 1823, he landed in Callao. Once in Lima, he hoped to put an end to the squabbling among the troops. He could not satisfy the Chilean reinforcements who returned home, nor could he get the Peruvian navy to listen to his commands. The last straw was the mutiny at Callao, whose perpetrators freed royalist prisoners and hoisted the Spanish flag. Undaunted, Bolívar and his Colombian troops attacked the royalists, although most of them fell prey to altitude sickness. The following August, he defeated the Spanish near Lake Junín, and on December 9, 1823, he took the remainder of the royalists at Ayacucho, accomplishing the liberation of the continent.

There were still royalists to hunt down, and Bolívar sent Sucre to find them. In the meantime, Bolívar and Santander commenced the creation of the first Pan-American meeting to be held in 1826. As ordered, Sucre pacified the remainder of Perú. Cuzco and southern Perú surrendered peacefully, but Sucre followed a number of diehards into Upper Perú. With the help of the people of La Paz, he finalized the conquest of Upper Perú in April 1825, although a new political problem had arisen. Both Perú and

Argentina claimed Upper Perú, but the majority of its people wished to be independent of both. Before Bolívar could come to a decision, Sucre declared the República de Bolivia a sovereign nation. Bolívar went to Bolivia (formerly known as Upper Perú) to receive its blessings and oversee the creation of its constitution. He placed Sucre in the presidency and left for Lima.

At Lima, Bolívar continued his governmental work, and Perú adopted the Bolivarian constitution. In 1826, he left Perú for Colombia in order to consult with Santander, who had faced considerable problems during Bolívar's absence. His first job had been the promulgation of a liberal constitution and its reforms. He instituted the gradual abolition of slavery and the end of Indian tribute. He hesitated to anger the elite landowners, so he divided Indian communal lands and seized church property for the government. While Santander's intentions were honorable, they exacerbated internal difficulties. Education expanded, but Indian lands, now available for purchase, were soon taken by wealthy landowners. The abolition of slavery became an affront to some, and to others it was not enacted soon enough. His attempts to coordinate government actions seemed too arbitrary and often smacked of authoritarianism. His handling of a huge British loan came into question because the money disappeared so quickly. Rumors of government corruption had already reached Bolívar.

In addition to governmental concerns, Santander had also been responsible for sending recruits and supplies to the army in Perú. In 1826, the task of organizing the first Pan-American congress at Panamá had fallen on his shoulders. Bolívar had not rushed back to Colombia. He spent time in the company of Manuela Sáenz while he oversaw the adoption of the constitution in Lima. While Bolívar lingered in Lima, Santander oversaw the reelection of Bolívar as president of Gran Colombia. Meanwhile, Bolívar became increasingly suspicious of Santander. Rumors of corruption were mixed with civil unrest. The most serious problem seemed to be the rift that had grown between Santander and Páez. Páez had refused a direct order to appear before the Congress in Bogotá, and conflict seemed imminent. Gran Colombia seemed more fragile than ever, a situation that posed a dangerous threat since Bolívar was contemplating the creation of a Federation of the Andes.

In Venezuela, Páez considered his options. As early as 1824, it had become apparent that Venezuela did not have equitable representation in Bogotá. Venezuelans were also uncomfortable with the new constitutional reforms. The slave owners were angered by the abolition law. Men like Páez, who constituted a large portion of the military, were angered and even insulted by its moderation. Factionalism divided the country along old lines. Eastern Venezuela, for instance, sided with Santander in the vice-presidential elections to antagonize its rivals in Caracas. Other Venezuelans distrusted Santander and believed the rumors of his corruption. The military was divided over the execution of one of its colonels on what it believed was a trumped-up charge. The Colombians seemed intent on removing Páez from office as rumors circulated that Santander intended to impeach his old friend.

In the midst of these problems, Páez acted to unify Venezuela. Accused of mismanagement and fearing that impeachment might exacerbate matters, he resigned in March 1825. Surprisingly, his resignation was denied, but within a year Santander began formal impeachment proceedings. In compliance, Páez resigned again but his supporters refused to accept a Colombian yoke. He suggested that Bolívar return and consider monarchy, but the people in Valencia proclaimed Páez their leader. Páez refused to appear before the Congress in Bogotá, and his refusal constituted rebellion.

The unrest in Venezuela pulled Bolívar away from Bogotá in December 1826. Once in the country, he issued a general amnesty for Páez and his men, secretly approving of Páez's actions and confirming his leadership. He attempted to solve Venezuela's economic problems by raising tariffs and refusing anything but cash payment. His attempts to fill the treasury only turned away the very merchants who had kept the country afloat. The *Libertador* also made plans for a national convention to reform Gran Colombia's current governmental policies, which immediately brought protests from Santander. These were followed by criticism in Colombia's newspapers. Bolívar, sensing a dangerous rift developing, left for Bogotá.

Once in the capital, the *Libertador* continued his plans for a Great Convention to be held the following year. He hoped to create a more conservative constitution and entertained ideas of a lifelong presidency and an Andean Federation. On April 9, 1828, the Great Convention met. The delegates were split between a *bolivariano* faction, made up of supporters of Bolívar, and a *santanderista* faction, made up of supporters of Santander. Neither side could come to an agreement, and the Bolivarian faction returned home, leaving the convention without a quorum. In the absence of any national consensus, President Bolívar assumed dictatorial powers.

The creation of a Bolivarian dictatorship drove Venezuelans to make a decision. Even the conservatives, who should have been happy with Bolívar's reforms, refused to remain subservient to Colombia. In November 1829, the Venezuelan Congress seceded from Gran Colombia. When the new convention, known as the *Congreso Admirable* (Admirable Congress), met in Bogotá in1830, Venezuelan independence had already taken place. The Federation of the Andes never materialized, and the new constitution they passed was extremely liberal. The Congress also appointed Páez (governed 1830–1834, 1839–1843) as Venezuela's provisional president, an act that the Venezuelan Congress confirmed in 1831. Bolívar never returned to Venezuela. The new Venezuelan government forbade their countryman ever to set foot in his homeland again.

SUMMARY

After 20 years of revolts, revolutions, and wars, Venezuela finally achieved its independence. Through the efforts of such notable leaders as Francisco de Miranda, Simón Bolívar, Rafael Urdaneta, José Antonio Páez, and Antonio José de Sucre, the colony was able to break away from Spain, unite with Colombia and Ecuador, and then break away on its own. By 1830, the new nation was ready to govern itself, although the power vacuums created by the years of fighting mandated the need for a strong leader to bring peace and prosperity. Thus, the rise to power of the *llanero* José Antonio Páez ushered in a series of *caudillos*, which ruled Venezuela for the remainder of the century.

5

The Age of Caudillismo (1830-1898)

Since the breakup of Gran Colombia in 1830, Venezuela has been a republic, governed by 27 different constitutions and 42 different heads of state. After the dissolution of Gran Colombia, José Antonio Páez set up a provisional government in Venezuela and assumed the presidency. With the selection of Páez as provisional president, Venezuela entered a period in which power was transferred from one *caudillo* to another, hence the name "Age of *Caudillismo*."

In his 1812 Manifesto of Cartagena, Simón Bolívar expounded upon the factors that led to the disaster of the first republican attempt in Venezuela. This document has been considered by many as the most convincing proof of Bolívar's militant anti-federalism. Bolívar firmly believed that a republic became weakened by a federal system of government. Both the 1819 and 1821 constitutions of Gran Colombia favored centralized governments controlled from Colombia, a system quite unfavorable to most Venezuelans.

In conjunction with the separatist movement, there was also a very strong anti-Bolívar movement in Venezuela. For example, the inhabitants of the city of Valencia petitioned Páez to "not allow in any way the return of General Bolívar to Venezuelan soil," while the citizens of Puerto Cabello requested that Bolívar's name "be condemned to oblivion." In regard to the exiling of Bolívar, Páez later noted that, difficult as it might be, the expulsion of Bolívar was the best way of forestalling a civil war. The separation from Colombia did little, however, for the consolidation of Venezuela. Regional entities continued to be autonomous, and the newly independent nation developed as a fragmented, rural country with strong regional identities.

From the capital city of Valencia, a new Venezuelan constitution was drafted, signed, and promulgated by the end of 1830. The new constitution reflected the times in its creation of a republican form of government with popular representation. As was the norm in nineteenth-century Latin America, voters and officeholders had to be men over the age of 21, literate, and either landholders or businessmen with respectable income. The legislative body was bicameral, with senators and representatives. The president was elected to a four-year term, and could not be reelected for a second consecutive term. Presidents were elected toward the end of one year and took office at the beginning of the next year. The constitution made only free men citizens of Venezuela, and slavery was allowed to continue.

In response to the dissatisfaction with the Colombian-centered governments, the Venezuelan nationalist movement gained strength. The federalist rhetoric gained impetus in a Venezuela that had become discontented with the Bogotá government and the inhabitants of Nueva Granada. This group of nationalists saw in General José Antonio Páez the image of the *caudillo* that was needed to advance the Venezuelan separatist movement. Although obviously not unbiased, Páez's autobiography pointed to the fact that Venezuelan independence was neither a single man's doing nor the result of a small party's actions. Its pages profusely document the petitions of the Venezuelan people calling for the nation's emancipation from the government of Bogotá. Twice elected president under the new constitution, Páez oversaw a period of prosperity and peace that lasted until 1847. Páez's election ushered in a period of conservative oligarchy, which ruled Venezuela from 1830 to 1848.

CONSERVATIVE OLIGARCHY

Whether as president or strongman, José Antonio Páez dominated the Venezuelan political scene between 1830 and 1848. As noted, he was elected president in 1830 and again in 1838, with the conservatives José María Vargas (1786–1854), José María Carreño (1792–1849), and Carlos Soublette (1789–1870) each serving portions of the presidential term 1835–1839. In the presidential election of 1842, the conservative candidate

Carlos Soublette won the election, although Páez continued to be the power behind the office.

Even today, Páez's name is a cause of controversy. Some blame him for betraying Simón Bolívar and for having sold out to the oligarchy. Others criticize Páez for founding the Venezuelan Republic, which both Francisco de Miranda and Simón Bolívar (both more revered in Venezuela than Páez) had failed to do. The truth is, however, Páez's government did have nationalistic goals and aspirations.

The most recent historical critiques view this period of republican life as a time of prudence and positive nation-building efforts. Páez placed Venezuela's affairs of state in the hands of individuals who had studied the necessary techniques for structuring a government. Of special concern was the need to build a nation out of the chaos and ruin of war. There was a modernizing effort to free the economy from absolutist state control, which was a relic of the Spanish colonial regime, and to further free the state from military and religious responsibilities.

An assessment of Páez's foreign relations is also a positive one. Relations between the United States and Venezuela, for example, were probably the most stable in the hemisphere. Between 1830 and 1848, the ties between the two governments were quite harmonious, a level of cooperation not experienced again until the Juan Vicente Gómez (1857–1935) dictatorship (1908–1935). Historian Judith Ewell (1996) pointed out that the principal gains of Páez's regime came about because of the faith in his administration by the United States, which relieved the North American nation of the need to meddle or otherwise intervene in Venezuelan affairs. In combining political authority and military power, Páez was able to maintain control over the aristocracy (both *criollo* and royalist), over Bolívar's followers, and over the supposedly "ungovernable" colored masses. This successful control allowed Páez to project an image of trustworthiness to the outside world.

Another view of Venezuela during this time was that of Sir Robert Ker Porter (1777–1842), consul of Great Britain in Venezuela from 1825 to 1842. In his detailed diary, Porter recounted his stay in Caracas, leaving a sometimes fatalistic impression. His diary entries clearly illustrate his disdain for the Venezuelans. In one entry he stated that the mix of Spanish, African, and Indian blood resulted in a "horrible mixture in the veins of these republicans."[1] Although quite biased, Porter's diary is valuable as a historical document and serves as a unique window into Venezuelan social life, as he was an exceptional witness to contemporary Venezuelan affairs by virtue of his close ties with Caracas's high political and social circles.

Porter's commentaries regarding Páez are no less revealing. He saw talent in the leader from the *llanos*, as well as public morality and a capacity for growth. At the same time, he faulted the general for not being harsh enough. He also lamented the ease with which the locals established pacts with rebels, and noted that Venezuelans tended to be all talk and little action. His diary also expressed the reality of the country's scarcity of resources and the personal tact of Páez. In a country that lacked a solid social structure and was in the midst of inescapable political limitations, it is not surprising to find in José Antonio Páez the most seemingly suitable solution to the country's pressing ills.

The demand for coffee outside of Venezuela provided the nation with a means of economic prosperity. Through the use of force and compromise, Páez maintained internal peace that fostered domestic prosperity. By using the funds generated by coffee exports, Páez oversaw the establishment of the country's social and economic infrastructures. The Caracas elite quickly diversified to form a commercial bureaucracy to serve as intermediaries between the foreign sources of revenue and the domestic producers of coffee and cacao.[2]

By the 1840s, coffee prices had dropped dramatically and President Páez began to lose his political support among some of the Venezuelan elite. For the most part, two major political factions emerged: the conservatives, who remained loyal to Páez, and the liberals, who opposed Páez. The official rupture among the elites occurred in August 1840, with the establishment of the Liberal party. Among the leaders of the Conservative party were Páez, José María Vargas, and Carlos Soublette; the Liberals were headed by the party founder, Antonio Leocadio Guzmán. These parties were not based on political ideology, but were rather two different groups trying to achieve political power. Guzmán carried out his attacks against the Conservative government through the weekly newspaper, *El Venezolano*.

LIBERAL OLIGARCHY

General José Tadeo Monagas (1784–1868) and his brother, José Gregorio Monagas (1795–1858), joined the Liberal party in its early days. After co-opting the federalists, the Liberals became known as the Yellow Liberals, although there was no specific policy program that the party followed. The Liberals first came to national political prominence in 1846, when Páez selected José Tadeo Monagas as his successor. The belief was that, once in power, Monagas's views would become more moderate. Monagas won the election, although he would eventually lose the support of both the Liberals and the Conservatives. In 1848, Monagas ousted the Conservatives from his government and sent former president Páez into exile, initiating 10 years of dictatorial rule by the Monagas brothers. The ensuing fiscal and economic disorder proved to be fertile ground for the proliferation of corruption and graft. José Tadeo Monagas, a war hero who had grown rich during the independence wars, was not a man who liked to share power with others, including those who had supported him.

José Tadeo Monagas used the political parties in order to govern as a dictator. He appointed inept bureaucrats from the eastern part of the country to high-ranking government posts, primarily because of their blind obedience to him. Opposition newspapers were closed down, and the Congress showed signs of submitting to Monagas's executive power. Throughout the republic's young life, the governments of the brothers José Tadeo and José Gregorio Monagas were the most defined examples of political personalism yet. Far from shoring up public order, the regimes of the Monagas brothers primarily served as a prelude to the upcoming chaos of the Federal War.

The administrations of the two Monagas brothers were noted for both positive as well as negative aspects. For example, during their tenure in office, slavery was abolished (1854) and the 1830 constitution was reformed (1857). At the same time, the economic downturn in Venezuela's export commodities created fiscal problems. These problems were further exacerbated by the actions of the central government, which reduced the autonomy and authority of the provinces and aggravated the existing tensions between the provinces and Caracas. The blatant self-enrichment and self-promotion tactics of the Monagas family forced a faction within the Liberals to join forces with Conservative groups under the slogan "*Unión de los venezolanos y olvido de lo pasado*" (roughly translated as "Venezuelans uniting and forgetting the past"). This collaborative movement eventually ousted the Monagas regime in March 1858.

FEDERAL WAR

The Conservative and Liberal factions failed to agree on a replacement for Monagas, resulting in 12 years of intermittent civil war. Between March 1858 and July 1863, local *caudillos* engaged in a chaotic power struggle known as the Federal War, stemming from the fact that the Liberals favored federalism. This civil war was also known as the *Guerra Larga* (Long War), the *Revolución Federal* (Federal Revolution), and the *Guerra de los Cinco Años* (Five Years War). It was, after the wars of independence, the longest civil war Venezuela has ever endured.

Background

In terms of its social and political undertones, which had remained unresolved since the separation of Venezuela from Gran Colombia, the Federal War constituted a continuation of the independence movement. With the birth of the Republic of Venezuela in 1830, a consensus arose among the victorious *caudillos* that the status quo had to be preserved, thus ensuring an oligarchic system of government. This government would then allow not only the ruling elites, or *mantuanos*, of colonial times to retain power, but would also include among its ranks the victorious military *caudillos* from the emancipation struggles. The privilege and prestige of these *caudillos* had been confirmed with the generous tracts of land they had been awarded after the transfer of lands of the colonial *latifundias* from the Spaniards to the emancipated *criollos* and *mestizos*.

As early as the first internal rebellions (1830–1831) fought in the eastern areas of the young nation, the regional *caudillos* attempted to erode the centralized power base of General José Antonio Páez in favor of a system that granted them greater authority. These insurrections represented the most ardent manifestations of the staunchly regionalistic *caudillo* system. Thus, these regional *caudillos* favored a federalist political system that would best allow them to maintain their regional control. The so-called *Revolución de las Reformas* (Revolution of the Reforms) of 1835–1836 constituted one of these efforts by the regional landowning *caudillos* to limit the centralized power of Páez and the ruling elites. These uprisings also sought to give the regional landowning *caudillos* greater political and economic autonomy.

The War

Following these decades of conflict, the revolution of 1858 set in motion the chain of events that would precipitate the Federal War. In the end, the war gruesomely confirmed the fact that Venezuela had not been able to identify itself with its institutions and laws, nor had the integrationist movement been forceful enough to prevail and take root. In addition, the Federal War gave rise to a new political leadership and put an end to generals who favored provincial secession, but it brought neither peace nor a nation-state. The Federal War was essentially a *guerrilla* war, and it did not involve all of Venezuela. During the conflict, the political debate in Caracas remained centered around the traditional opposition between liberalism and conservatism. For the most part, the Liberals were federalists and the Conservatives were centralists.

The leadership of the federalists originally rested on the shoulders of such military men as General Ezequiel Zamora (1817–1860), whose program was essentially intellectual and political and more radical than moderate. However, the *"grito de la federación"* ("cry of the federation") would bring with it once again the disruptive participation of the *llaneros*. The traditional confrontation between the egalitarian ideals of the *llanero* culture and the regimented ideals of hierarchical culture was at the core of the Federal War. More than a mere rebellion of *campesino* and rural values, the Federal War became an attempt to unite two separate Venezuelan realities: that of white Venezuelans in power and that of racially mixed Venezuelans from the hinterlands. However, in the end, the war did not change the existing structure of the traditionally agrarian society. As such, the war's social impact was ultimately insignificant. The political leadership of the federalist insurrection forces, especially after the death of General Zamora in January 1860, was exercised by various groups, including landowners, members of the urban middle class, and *caudillos* of a bourgeois ideology. This varied leadership helps explain the gap between the reasons given for rebellion and the popular reaction those reasons received.

The heaviest fighting took place in the *llanos* region, in the modern-day states of Barinas, Portuguesa, Cojedes, Apure, and Guárico. Scattered *guerrilla* fighting also took place in the central part of the country—in what are now the states of Falcón, Lara, Yaracuy, Carabobo, and Aragua—as well as in the eastern part of the country, especially in modern-day Anzoátegui and Sucre states. Entire areas of the country, such as the Andes, Guayana, and the areas in what is now the state of Zulia, remained unaffected by the armed conflict. Livestock farming was the worst hit agricultural sector; other sectors were not nearly as adversely affected.

Once the initial consensus of the revolution of March 1858 was lost, President Julián Castro (1805–1875) (governed 1858–1859) sought whatever favorable alliance he could that would allow him to remain in power. His political machinations precipitated his downfall, and his eventual replacement with the conservative-leaning governments of Pedro Gual (1783–1862) (governed intermittently from 1858–1861) and Manuel Felipe de Tovar (1803–1866) (governed 1860–1861). Within the conservative party, however, two factions emerged: the constitutionalists or legalists, who favored a civilian government and supported Pedro Gual and Manuel Felipe de Tovar; and the dictatorials, led by Pedro José Rojas (1818–1874), who supported José Antonio Páez as the only viable leader who could reestablish the peace.

While continuing to confront the Liberals, the 78-year old Gual was unable to control the conspiracies of the *paecistas* (supporters of Páez); he fell from power in August 1861, was arrested in his home, and exiled. As such, José Antonio Páez returned to the presidency in March 1861, which increased the political tensions that led to the ouster of President Gual. While Páez served as president, real power resided in Pedro José Rojas. During this time, the Conservative party was reduced to various groups that lacked any sense of direction and any specific agenda. Páez sought negotiations with the federalist leader Juan Crisóstomo Falcón (1820–1870) in hopes of reaching common ground. Such attempts at bridging the gap between the Conservatives and the Liberals came to naught, and the armed struggle continued until the centralist (Conservative) surrender through the Treaty of Coche was negotiated in April 1863.

It is difficult to determine the human impact of the Federal War. Some estimates place the death toll between 150,000 and 200,000, which meant a loss of between 8 and 11 percent of the nation's overall population. Diseases, such as malaria and dysentery, accounted for a greater proportion of those deaths than did fighting. Demographically speaking, the Federal War resulted in massive migrations. Not only in terms of the combatants displaced within the theaters of war, but also in terms of the civilian masses who sought refuge in other areas of the country. Particularly relevant was the migration of people from what are now the states of Barinas and Portuguesa toward the Andean states of Táchira, Mérida, and Trujillo.

The conciliatory peace forged in the Treaty of Coche meant only a nominal triumph for the federalist cause. In reality, the aspirations of a federation never became anything more than mere ideals. Juan Crisóstomo Falcón shared the spoils of war with his closest circle of cronies, so one type of corruption was merely replaced by another. In the end, the basic foundations of Venezuela's oligarchic society remain unchanged. The spirit of the Federal War as a racial war or as a war for social equality never amounted to more than mere rhetorical debate among the country's political elite.

THE FEDERAL EXPERIMENT

In the end, the Liberals triumphed and General Juan C. Falcón was named president, with Antonio Guzmán Blanco as his vice president. The federal constitution of 1864, drafted under the direction of Guzmán Blanco, granted greater federal participation to the general population and the individual states. However, it also created many of the very problems that undermined the consolidation of state institutions. For example, the constitution allowed two or more states to unite and form a separate unit or secede if they saw fit. Despite the constitution's failings, national and state legislators managed to disregard and work around the fact that the regional and local *caudillos* often refused to relinquish their territorial powers, a fact that inevitably led to further conflict. Other factors also contributed to the unlikelihood that a liberal state would take root. The historical facts tend to support the view that the concept of a unified state in Venezuela was nothing more than a fictional ideal promoted by the elite class. The regionalist sentiment was forcefully prevalent and accounts for the reasons why Coro, Guayana, and Maracaibo did not join the Republican cause in 1810. The latter two regions, both important economic centers in their own right, openly challenged the authority of Caracas on several occasions.

Inheriting an economy in shambles and a country in chaos, the federalist government was far from peaceful. At the end of 1867, President Falcón was faced with the *Revolución Azul* (Blue Revolution), so named because the revolutionaries adopted a blue badge as their sign, and led by former president José Tadeo Monagas. After driving Falcón from Venezuela, the *azules* (the Blues) supported Monagas until a new government could be chosen. Later that same year, José Tadeo Monagas died, and his son, José Ruperto Monagas (1831–1880), was named his successor by the Congress in 1869.

In many Latin American nations during the nineteenth century— Venezuela being no exception—the majority of the chief executives assumed the principles of personalism, whereby their actions did not follow the dictates of the law, but rather the will of the ruler. In Venezuela, personalism *(personalismo)* had its roots in colonial society, manifesting itself during the War of Independence, and further developed after 1830 through a staunch "good old boy" network of friendships and client-based relationships. A strong central government was finally restored in 1870 by President Falcón's aide, Antonio Guzmán Blanco, who established a dictatorship that endured for 18 years.

THE GUZMANATO

Dissatisfied with the government of José Ruperto Monagas (governed 1869–1870), General Antonio Guzmán Blanco and the Yellow Liberals were successful in ousting the government in April 1870. From then until 1887, Venezuela was ruled—directly or indirectly—by Guzmán Blanco, who was president on three occasions: *el septenio* (1870–1877), *el quinquenio* (1879–1884), and *la aclamación* or *bienio* (1886–1888). During his administrations, cities were transformed and modernized, especially Caracas.

Many public buildings and monuments, such as the Capitol, Plaza Bolívar, the Caracas Municipal Theatre, and the National Pantheon, were built. In addition, the transportation infrastructure was improved to include a Caracas–Valencia road, the development of the ports of La Guaira and Puerto Cabello, and the establishment of the first railroad system. The government also built an aqueduct to supply Caracas with water.

In terms of domestic issues, primary education became free and compulsory, and Venezuelan currency was standardized in order to facilitate commerce. Prior to 1871, different coinage circulated in different regions of the country. However, in that year, the *venezolano* or *peso fuerte* was created as the national currency, bearing the image of Simón Bolívar on one side and the national seal on the other. Political and economic power became centralized in order to facilitate control over the nation and to undermine the power of the regional *caudillos*. In addition, the number of states was reduced from 20 to 9.

In effect, Guzmán Blanco was able to vanquish all other *caudillos*. He removed disloyal conservative *caudillos* by force and replaced them with loyal liberal regional strongmen. Through the benefits of a rapid expansion of coffee production and foreign loans, "The Illustrious American," as he was called, had at his disposal considerable resources to maintain his supporters. As a consequence, Guzmán Blanco brought nearly two decades of peace to Venezuela.

In 1877, after his first term in office of seven years or *septenio*, Francisco Linares Alcántara (1825–1878) assumed power and took actions contrary to Guzmán Blanco's wishes. Open conflict ensued between the *guzmancistas* and the *alcantaristas*, and this is what came to be known as the *Revolución Reivindicadora* (Vindicating Revolution). The *guzmancistas* were victorious and marched into Caracas, with Guzmán Blanco returning to power once again. This time, he was in power for a five-year term, *el quinquenio*, at the end of which General Joaquín Crespo (1841–1898) assumed power. Crespo was a loyal follower of Guzmán Blanco and ruled during the new constitutional period, which had been reduced to two years, from 1884 to 1886. In 1886, Guzmán Blanco was unanimously acclaimed by the Federal Council (comprised of one senator and one deputy from each state) to rule for another two years.

The most vigorous attempt to create a national state in the nineteenth century occurred during the regime of Antonio Guzmán Blanco. This was only the second time in Venezuelan republican history during which the affairs of state followed a peaceful and well-intentioned course. By the end of his third and last administration, Venezuela possessed public works, modern laws, national symbols and sentiments, and an administration that was capable of expanding its control throughout the entire nation. Through successful military campaigns, Guzmán Blanco defeated the *caudillos'* armed opposition and, consequently, announced his intent to enforce respect for the centralized government throughout the republic. Above all, however, thanks in part to his agreements with regional leaders, he enacted a significant campaign of modernization that required the fulfillment of the conditions necessary for the establishment of a state along with an impetus to economic development.

Despite his dominance and efforts at modernization, many of the achievements of the Guzmán Blanco regime did not survive the test of time. Perhaps it was because the goal of building a nation was undermined by a succession of minor *caudillos.* Or perhaps it gave priority to the essentially personalistic nature of such leaders, thus preventing the continuance of reforms beyond the time the leader is in power.

The four years that followed Guzmán Blanco's rule were marked by several failed attempts to consolidate a civilian government. In 1888, Juan Pablo Rojas Paúl (1826–1905) (governed 1888–1890) was elected president, followed by Raimundo Andueza Palacio (1846–1900), who governed from 1890 to 1892. Rojas Paúl and Andueza Palacio were the only two civilian presidents since 1835, with the exception of the two brief terms of Pedro Gual and Manuel Felipe de Tovar during the Federal War. Andueza Palacio attempted to make significant changes in the constitution, which created a political storm across Venezuela. Under the banner of the *Revolución Legalista* (Legalist Revolution), former president Joaquín Crespo marched on Caracas in June 1892 and took control of the government until 1898. The winner of the 1898 elections was the government's candidate, Ignacio Andrade (1839?–1925) (governed 1898–1899), who defeated his main rival José Manuel Hernández (1853–1921). Hernández accused Andrade of having won because of governmental favoritism, and he challenged the election results. General Joaquín Crespo himself joined in the fight against Hernández, and lost his life in the conflict. In 1899, while Andrade was preparing for reelection, he was overthrown by General Cipriano Castro (1858–1924).

BOUNDARY DISPUTE

One issue that dominated Venezuelan foreign policy during the latter half of the nineteenth century was the boundary dispute between Venezuela and Great Britain. The involvement of the United States in the matter also created diplomatic tension between Great Britain and the United States during much of the same time. At the core of the dispute was the exact boundary between Venezuela and British Guiana (modern-day nation of Guyana). The Venezuelan claim, extending east to the Essequibo River—thus taking in most of the settled areas of British Guiana—had been inherited from Spain. The British claimed the land they had acquired from the Dutch in 1810, stretching west from British Guiana to the Orinoco River. The dispute took on added significance in the 1840s, when the discovery of gold in the region intensified the claims. Great Britain refused to arbitrate the dispute, while Venezuela maintained that the British were simply delaying a resolution so they could advance their settlements farther into the disputed area. Venezuela sought assistance from the United States and eventually (in 1887) broke off diplomatic relations with Great Britain. U.S. President Grover Cleveland's first administration (1885–1889) attempted negotiations, but without success.

Into the mix stepped U.S. Secretary of State Richard Olney, who issued his "Olney Declaration" in 1895. His position was a broad interpretation of the Monroe Doctrine, which argued that the United States had dominance in the Western Hemisphere. Olney demanded that the parties involved use arbitration to resolve the issue, stating the position that the Monroe Doctrine gave the United States the right to intercede if necessary. The British government offered to submit resolution of some of the disputed area to arbitration but refused to have the entire region available for discussion. In what was perceived as a rebuff to Secretary Olney, the second Grover Cleveland administration (1893–1897) sent a message to Congress (December 17, 1895) that denounced the British refusal to arbitration. The administration also maintained that it was the responsibility of the U.S. government to take steps to determine the boundary, as well as to resist any British aggression beyond that boundary once it had been set.

In an effort to avert war and deal with more pressing international issues, the British government eventually sent a conciliatory note accepting Olney's interpretation of the Monroe Doctrine. An American commission was appointed, and the boundary was determined in 1899. As it turned out, the determination was favorable to Great Britain. The granting of independence to Guyana in 1966 further sparked the boundary controversy. Venezuelans refer to the disputed region as the *Zona en Reclamación* (Contested Zone), and the country has occasionally attempted to restate its claims to the disputed territory, most recently in 2000.

SUMMARY

The personalization of political action, along with the reemergence of regional identities were two elements that persisted throughout the nineteenth century in Venezuela. The lack of a definitive explanation for these tendencies renders it essential to review once more the causes leading to such a state of affairs. Geography alone cannot sufficiently explain the regional peculiarities, nor can it explain the configuration of political personalism.

The issue posed above is not an original one. It is a fairly common historical problem in the formation of a state and of a nation. When the ties with Spain were broken in Latin America during the first two decades of the nineteenth century, a power void was created. In Venezuela, as in many other Latin American nations, the void was filled by a multitude of power centers, which basically replaced the Spanish colonial political and administrative jurisdictions.

The most common response to this disunity throughout Latin America was the success of the *caudillo* and the imposition of a dictatorial order. In this sense, Venezuela was no exception. In fact, the issue that sets Venezuela apart is the comparatively late construction of its national state. Personalism in the exercise of power and the push for regional autonomy during the nineteenth century were elements that reflected the absence of an effective state-building machinery, as well as the lack of a deep-rooted concept of nationhood. If the push for regionalism was the result of the very brief but integral Spanish control over the whole of the Venezuelan provinces, then political personalism was the answer that sought to find order amid unfavorable and even adverse social and economic conditions. The regional differences in the concept of personalism probably appeared in republican life as an extension of the traits present in the earlier Spanish colonial order.

Such an inheritance was reinforced by the effects of the wars of emancipation. However, the development of the historical process did not take place uniformly. Historians such as Tulio Halpering Donghi point out that, in the Andean region of the country, armies formed as a result of the Wars of Independence, which were powerful enough to impose upon the state and society the burden of supporting them. Throughout Latin America, the process evolved differently. Venezuela arrived at the end of the independence conflict with a great deal of its military outside its national borders, a fact that favored the enterprise of eliminating the military from national power. However, demobilization did not bring with it a lasting reduction of *caudillismo*. The new republican life was far from being able to block the development of the *caudillo* phenomenon. Its presence accounts for the fact that, between 1830 and 1945, the country was unable to experience eight continuous years of civilian government.

It is not accidental that the rebellious Venezuelan provinces adopted a federal system of government. It is worth noting that the appearance of federalism in Venezuela at the turn of the nineteenth century was not the result of an effort to simply imitate the constitutionalism of the United States. The predisposition to favor a federal form of government had a historical foundation that had its roots in colonial government.

Historian Manuel Pérez Vila expressed a view held by many Venezuelans when he remarked (1984) that, if nationalism preceded nationhood in Venezuela, then the nineteenth century can be viewed as a long arduous road toward the building of a nation. The unsuccessful efforts at developing a national unity in 1830, 1864, and 1898 were characterized by a dif ference in mentality, by a diversity of regional interests, and by the lack of an adequate means of internal communication.

Political life in nineteenth-century Latin America was characterized by competing networks of friends and followers, the so called *patronazgo* structures. Upon examining the statistics, the facts seem horrendous. In the whole of the nineteenth century, there were only 16 years of peace (1837–1846 and 1885–1892). The averages are also quite telling: 12 acts of war per year, which averages out to one war per month. Given such data, the skepticism mentioned above seems to be a legitimate reaction. Venezuelan historian Guillermo Morón noted a curiosity of 1873 Venezuela that sheds light on these statistics: In that year, the Venezuelan state of Carabobo alone had 449 generals, 627 colonels, 967 majors, 818 captains, 504 lieutenants, and 85 second-lieutenants. These staggering numbers comprised 15 percent of the active male population of the state who were over the age of 21. Thus, the frequency of revolution in Venezuela seems fairly logical.

As we will explore in the next chapter, a fundamental turnaround began to take place in Venezuelan political life in 1899, with the emergence of Cipriano Castro. From the Andean state of Táchira, Castro rose up in rebellion against the constitution of 1893. Through the liberal *Revolución Restauradora* (Restorative Revolution), Castro fought to defend the principles of the federation, although the revolution would give rise, paradoxically, to a heavily centralized state. An observer who views Venezuela in the final years of the nineteenth century with the hope of organizing and understanding the multitude and variety of issues facing the region, could legitimately inquire as to whether there was a political order that guaranteed a course for collective life.

In conclusion, it is understandable how Venezuela became unified so late in its political existence. There was, after all, no political unity in Venezuela upon the Spaniards' arrival. There was no single great center of power among the various culturally underdeveloped pre-Columbian tribes who populated the national territory. The first instance of political unity occurred only three decades prior to the independence movement when the Spanish Bourbon King Carlos III decreed the establishment of a captaincy-general at Caracas. Neither the War of Independence nor the Federal War was able to generate the creation of a national state. This failure was, in no small part, a result of the phenomenon of regional divisionism in Venezuela throughout the entire nineteenth century. The creation of a national state in Venezuela did not follow the course of negotiation and compromise. There was never a compromise that might have allowed federal states to voluntarily cede some of their sovereignty to a central government in order to form a greater national unity. Without a voluntary compromise, the problem was solved by force. The state was created by the work of despots who maintained national unity not in the face of a foreign enemy, but rather as an instrument for combating the tendencies caused by regional differences.

NOTES

1. Robert Ker Porter, *Diario de un diplomático británico en Venezuela, 1825–1842* (Caracas: Fundación Polar, 1997), 242.

2. John Martz and David Myers, *Venezuela: The Democratic Experience* (New York: Praeger, 1977), 13.

6

Restoration and Rehabilitation (1899–1935)

A fundamental turnaround began to take place in Venezuelan political life in 1899, with the arrival to power of Cipriano Castro (governed 1899–1908) and his lieutenant, Juan Vicente Gómez. Even though Cipriano Castro fought to defend the principles of federalism, his revolution gave rise to a heavily centralized Venezuelan state. During Castro's administration, Venezuela experienced a transition whereby it was finally able to shed the turmoil of the nineteenth century. This transition would allow the country to enter the twentieth century under an aura of modernization and order. Among the most influential phenomena that forced the country to seize its new modern outlook were the end of political fragmentation, the influx of a forward-looking mentality into leadership roles, and the development of a nationalistic identity. During the administrations of Cipriano Castro and Juan Vicente Gómez, Venezuela's social structure was radically transformed, a regular army was established, and a national bureaucratic administration was created. In addition, after 1918, Venezuela became the beneficiary of an autonomous source of revenue from the exploitation of its oil resources, with which the nation generated its own economic base.

CASTRO'S RESTORATION

Castro's government consisted of a transitional period between the so-called yellow liberalism of the *caudillo* past and a more participatory government. Similar to his predecessor, Castro's tenure was one of personalism, as well as a regime marred by corruption in top administrative levels. Castro's liberal *Revolución Restauradora* (Restorative Revolution) was, in fact, the direct result of the decentralization and turmoil brought about during President Ignacio Andrade's administration (1898–1899), upon the death of General Joaquín Crespo (1898), his most powerful military supporter. The sudden loss of Crespo's support, coupled with rising international pressure to repay the country's foreign debt, led to a period of domestic strife and dissension. This domestic turmoil paved the way for General Castro's eventual overthrow of the Andrade government.

Under Castro's banner of radical change, new men, new ideas, and new procedures became the building blocks of a new revolutionary era in the country's development. The *Revolución Restauradora* owed its success to the imposition of the will of an aggressive and united leadership against various military and political figures. In the end, several opposition leaders fled into exile, including President Andrade. Upon Andrade's departure, Cipriano Castro began to forge alliances with the remaining *caudillos*, some of whom had originally opposed him. This move essentially put an end to the country's long tradition of *caudillismo* and political fragmentation.

President Castro also enjoyed the ever-increasing support of an inner circle of sympathizers, known as the *Círculo Valenciano* (Valencian Circle), whose members were long-time supporters of Castro and had accompanied his triumphant entry into the Venezuelan city of Valencia. Castro came to power leaving Colombia with 60 men under his command, and marching into Caracas on October 22, 1899, with over 2,000 followers. He was first named provisional president, until the constitution was modified in 1904, after which he was named president for the period 1904–1911. His vice president was Juan Vicente Gómez, who was one of the original 60 men who started the movement with Castro.

During his time in office, Castro faced both internal and external enemies. Within Venezuela, his opponents included the *latifundistas* (large landholders), financed by some within the banking sector. This movement came to be known as the *Revolución Libertadora* (Liberating Revolution).

Naval Blockade

Not highly regarded by the international community, Castro's government is best known for the 1902 naval blockade by British, German, and Italian units seeking redress for the claims of their citizens against Venezuela. According to Kelvin Singh (1999), British imperialist interests in Venezuela included the desire to acquire as much of the gold-bearing area of the disputed Venezuela–British Guiana region as possible; the desire to ensure free navigation of the Orinoco River, which would facilitate the development of expanded British trade with Venezuela, Colombia, and Northern Brazil; and the hope to secure the abolition of the 30 percent surtax on goods shipped from the British and Dutch Antilles, particularly Trinidad and Curaçao. The French and German interests were primarily financial, largely diplomatic claims and debts owed to their bondholders and companies operating in Venezuela.

Singh also pointed out that these interests were interwoven with the geopolitical advantages that these powers already had or aspired to in the Caribbean region. The conflict was finally resolved thanks to public pressure in England, Germany, and France. Added to this public pressure was the intervention in 1903 of U.S. President Theodore Roosevelt, who offered to serve as mediator. Under pressure from Roosevelt, Venezuela promised to pay its debt, and the European powers agreed to end the blockade and return the Venezuelan ships they had seized. Apparently, Castro had not learned his lesson, as several more international incidents occurred during the remaining five years of his presidency. In the end, Cipriano Castro had the same motives as had previous *caudillos*: ambition for power.[1]

In November 1908, President Castro traveled to Europe for medical treatment of a kidney ailment. The next month, Vice President Juan Vicente Gómez seized upon the opportunity to overthrow the Castro administration. In a few very well-planned maneuvers and troop rotations, Cipriano Castro's *Restauración* was replaced by Juan Vicente Gómez's *Rehabilitación*, with the slogan of *Paz, Unión, y Trabajo* (Peace, Union, and Work). After pledging to the international community that his government would honor Venezuela's commitments to them, Gómez received diplomatic recognition and international support. In fact, when former president Castro attempted to return to Venezuela and depose Gómez, U.S. President William Howard Taft ordered a U.S. warship to Venezuela to protect Gómez.

GÓMEZ'S REHABILITATION

Juan Vicente Gómez became the ideal Venezuelan *caudillo*. He retained de facto absolute power from 1908 to 1935, alternating between the posts of president, president-elect, and minister of war. At all times from 1908 to 1935, he remained commander-in-chief of the military. During his rule,

Venezuela experienced repression and torture. Without a doubt, the rise of Gómez signaled the end of the era of the regional *caudillo*.

The Gómez era witnessed an expansion in the Venezuelan economy. At first, a boom in coffee exports provided increased revenue for the nation. After 1918, the exploitation of Venezuela's petroleum reserves began to provide the government with revenues in amounts previously unknown in the South American country. It is because of this relationship between the repressive regime and its utilization of the newly found revenue generated by the petroleum industry that the Gómez tenure has also been called a "petroleum dictatorship." The Gómez government granted infinite incentives to the petroleum exploration enterprise, and a small circle of the dictator's friends enjoyed this national resource as if it were their own. The enormous increase in national revenue allowed Gómez to pay off Venezuela's foreign debt and undertake a massive public works program. It was during this time that an urban middle class emerged in Venezuela, primarily associated with the petroleum industry. For most Venezuelans, the petroleum era did not bring with it additional jobs, increased wages, or an improvement in their standard of living. Instead, the oil boom brought about a decline in domestic agriculture, an increase in imports, and inflation. In addition, public education and health care witnessed little improvement during this time period.

As noted above, the true beneficiaries of the petroleum industry bonanza were Gómez and his associates and cronies. This is especially true for those who hailed from Gomez's home state of Táchira, located in the Andes Mountains. Gómez also used the increased revenue to reshape the Venezuelan army into a force dominated by fellow *tachirenses* (people from Táchira). Thus, the army became a beneficiary of the petroleum revenue and, at the same time, an instrument of power for President Gómez. Through his indiscriminate use of the army, Gómez eliminated his regional foes and political opponents. Another important instrument of Gómez's dictatorship was his omnipresent secret police force, known as *la Sagrada*. At the hands of the army and the secret police, tens of thousands of Venezuelans were routinely imprisoned and put to death by starvation or torture.

The Great War

On July 28, 1914, the Austro-Hungarian Empire declared war on the Kingdom of Serbia. This declaration—sent via telegram—started what came to be known as The Great War (after 1939, this war became known as World War I) between the Central powers (Germany, Austria-Hungary, Ottoman Empire, and Bulgaria) and the Allied powers (France, Russia, England, Italy, United States, and so forth). Of the 20 Latin American republics, 8 eventually declared war, 5 simply severed relations with the Central Powers, and 7 officially opted for neutrality. Thus, slightly more than half of Latin America voiced in some official manner its solidarity with, and sympathy for, the United States and/or the Allies. Of the 8 countries that declared war, only 2—Brazil and Cuba—took an active part in the global conflict.

Throughout World War I (1914–1918), the Venezuelan government pursued a policy of strict neutrality. This foreign policy was based primarily on two considerations. First, Gómez feared that any military support that Venezuela could provide would militarily weaken his regime at home and possibly give rise to revolution. Second, Venezuela was apprehensive of intervention. If Venezuela sided with the Allies, there was an expectation that Germany would intervene in Venezuela. At the same time, if Venezuela sided with Germany, it was believed that the Allies would depose Gómez and establish a government more favorable to them.

It thus became very important for the Venezuelan government to walk a thin, and often dangerous, line of neutrality. To Venezuela, neutrality clearly became a national imperative, and to Gómez it became a righteous vehicle that might allow him to remain in power. Accordingly, Venezuela constantly reiterated its policy of neutrality, spelling out very clearly the country's duties and obligations in this respect. In fact, the Venezuelan government proposed that a Congress of Neutrals be organized to consider the rights and duties of neutrals with regard to modern warfare. In turn, this Congress would submit its conclusions to a conference of all nations, which would incorporate these findings into the laws of nations as an effective assurance for peace in the future.

There was also financial pressure upon Gómez, which was reflected in American-Venezuelan relations, especially at the time when the United States broke off diplomatic relations with Germany. It was further felt by the German colony in Venezuela—and in some sections of the native population—that, since German citizens and sympathizers were unable to enlist in active support of Germany, measures would have to be taken to prevent supporters of the Allies from fighting on their side. Accordingly, it was decreed that Venezuelan citizens enlisting in belligerent armies would forfeit their diplomatic protection. This decree was actually aimed against the Allies, since they ruled the seas and no Venezuelan sympathizer could reach Germany.

Even though Venezuela remained neutral, Gómez found the spirit and practice of the German system of government congenial and worthy of emulation. Thomas Rourke noted in his biography of Gómez that when the war erupted, the Venezuelan dictator's uniforms became very German, as evidenced in pictures of him wearing a spiked helmet, carrying a sword, and his mustache trained upward like the German kaiser's. Although Gómez, personally, was apparently pro-German, not all members of his government supported the German position. In fact, many officials were ardent advocates of friendship and support of the United States.

Venezuela adhered to its policy of strict neutrality. In fact, the foremost principle that guided the Venezuelan government was consistency. On the whole, it can probably be concluded that the status of Venezuela as a neutral nation was not significant to the overall war effort. The country was separated by an ocean from warring Germany and was effectively prevented from sending any appreciable amount of goods to the Central powers by an Anglo blockade. In fact, this was the main reason why U.S. export controls were applied much less stringently to Latin American neutrals than to European neutrals.

A Changing Economy

The Venezuelan economy shifted after World War I from a primarily agricultural base to an economy centered on petroleum production and export. As noted previously, the only viable sector of the Venezuelan economy was coffee production. By 1914, Venezuela harvested over one million bags per year and exported more coffee than any other country except Brazil. At the same time that coffee exports were increasing, exports of cacao and cattle hides were decreasing. Prior to World War I, the truth of the matter is that Venezuela was not commercially significant in the global economic system.

As noted in chapter 1, the native inhabitants of Venezuela knew of the petroleum deposits long before the arrival of the Europeans. The natural seepages of crude petroleum had been occurring around Lake Maracaibo for centuries, and the early Spanish explorers noted that the natives used crude oil to caulk and repair their canoes. Centuries later, when the United States began to utilize petroleum on a larger scale, Venezuelans saw the commercial possibilities. The first commercial oil well in Venezuela was drilled in February 1914, and three years later Venezuela began exporting petroleum. By 1926, the country was exporting about 37 million barrels of oil per year; by 1928, it was exporting slightly more than 100 million barrels a year, more than any other country in the world.

Domestic Unrest

Although General Gómez was able, for the most part, to maintain domestic tranquility through the use of force and intimidation, there were over 20 notable armed revolts during his tenure. Among the more important revolts were those led by Emilio Arévalo Cedeño (1882–1965), José Rafael Gabaldón (1882–1975), Román Delgado Chalbaud (1882–1929), Horacio Ducharne (1865–1915), and Juan Pablo Peñaloza (1855–1932). At the same time, there were several student-led protests against the Gómez dictatorship, most notably the protests of 1912, 1917, 1921, and 1928.

Of these protests, the February 1928 student movement at the Universidad Central de Venezuela (Central University of Venezuela) in Caracas, stands out as a watershed event in modern Venezuelan history. Familiar with successful anti-totalitarian regimes in other countries, such as the Mexican Revolution of 1910, the student leaders attempted to initiate a movement to free Venezuela from the tyranny of Gómez. The protest movement began when Jóvito Villalba (1908–1989) and two other students were arrested for publicly speaking out against the government. To protest these arrests, more students joined the antigovernment activities and were also arrested. A popular demonstration followed and was met with a forceful response from the government, in which numerous participants were killed and wounded. Gómez responded by closing the university and rounding up the students, many of whom went to prison. Some of the student leaders of this protest movement—known as the "Generation of 1928"—died in prison, others escaped into exile. Among this group of students were some who would become Venezuela's major political leaders, such as Rómulo Betancourt (1908–1981), Jóvito Villalba (1909–1989), and Raúl Leoni (1905–1972).

SUMMARY

The twentieth century began for Venezeula when Cipriano Castro assumed power in 1899. The Castro administration began the process of centralization for Venezuela, and Castro's efforts allowed his successor, Juan Vicente Gómez, to bring about the process of modernization. For over 25 years, Gómez ruled the nation as a brutal dictator, utilizing resources from the coffee and petroleum industries to carry forward his plans for growth and modernization. When Gómez's death was announced in December 1935, the majority of Venezuelans were in disbelief. Only after the newspapers published photographs of Gómez lying in his coffin did throngs of elated Venezuelans dare to shout "the catfish is dead!" It was now official; the nineteenth-century model of *caudillismo* was dead.

NOTE

1. Guillermo Moron, *A History of Venezuela* (London: George Allen & Unwin, 1964), 183.

7

The Emergence of Modern Venezuela (1935–1958)

The goal of modernization has been very important for Latin Americans in general, and Venezuelans in particular. In a sense, humans become anguished at the thought of being left behind and excluded by progress. Civilization versus barbarism, rural versus urban, federalism versus centralism, and democracy versus dictatorship are but a few of the conflicts in which this anguish is expressed. As such, the concept of modernization becomes a point of convergence for rivals. The goal of modernization was led by several distinct social elements within Venezuela, each of which carried out a very different version of what it viewed as modernization. For example, modernization has been led by an educated civil-military elite (Eleazar López Contreras [1883–1973] and Isaías Medina Angarita [1897–1953]), a peoples' party, *Acción Democrática* (Democratic Action) (AD), a working-class party, the *Partido Comunista de Venezuela* (Venezuelan Communist Party) (PCV), and a conciliatory party, the *Comité de Organización Política Electoral Independiente* (Committee for Independent Electoral Political Organization) (COPEI). In addition, there are social elements such as the armed forces and a populist modernization effort that involved an alliance of Venezuelan elites.

TRANSITION TO DEMOCRACY

During transition from dictatorial to democratic rule, new political institutions developed as power transferred from the military to civilians. However, the military was still very dominant, and the death of General Gómez left a leadership vacuum that could only be filled by another *tachirense* military leader. On the day after Gómez's death, the Council of Ministers appointed General Eleazar López Contreras as the new president (governed 1935–1941). López Contreras had been a long-time supporter of Gómez, having arrived in Caracas with Castro and Gómez at the end of the nineteenth century.

As president, López Contreras introduced significant changes in governmental administration that allowed, among other things, for the founding of new political organizations. Indeed, the foundations of modern political organizations and media, the opening of debates among the different ideologies, a greater sensitivity by the government to the various protests and uprisings, and a renewed interest in institutional management all constituted building blocks of a process referred to as "democratic learning" or "evolving democracy." Utilizing the slogan *sembrar el petróleo* (sowing the seeds of oil), López Contreras also undertook efforts to modernize the Venezuelan economy. These efforts included establishing a central bank in 1939 and opening new petroleum fields for exploitation. The López Contreras administration also placed a greater emphasis on higher education and public works projects.

The first three years of López Contreras's administration were very important politically. Although these years were marred by general strikes in 1936 and 1937, there were some significant political advances. For example, several political parties were either founded or reorganized during this time, including the *Movimiento de Organización Venezolana* (Movement for Venezuelan Organization) (ORVE), the *Partido Democrático Nacional* (National Democratic Party) (PDN), and the seminal organization that eventually became the *Comité de Organización Política Electoral Independiente*.

The ORVE had a nationalistic and multiclass agenda, and during its early years sought nothing more than to aid in the government's effort to create a modern Venezuela. Over time, however, its moderate tone became much more aggressive. In its first phase, the ORVE was led by Alberto Adriani (1898–1936) and Mariano Picón Salas (1901–1965). By June 1936, Rómulo Betancourt (1908–1981) assumed control, and the organization was restructured. Following Betancourt's rise in the party, Adriani became a member of López Contreras's cabinet, and Picón Salas took a diplomatic post overseas. With this change in party leadership, the ORVE turned from a "hesitant and intellectual" party to a "combative party with a concrete agenda, defined tactics, and a controversial feel."[1] The PDN was the result of the fusion of various leftist groups, including the *Federación de Estudiantes de Venezuela* (Federation of Venezuelan Students) and the *Movimiento de Organización Venezolana*. As stated in its founding documents, the leadership of this new party was committed to the installation of an authentic democratic regime, to which end it was imperative to establish universal and direct suffrage with a secret ballot. The new party also proposed eradication of *gomecista* [pro-Gómez] practices by bringing to trial those of his accomplices who were more directly responsible for the old regime's crimes. The PDN also called for the persecution of the vices inherited from the Gómez era, especially corruption, abuse of authority, favoritism, and nepotism.[2]

The PDN was not yet legalized by the López Contreras government, and after the oil industry strike of 1936, many of the party's leaders were expelled from the country (under charges of being communist sympathizers or anarchists). Rómulo Betancourt, one of the PDN's more significant members, eluded persecution and dedicated himself in exile to reorganizing the party. Among the more important and immediate goals was to establish a clear and safe distance from the communist movement. The PDN received official status in 1939, and Betancourt's faction embarked on a new party mission. The PDN declared itself the only national party capable of leading the people in their struggle for a democratic and anti-imperialist revolution. The party defined itself as a leftist, multiclass, and progressive party, in contrast to the reactionary, centrist, and class-based parties. In 1941, the PDN launched the symbolic presidential candidacy of Rómulo Gallegos, seeking to both chart the course of an extensive mass movement and broaden the base of support to transform the PDN into a national party. The success of this 1941 initiative made Gallegos and Betancourt the de facto leaders of the opposition against President Isaías Medina Angarita (governed 1941–1945).

The Venezuelan communist movement had its organizational foundations in the *Partido Revolucionario Venezolano* (Venezuelan Revolutionary Party), founded in Mexico in 1926. Among the leaders of this early communist movement were Salvador de la Plaza (1896–1970) and Gustavo Machado (1898–1983). In 1931, the *Partido Revolucionario Venezolano* became the *Partido Comunista de Venezuela*, by which point the party was already active in the international communist movement. Upon President Gómez's death (1935), the communist leaders returned to Venezuela and clandestinely reorganized themselves under the name *Partido Republicano*

Progresista (Republican Progressive Party), because the 1936 constitution banned all communist groups from political discourse. After brief unifying experiences with other parties, the communists sought to deepen their social base, especially among the working class and students, and to consolidate their organizational structure throughout the country. By the time of the 1941 elections, the clandestine communists had formed two legal political organizations.

On September 1, 1939, German armed forces invaded Poland, starting the Second World War (1939–1945). From the outset, the López Contreras government remained neutral. However, following the Japanese attack on Pearl Harbor, Venezuela broke diplomatic relations with the Axis powers. While Venezuela would eventually join with the Allies, it did not provide military forces nor engage in military operations. However, Venezuela did aid the Allied cause. According to Venezuelan historian Guillermo Morón, almost all of the oil used by Great Britain during the war came from Venezuela.

The year 1941 was an important one for political activities in Venezuela. General Medina Angarita, another *tachirense*, was selected president by the Venezuelan National Congress through a dubious election process that, given Congress's membership, left little doubt as to the eventual outcome. Hence, the "symbolic" nature of Rómulo Gallegos's candidacy. In addition, the year marked the return of many of the exiles of the Gómez and López Contreras era. Significantly, the year also marked the foundation of *Acción Democrática* or, more accurately, the transformation of the *Partido Democrático Nacional* from an outlawed party to a new and officially recognized party.

Acción Democrática was the result of a 10-year process of fine-tuning and consolidation of a peculiar political style and ideology. In this regard, the *Movimiento de Organización Venezolana* and the *Partido Democrático Nacional* were early stages in the development of a modern instrument for political and social struggle (i.e., *Acción Democrática*), through which the traditional relations between state and society would be transformed. From the outset, *Acción Democrática* proved to be a well-oiled nationwide political machine, with every district and municipality assigned a party leader. The party was capable of raising funds and was managed by a board of professional politicians. It was a party that aspired to lead the masses, a goal that it achieved after the *golpe* of 1945, through a Leninist structure whose operations were inspired by democratic centralism. *Acción Democrática* viewed itself as a leftist-revolutionary, nationalist, populist, multiclass, anti-imperialist party that sought to carry out the dictates of social democracy.

General Medina Angarita assumed the presidency at the very moment that the country was experiencing a variety of new social forces. In particular, Venezuela now had socially indoctrinated and structured political parties, an economy based on the petroleum industry, a public administration apparatus that was fairly well organized, and social advances in the areas of health and education. Finally, Medina Angarita presided over a Venezuela where the earlier restrictions on freedom and political rights were eased. These substantive changes were, in large part, the result of popular demands and domestic changes. For example, as noted, Venezuela became a reliable oil provider for the Allies during the Second World War, and the Allied campaign of exalted democratic values had profound repercussions in Venezuela. During the administration of President Medina Angarita, initiatives were put forth in favor of institutional modernization. Important reforms were carried out in a number of key areas, including income taxation, hydrocarbons, social security, and agrarian reform. The political arena was characterized by an atmosphere of tolerance.

Even with the many reforms, the opposition demanded more: direct and secret universal suffrage, the modernization of public service agencies, the eradication of corruption, a greater national participation in the benefits of the oil revenue bonanza, and the reinvestment of a greater amount of revenue capital. The leftist opposition made democracy its war cry, and, to that end, it pursued the organization of the masses and command of the streets. President Medina Angarita represented the apex of a power structure in which an elite leadership (hardly reflective of the masses they represented) took on the task of modernizing the country's infrastructure as its loftiest goal, superseding the establishment of democracy itself. In that regard, the idea of modernization that formed the basis of the national projects during Medina Angarita's administration actually lacked a popular base of support.

Besides *Acción Democrática*, the political arena also consisted of representatives of several other groups. Among them were the supporters of the Medina Angarita government, specifically the *Partidarios de la Política del Gobierno* (Supporters of Government Policy) and the *Partido Democrático Venezolano*. Additionally, there were the Catholic-dominated *Acción Nacional* (National Action), the communist-dominated *Unión Municipal* (Municipal Union), the *Unión Popular Venezolana* (Venezuelan Popular Union), and the *lopecistas*, followers of former President López Contreras, who sought his return to the presidency.

Against this backdrop of sociopolitical growth and reform, municipal and state legislative elections were held in October 1944. The results of these elections would determine the composition of the national Congress, which would elect the next president in April 1946 (for the term 1946–1951). At this time in Venezuela, voters elected the members of the municipal councils and the members of the state legislative assemblies. In addition, they chose the national senators, who then elected the president.

By 1944, the Venezuelan communists adopted a stance radically different from that of three years earlier. In 1941, the communists rejected Medina Angarita's candidacy because of what they perceived to be fascist tendencies. By the end of 1944, the communists (i.e., members of the *Unión Popular Venezolana*) and the *medinistas* (supporters of Medina Angarita) reached a compromise through which they decided to join forces in the Caracas municipal elections. This alliance won the elections. *Acción Democrática's* defeat convinced its leadership of the need to modify the nation's electoral rules and procedures. At that time, only literate adults older than 21 years of age were eligible to vote, and AD realized that under such electoral conditions it would be next to impossible for the party to gain power in the short term. The opportunity to bring about this change presented itself in the form of the *Unión Patriótica Militar* (Patriotic Military Union) (UPM), an organization of junior military officers. The organization expressed discontent at the slow pace of modernization and advancement within the military service. This clandestine group of officers was also unhappy with the lack of professionalism among senior military officers, most of whom were from the state of Táchira.

THE TRIENIO

Modern politics in Venezuela began with the October 1945 *golpe de estado* by *Acción Democrática* and the *Unión Patriótica Militar*. As a result of the October Revolution, the *Junta Revolucionaria de Gobierno* (Revolutionary Government Junta) was established and assumed power. The *junta* was presided over by *Acción Democrática* leader Rómulo Betancourt and included civilian members Raúl Leoni, Luis Beltrán Prieto Figueroa (1902–1993), Gonzalo Barrios (1902–1993), and Edmundo Fernández (1905–1979). Representing the military were Carlos Delgado Chalbaud (1909–1950) and Mario Ricardo Vargas (1913–1949). *Acción Democrática* controlled the government, and the UPM controlled the armed forces.

From the onset of the October Revolution—October 18, 1945—until its collapse in November 1948, the country experienced a period of great political change. New parties were formed and democracy was institutionalized by universal, direct, and secret balloting. The previous modernization efforts were revitalized and intensified, thus paving the way for the effective democratization of Venezuelan political life. In economic matters, the *Trienio* (1945–1948), as this time period came to be called, witnessed a process by which capitalism became the only viable road to national development. Additional laws were passed that reinforced the course of modernization at the national level, emphasizing social reform. During the *Trienio*, national-level participation and control was increased. For example, the state reached a 50-50 arrangement with the petroleum companies; it decreed several significant education measures; it created a national economic council; the Venezuelan Development Corporation was founded; plans for simultaneous national industrialization were drawn up; and unionization was promoted by both the government and the major political parties. *Acción Democrática* especially promoted unionism, as it viewed labor unions as a source of power, as well as political and social legitimization. Efforts were also undertaken to reform the armed forces, although the slow pace of the reforms and the modest changes they brought about would later cause political problems for the government. In addition, a program of agrarian reform was undertaken, and the government began a program of land distribution with a plan to expand the program into full rural development in the Agrarian Reform Law of 1947.

The *Acción Democrática*–headed government undertook additional steps that drew support from the Venezuelan peasantry, or *campesinos*, who accounted for about 50 percent of Venezuelan families in 1945. Scattered throughout the country, the *campesinos* led a marginal existence on meager incomes and often displayed a high level of insecurity due to their tenuous claims to the lands they cultivated. They also generally lived in rural communities of fewer than 1,000 residents. Although they shared common economic conditions, the Venezuelan *campesinos* lived in three diverse geographical and ecological areas: the plains, the mountains, and the jungles. Many *campesinos* received land under the Agrarian Reform Law of 1947, which transformed them from sharecroppers and tenant farmers to land owners.

Also of importance during the AD-headed administration were the organization and reorganization of several political parties and labor unions. Among the more important parties were the *Comité de Organización Política Electoral Independiente*, the *Unión Republicana Democrática* (URD), and the *Partido Comunista de Venezuela*. Labor organized itself into the *Confederación de Trabajadores de Venezuela* (Confederation of Venezuelan Workers), and the various state and local *campesino* unions, which had been formed in 1936, banded together to form a national peasant federation, the *Federación Campesina de Venezuela* (Peasant Federation of Venezuela).

The leaders of the unions were not only labor leaders but also political party leaders, and, not surprisingly, the party roles assumed by the leaders were directly related to their union positions. Many of them served on local, state, and national agrarian bureaus or as agrarian secretaries of various party committees. The *campesinos* as a group actively participated in partisan activities. The *campesino* union leaders accepted applications for land and submitted them to the next step in the process of agrarian reform. Leaders at all levels established a system of contacts with the executive and legislative branches of the government, and it was because of these roles that the *Federación Campesina de Venezuela* leaders had been able to become involved in the various levels of decision-making.

The *campesinos* engaged in their first significant political activity after *Acción Democrática* assumed power in 1945. The co-optation of the peasants into politics began immediately. The peasants gained political and social acceptance and prestige and were successful in achieving some of their goals. *Acción Democrática* and its leaders gained new political and financial support, as well as increased political resources. The close ties between *Acción Democrática* and the *campesinos* surprised few, since many of the AD leaders who had founded the party had participated in the earlier formation of the local *campesino* unions in the mid-1930s.

The path that the new government pursued was not a smooth one. With the introduction of the various political, economic, and social reforms came additional problems, from both the political Left and the Right. In addition, the events of the October Revolution are not explained fully by the ambitions of the leaders of *Acción Democrática*. One must also take into account the dubious manner of the presidential succession that faced Generals López Contreras and Medina Angarita. In addition, one must consider the significance of the differences within the military between a generation of military academy–trained officials (with solid technical and professional backgrounds) and the old guard officers, especially the *tachirenses*, who had risen through the ranks under Gómez.

The Rómulo Betancourt–led *junta*, which took power as a result of the 1945 *golpe*, committed itself to the establishment of a democratic and nonpartisan foundation of political discourse. The *junta* also set out to eradicate the corrupt practices of public officials. To no surprise, the government undertook several cases of political corruption against public officials who had served in the Gómez, López Contreras, and Medina Angarita administrations.

Faced with the task of formalizing the new political guidelines, a national assembly was needed to draft a new constitution. *Acción Democrática* won an overwhelming majority in the assembly, whose deliberations eventually led to the constitution of July 5, 1947. This constitution assigned the state more active roles in solving the country's socioeconomic ills and fostering national development.

In the December 1947 elections, Rómulo Gallegos (governed 1948), the *Acción Democrática* candidate, was elected president in the first universal, direct, and secret elections held in Venezuela. *Acción Democrática* also won a majority of seats in the congressional elections. The hope of many was that the political process initiated on October 18, 1945, could finally be consolidated. To such an end, initiatives were put forth in the areas of foreign policy, public education, and agrarian reform. The overall goal of these measures was to refine the master plan laid out during the government of the Betancourt-led *junta*.

The modern Venezuelan political party system was formed during the three years when *Acción Democrática* was in power. These years witnessed the phenomenon of political parties accounting for their differences, based not only on the democratic model imposed by *Acción Democrática*, but also by realizing the responsibility of negotiating accords. In doing so, the various political parties could ensure their viability, a rationale that, unfortunately, led many parties to face each other off and, in the process, bury the lessons of the 1945–1948 experience. As a consequence, Venezuela developed a system with one predominant party, *Acción Democrática*. In the popular elections held during the *Trienio* (October 1946, December 1947, May 1948), AD achieved undeniable victories, receiving over 70 percent of the votes in each election. With the exception of the armed forces and the Catholic Church, by 1947 *Acción Democrática* had become the most important element of power. As a result, the formation of an opposition movement was to be expected.

One such movement was the *Unión Republicana Democrática* (URD), which had been founded in December 1945 as a conservative group. The party was founded by Isaac Pardo, Elías Toro (1871–1918), and Andrés Guzmán Otero, and would later be joined by Jóvito Villalba and an array of personalities from the *medinista* faction of the *Partido Comunista de Venezuela*. In its platform, the *uerredistas*, as URD party members are known, pointed out that the *Unión Republicana Democrática* was not a political party but rather a combination of democratic forces. Furthermore, once their goals were achieved, the organization would cease to exist and its followers would be free to come together under different political banners. The URD perceived itself as a broad front and the most adequate vehicle for those Venezuelan sectors that had not yet organized. They encouraged those sectors to come together and express their will in an effective way, such as in the elections for a constitutional assembly and president. Among the goals of the URD was no mention of perpetuating the organization, but rather of taking measures to avoid an AD monopoly in the elections of 1946 and 1947. Thus, for URD, it was a matter of creating a political force that could counter *Acción Democrática*.

Another important political party that was formed during the *Trienio* was the *Comité de Organización Política Electoral Independiente*, commonly known as COPEI, founded in January 1946. Its formation was the result of the need by many Venezuelan Catholics to confront the advances of the leftist movement. In fact, in response to the socialism and Marxism displayed by the more important political groups in Venezuela after Gómez's death, there emerged a social and political preoccupation with Catholic overtones, which came to life in different political, organizational, and ideological initiatives. COPEI is one example of the political expression of such a Catholic concern.

In the beginning, COPEI denied that it was a political party. The members traveled the country to spread their message and establish solid bases of support, especially in the Andean region. The leadership of COPEI attempted to design a unique ideological framework based on Christian humanism and sought to gain the power through which they could impose their ideas. During these early years, the group's ideological overtones became quite clear and decisive. Out of the youthful founders of COPEI, one stood above the rest: Rafael Caldera (1916–). He played an influential leadership role among the party's youth, and COPEI members recognized in him a preeminent and well-respected authority. Caldera was a political intellectual and strategist and would twice be elected president of Venezuela (1968 and 1993).

On February 15, 1948, Rómulo Gallegos was inaugurated as president. His administration undertook renewed efforts at agrarian reform, as well as measures to reduce the influence of the military. In the midst of these political actions, the legitimately elected government of President Gallegos was overthrown in a military *golpe*. With that one event, the political system was annulled, legitimate elections and political guarantees were interrupted, and the constitution of 1947 was renounced. The new military government unleashed a repressive effort against *Acción Democrática* and the unions, and eventually the regime targeted the communists and the media. The democratically elected Congress was dissolved, as were the municipal councils and the regional electoral *juntas*. Perhaps naively, COPEI and URD, trusting in the *golpe*'s good intentions to correct the course of action that *Acción Democrática* had started, waited in vain for the restoration of democratic freedoms, until even they were banned by the new military regime.

Although there may be numerous reasons for the *golpe* against President Gallegos, one stands out above all others: the rupture of the alliance between *Acción Democrática* and the armed forces. Notwithstanding AD's political power and President Gallegos's personal prestige and seriousness, the institution of democracy rested squarely on the shoulders of the military; and the military understood this from the very beginning. However, the political dynamic unleashed by *Acción Democrática* temporarily bestowed a mantle of loyalty upon the military, compelling the latter to adhere to the idea that the armed forces should remain faithful defenders of the constitutional government and, thus, form a united front to jealously guard the ideals of the October Revolution, a concept also referred to as *octubrismo*.

The rumors of a military *golpe* against *Acción Democrática* began to circulate almost from the very dawn of the October Revolution. As mentioned above, the road to reform was not an easy one for *Acción Democrática*, and the military was part of the problem. One important military uprising took place in December 1946, and rebels temporarily dominated important areas in the central part of the country. Consequently, the threat of a *golpe* hung like a cloud over *Acción Democrática* during the *Trienio*. Yet the party, which had been accused of monopolizing politics, was unable to get its political opposition fired up enough to come out in defense of the constitutional and legitimately elected government that had come to power just ten months before. In effect, the people's party had no one to defend it.

MILITARY DICTATORSHIP

Acción Democrática had little time to consolidate or implement its far-reaching reforms. The military *golpe* of 1948 cancelled and reversed the programs. For the next 10 years, the right-wing military dictatorship systematically dismantled any democratization efforts. Three military officers who participated in the 1945 *junta* assumed power through the new *Junta Militar de Gobierno:* Minister of Defense Carlos Delgado Chalbaud, Chief of the General Staff Marcos Pérez Jiménez (1914–2001), and Assistant Chief of Staff Luis Felipe Llovera Páez (1913–1977). The *junta* appointed a cabinet of four military men and eight civilians, and elevated Delgado Chalbaud to the presidency. As noted previously, the 1947 constitution was voided, and the 1936 constitution was brought back into force.

Many of the early acts of the new *junta* impacted *Acción Democrática* and its members. The right-wing regime refused to co-opt the leftist groups. On December 7, *Acción Democrática* was officially dissolved and its leaders were either forced into exile or arrested. Many AD members were imprisoned at La Guasina, the new prison camp built almost exclusively to house political prisoners. During 1951 and 1952, thousands of *Acción Democrática* members were put in prison. Many of them, including such leaders as Alberto Carnevali (1914–1953), died from torture, overwork, malnutrition, and disease. The government seized the party's property and printing presses and terrorized its supporters. In addition, it arrested many of the *campesino* union leaders. Most of the *campesinos* who had received land during the *Trienio* were removed from their property. Many labor syndicates and peasant unions were abolished because of their domination by *Acción Democrática* party members. The Delgado Chalbaud–led *junta* had every intention of keeping the armed forces behind it and rarely made important decisions without consulting the *Gran Consejo Militar* (Grand Military Council), which consisted of the defense ministry's top officials, the general staff, and the commanders of the four branches of the service.

The years from 1949 to 1952 were turbulent in Venezuela. The governing *junta* disbanded the *Confederación de Trabajadores de Venezuela* after it called for a general strike against the government, and it closed the campus of the Universidad Central de Venezuela because of student riots against the regime. The *junta* repealed *Acción Democrática's* 1948 education law, and teachers known to be sympathetic to AD were dismissed, exiled, or jailed. In November 1950, President Delgado Chalbaud was assassinated, and many Venezuelans claimed that Marcos Pérez Jiménez had a hidden hand in the plot. Even today, Pérez Jiménez's involvement remains unclear. Germán Suárez Flamerich (1907–1990), a Caracas lawyer who had been serving as Venezuela's ambassador to Perú, headed a new *junta* with Pérez Jiménez and Llovera Páez. Pérez Jiménez served as minister of defense and Llovera Páez as minister of interior relations.

Even though Germán Suárez Flamerich was head of the governing *junta*, Marcos Pérez Jiménez became the de facto leader of the country. Pérez Jiménez was the most recent of the great Andean strongmen in Venezuelan history. Following in the footsteps of Generals Cipriano Castro and Juan Vicente Gómez, Pérez Jiménez participated in a *golpe de estado* that eventually led to his assumption of dictatorial powers, as had his two great Andean precursors. Pérez Jiménez was, however, possibly the most ruthless of the three, and arguably the most ruthless of any leader in Venezuelan history. Born in Táchira in 1914, Pérez Jiménez attended secondary school in Colombia, followed by military training at the *Escuela Militar de Venezuela* (Venezuelan Military Academy), where he graduated in 1934. He completed his military studies in Perú at the

Escuela de Aplicación de Artillería (School for Artillery Applications) and the *Escuela Superior de Guerra* (War College), undertaking advanced military training. Upon his return to Venezuela, he became involved in the *Unión Patriótica Militar.*

Under popular pressure, Pérez Jiménez announced plans for a new presidential election to be held in November 1952. He seemed certain that he would win the presidency and, therefore, had nothing to lose by holding the election. Jóvito Villalba of URD and Rafael Caldera of COPEI opposed Pérez Jiménez, who ran on the *Frente Electoral Independiente* (Independent Electoral Front) ticket. Although the two parties were allowed to campaign, they had to furnish detailed information to the government regarding party-sponsored public meetings, membership rolls, and finances. The government also censored the press coverage of Villalba and Caldera. Both *Acción Democrática* and the *Partido Comunista de Venezuela* were barred from participating, because they had been previously outlawed by the government. Even so, *Acción Democrática* clandestinely supported Villalba. By most accounts, the balloting on November 30, 1952, was fair and orderly; the results, on the other hand, were not.

After the initial returns showed Villalba leading by a large margin, Pérez Jiménez had the news coverage of the returns halted. No further results were announced until December 2, 1952, when Pérez Jiménez announced that the results were as follows: FEI 788,086; URD 638,336; COPEI 300,309; Others 41,259.30. The members of the *junta* resigned and turned power over to the military, which in turn named Pérez Jiménez as provisional president. In addition to the presidency, Pérez Jiménez's party claimed a majority in the Constituent Assembly.

When the Constituent Assembly met on January 9, 1953, it ratified the election returns and declared Marcos Jiménez the Constitutional President of Venezuela. It also adopted a new constitution, which, among other things, made governorships appointed positions and authorized the president to take whatever measures he may deem necessary for the preservation of the security of the nation, the protection of social peace, and the maintenance of public order. The constitution, promulgated in April 1953 also reinstated the procedure whereby the president was elected by the legislature. The new government repressed secondary and university students, although it did promise modernization, economic development, and order. The Pérez Jiménez government used force to ensure order and compliance. Its *Seguridad Nacional* (National Security police) rounded up and imprisoned the opposition. By most accounts, thousands of Venezuelans were tortured and murdered during his administration. The right-wing Pérez Jiménez government also outlawed labor unions, censored the press, and shut down universities when they became too antigovernment.

Among other things, Pérez Jiménez's administration, the *Nuevo Ideal Nacional* (New National Ideal), called for a transformation of the nation's communication and transportation infrastructure, for rapid urban construction, and for major defense expenditures, all at the expense of the political process. Between 1950 and 1955, the Ministry of Public Works spent over 33 percent of the total government expenditures, with much of the money going to contractors with close government ties. The money for this material transformation came from the ever-increasing petroleum revenue. While Caracas gained many monuments to Pérez Jiménez's vision of modernity, the nation received little in the way of expansion of human resources, health care, and education. There was also, of course, rampant corruption that stole millions from the Venezuelan treasury.

Another aspect of the Pérez Jiménez administration reflected the realities of the late 1940s and 1950s: the support of anticommunist regimes by Western democracies. The staunch anticommunist stance of the Venezuelan government drew strong support from the United States. This relationship was also reflected in the continued favorable dealings between the Venezuelan government and foreign oil companies, such as Esso, Dutch Shell, and Gulf.

Pérez Jiménez attempted to confirm the legitimacy of his rule by holding a plebiscite in December 1957. The results of this poll announced that 85 percent of the population were in favor of Pérez Jiménez retaining power. To most Venezuelans, the results were obviously fraudulent, and the military began to take actions against the dictator to force his resignation. Earlier in the year, representatives of the major opposition groups, including AD, COPEI, PCV, and URD, had organized the *Junta Patriótica* (Patriotic *Junta*), under the leadership of Fabricio Ojeda (1929–1966) and Guillermo García Ponce. Ojeda was a young journalist; García Ponce, a member of the PCV. The *Frente Universitario* (University Front) (FU) was a clandestine youth organization founded by Américo Martín and Germán Lairet in 1956. By the end of 1957, these groups began to call for popular strikes against the regime. Moisés Moleiro, an AD youth member, worked with the FU and other radical youth movements, thus linking them to the overthrow efforts. Many of the students prominent in the ousting of Pérez Jiménez would eventually become involved in organizing *guerrilla* movements against later governments.

In mid-January 1958, students began rioting in Caracas, and the popular uprisings led to the end of Pérez Jiménez's 10-year regime. These riots followed an air force rebellion on January 1, 1958, although that *golpe* attempt amounted to an insurrection of little consequence. Eventually, the Church, press, and politicians united with the air force and navy to over-throw the despotic Pérez Jiménez. There was street fighting in Caracas on January 21, 1958, and two days later, on January 23, army officers forced Pérez Jiménez to resign and flee the country. The 1958 *Junta Militar de Gobierno*, headed by Rear Admiral Wolfgang Larrazábal (1911–2003), was immediately established. The *junta* consisted of five military members. With the replacement of two members by civilians on the same day, the *junta* changed its name to the *Junta de Gobierno*. Composed of Admiral Larrazábal, Dr. Edgar Sanabria (1911–1989), Colonel Carlos Luis Araque, Colonel Pedro José Quevedo, and Dr. Arturo Sosa (1924–1996), Jr., the *junta* promised open elections within a year.

The overthrow of Pérez Jiménez's dictatorship is significant. The *Movimiento 23 de enero* (23rd of January Movement) laid the foundations for a democratic regime that would eventually become one of Latin America's longest. In effect, on January 23, 1958, the opportunity arose for Venezuela's major political and social forces to create a new democratic and representative political system. The leaders agreed to make political consensus a top goal, to limit conflicts to a minimum, and to preserve the new democratic political regime at any cost.

On December 7, 1958, elections were held to elect a president as well as members of the national Congress, the state legislative assemblies, and the municipal councils throughout Venezuela. Eight political parties partici-pated in the 1958 national elections: *Acción Democrática, Unión Republicana Democrática, Comité de Organización Política Electoral Independiente, Partido Comunista de Venezuela, Movimiento Electoral Nacional Independiente* (MENI), *Integración Republicana* (IR), *Partido Socialista de Trabajadores* (PST), and the *Partido Socialista* (PS). Philosophically, the extreme Left included the PCV; the constitutional Left included the AD, URD, and MENI; center-Left included the PST and COPEI; and center included the IR. Only two par-ties stood on the Right: The URD contained a faction that extended to the Right, and COPEI contained a faction that could be considered extreme Right.

The final vote count for the presidential election was as follows: AD 49.18 percent, URD 30.66 percent, COPEI 15.17 percent, PCV 3.23 per-cent, MENI 0.70 percent, IR 0.59 percent, and PST 0.43 percent. The PS did not run its own candidate for the presidency. Based on political ide-ology, the breakdown was extreme Left 3.23 percent, constitutional Left 80.55 percent, and a combined total of the center Left, center, Right, and extreme Right of 16.20 percent. Rómulo Betancourt, the AD candidate, won the election with a plurality of votes.

SUMMARY

The period from the death of Juan Vicente Gómez (1935) to the fall of Marcos Pérez Jiménez (1958) is fundamental to understanding contemporary Venezuela. The social and economic structures were radically transformed and the major political forces took shape. The period was marked by important agreements and disagreements. Overall, despite the main players' impulsiveness and varied positions, they did not hinder the constant effort to modernize the country. The governments of General Eleazar López Contreras (1935–1941) and General Isaías Medina Angarita (1941–1945) represented a transformation toward political liberalization. Their regimes were characterized by efforts to take full advantage of the revenues from the oil boom. The democratic *Trienio* (1945–1948) was a period of significant political change. New parties were formed, and democracy was institutionalized by universal, direct, and secret balloting. The previous modernization efforts were revitalized and intensified, and the state reiterated that capitalism was the only viable road to national development.

The Pérez Jiménez dictatorship utilized force to ensure order and compliance, particularly through its *Seguridad Nacional*. While not supported at home, the Pérez Jiménez administration enjoyed the anticommunist support of Western democracies. Several days of popular uprisings led to the end of Pérez Jiménez's 10-year regime, and the former dictator fled the country. The 1958 *Junta Militar de Gobierno* delivered open elections within a year, which allowed the nation's political and social forces to create a new democratic and representative political system.

NOTES

1. Manuel V. Magallanes, *Acción Democrática: Partido del Pueblo* (Caracas: Ediciones Adeven, 1993), 2.

2. Ramón Rivas, *Historia y doctrina de Acción Democrática* (Mérida: Universidad Popular Alberto Carnevali, 1994), 78–79.

8

The Return of Democracy (1959–1963)

Most historians and political scientists agree that the presidency of Rómulo Betancourt (1959–1964) had three major achievements. The first significant accomplishment was the establishment of a coalition-style government. The second major achievement was the successful completion of the December 1963 national elections. The third feat was the transfer of power from one constitutionally elected president to another constitutionally elected president. Although there were many achievements of the Betancourt regime, these three elements are the focus of this chapter.

Adhering to the *Pacto de Punto Fijo* (Pact of Punto Fijo), a pre-electoral agreement by which the leaders of *Unión Republicana Democrática* (URD), *Acción Democrática* (AD), and the *Comité de Organización Política Electoral Independiente* (COPEI) had pledged to support the winner of the election, the victorious parties structured a coalition government. This new coalition represented a national unity in which most sectors of Venezuelan society were represented, and President Betancourt made coalitions and institution-building his immediate goal. Betancourt's first cabinet included two members of AD, three members of the COPEI, three members of the URD, one member of the armed forces, and four independents. In addition to the *Pacto de Punto Fijo*, the leaders also formulated the *Declaración de Principios* (Declaration of Principles) and a *Programa Mínimo de Gobierno* (Minimum Program of Government), which laid out political and economic programs.

The Venezuelan political system has been referred to as a populist system of conciliation, referring to a political system in which a large coalition of diverse political and social groups is essential. This spirit of cooperation among the various groups in support of democracy is often called the "spirit of the 23rd of January," referring to the date of the overthrow of the military dictatorship of Marcos Pérez Jiménez. Based upon the recognition and legitimacy of the interests it covers, a coalition creates a system of negotiations, transactions, compromises, and conciliations among the groups. According to Juan Carlos Rey, a new political style was put into practice that emphasized and employed utilitarian mechanisms and, at the same time, used ideological and/or coercive mechanisms. The particular coalition or alliance was expressed through a group of institutions and rules of play, which constituted the legal base by which the different political players, including the government, had to abide.[1]

THE BETANCOURT PRESIDENCY

When Rómulo Betancourt, the mantle bearer of *Acción Democrática*, was elected president, many on the Left had great expectations. As previously noted, *Acción Democrática* viewed itself as a leftist-revolutionary, nationalist, populist, multiclass, anti-imperialist party that sought to carry out the programs of social democracy. Even Cuban leader Fidel Castro (1926–) viewed the Venezuelan election with optimism. While in Caracas to visit with Rómulo Betancourt three weeks before he officially took office, Castro declared his solidarity with Venezuela. Much to the surprise of Castro and others, the subsequent Betancourt coalition did not include representatives of the extreme Left. In his inaugural address, President Betancourt declared that the development of Venezuela and the communist philosophy were not compatible. The communists felt betrayed by the actions of Betancourt. Communist party members had contributed much toward the *golpe* activities of January 1958. Their presses and radio stations had broadcast anti-Pérez Jiménez propaganda, and they had helped organize the street demonstrations and worker strikes.

When Betancourt assumed the presidency, he inherited an economy with significant problems. First and foremost, the national treasury was empty. Although this was partly due to the excessive spending of Pérez Jiménez, the primary reason was the graft and corruption of the former dictator and his allies. Another problem for President Betancourt was unemployment. As noted in the previous chapter, from 1950 to 1955, over one-third of national expenditures went to public works projects. As such, the sector with the highest employment rates were the petroleum and construction industries, with most of the construction jobs located in Caracas. As a consequence, employment rates in other sectors and in other regions of the country were considerably lower. When Betancourt took office in 1959, the unemployment rate for the nation was almost twice what it had been only five years earlier.

Another problem for the new democracy was the national debt. In January 1958, the foreign debt was already over U.S. $500 million ($3.4 billion in 2005 U.S. dollars). As noted in chapter 1, petroleum prices during the 1950s and 1960s remained relatively low. The increase in petroleum-related revenue throughout this period was due to increasing amounts of petroleum sold, not in prices per barrel. Thus, the Betancourt administration was servicing the debt already owed while trying to acquire additional funds to bring about economic recovery.

Betancourt fulfilled many of the elements of the government's plan for modernization. This plan was based, in part, on the concept of rentism—the principle by which national income from oil revenue was assumed to be an extraordinary and transitory source of income that must be invested into the creation of a non-oil-dependent society and economy. In doing so, it would allow Venezuela to reach high levels of prosperity and development, while continuing to maintain those levels once the oil revenues were gone. Thus, it becomes necessary to exploit the oil resources in the present in order to derive the maximum benefit possible for the future.

During the Betancourt regime, the state's interventionist role was solidified, the expansion of a decentralized public administration was encouraged, and several new state-run enterprises were created. Additionally, support for the basic industries was strengthened, and the industrialization process was reinforced in an attempt to offset imports. In oil exploration, a policy of "no more concessions" was embraced. At the social level, agrarian reform was aggressively pursued, as well as heavy government investment in the areas of health care services, public education, and sanitation. The *Acción Democrática* government also took steps to ensure that it did not repeat the errors of the *Trienio*. For example, the military was appeased by improved equipment and amnesty for certain crimes committed during the 1948–1958 military dictatorship.

President Betancourt also oversaw the drafting and promulgation of a new constitution. The 1961 constitution included modern and fundamental political, economic, and social principles, which established the foundations for how the state would function. The document also firmly established the basic rights of the Venezuelan people, both individually and collectively. This constitution would remain in force for eight presidential administrations before it was replaced in 1999.

Because of its actions in office during the *Trienio* (1945–1948), *Acción Democrática* enjoyed a reputation for extensive agrarian reform and gained a solid political base in the rural areas of the country. By 1958, Venezuelan peasants comprised 30 percent of the population. During the 14 years since the *Trienio*, many of the *campesinos* moved into urban areas in hopes of finding a better standard of living. Even though the *campesino* population had decreased, it has been estimated that, in 1958, *campesino* voting accounted for half of the votes for *Acción Democrática*.

In keeping with its earlier land reform program, the AD-headed government introduced an agrarian reform package to the Congress shortly after taking office. The minister of agriculture presented the comprehensive proposal in August 1959. The proposal's broad and ambitious objectives addressed not only the issue of land tenure, but other aspects of a broad agricultural program as well. It contained provisions for the implementation of graduated land taxes, farm credits, extension services, and land distribution and development. The goal of the program was to create small family farm owners. Congress adopted the Agrarian Reform Law in February 1960, and the final version of the law received the support of all political factions except the communists, who favored a more radical program. President Betancourt signed the law into effect on March 5, 1960.

The law provided for the government purchase of large estates and for the division and distribution of land among the *campesinos*. Under the guidelines established, three categories of land could be expropriated by the government: uncultivated lands; farms worked by tenants and/or sharecroppers; and pasture lands appropriate for crops. The landowners were to be paid market value for their properties, receiving between 10 and 30 percent immediately in cash and the balance in long-term bonds. The law limited the expropriation of private lands to those areas where no public land was available for distribution. Much of the public land that was available had been obtained by the government following the death of General Juan Vicente Gómez in 1935.

The Agrarian Reform Law of 1960 demonstrated the cooperation between the Ministry of Agriculture, the *Banco Agrícola y Pecuario* (Agricultural and Livestock Bank), and the *Federación Campesina de Venezuela*. The new program was of such magnitude that it has been cited as the most extensive non-revolutionary land reform program in the Western Hemisphere.[2] The program also provided for the establishment of rural settlements, called *asentamientos*, and the expansion of infrastructure into these settlements.

President Betancourt promised enormous government investment in the program to finance the distribution of land and create the necessary infrastructure, such as schools, electrification, and roads. Betancourt addressed the need to equip the *campesinos* not only with land, but also with the infrastructure and modern machinery to work it.

The impoverished urban population, less affected by the agrarian reform program, also made gains during the Betancourt administration. To most *barrio* (urban slum neighborhood) dwellers in Latin America, the government is perceived as having two functions: to provide the necessary elements to their social and economic advancement and to serve the partisan interests of the officials who administer the government. This paternalistic view was reinforced in the minds of *barrio* dwellers by the actions of the government during the administration of Pérez Jiménez.[3] The poor began to reside in the *superbloques* (housing projects) for little or no rent. For many, government-subsidized housing was one of the major benefits of living in a petroleum-rich country.

The municipal councils were directly responsible for the *barrios*. Like state and national politicians, municipal politicians were political party representatives elected by virtue of their positions on the official party list and not by direct candidate ballot. Voters cast their ballots for the political party of their choice, and when the votes were tabulated and the number of seats were calculated, then that number of candidates was selected from the official party list for that municipal council. For example, if *Acción Democrática* had won three seats on a council, then the top three names on the AD list would take office. Thus, the paternalistic benefits that *barrio* dwellers received originated from the political party, not necessarily from the council official. *Barrio* dwellers usually found that their treatment was commensurate with their support for the dominant political party in the area.

Labor also benefited from *Acción Democrática*'s actions in the first year of power. The *Confederación de Trabajadores de Venezuela*, having been disbanded by Pérez Jiménez in 1952, renewed operations in 1959. The government also enacted a new labor code, which ensured the right of association and collective bargaining.

Venezuela experienced many changes during the 14 years that separated the two governments of *Acción Democrática*. The country had moved from an oligarchic regime, through a social-democratic revolution, which lost out to a tyrannical dictatorship, and finally into a liberal democracy. New civilian organizations and political parties were established, thus creating channels of political participation for the Venezuelan population. The liberal democracy, still untested in 1958, attempted to create a political base within both the labor and agricultural populations.

By the end of 1960, the government had relatively stable political and economic conditions, which were deemed acceptable to the majority of the population. In foreign affairs, the Venezuelan government refused to recognize any regime that came to power by military force. This philosophy came to be known as the Betancourt Doctrine. The government had also founded the *Corporación Venezolana del Petróleo* (Venezuelan Petroleum Corporation), designed to oversee the national petroleum industry. In addition, the Betancourt administration was active in the creation of the Organization of Petroleum Exporting Countries (OPEC), the international oil cartel that Venezuela established in partnership with Kuwait, Saudi Arabia, Iraq, and Iran. As noted in chapter 1, petroleum prices during this period remained relatively low, thus the Betancourt administration did not have the generous source of revenue that later administrations would enjoy.

The Venezuelan political system had to overcome some obstacles during the period from 1958 to 1968, and its leaders had to be creative, firm, and willing to negotiate. The years 1960 through 1963 proved to be particularly trying for the Betancourt government, because certain factions within the military were annoyed with the government and what it perceived as actions designed to curtail the power of the armed forces. The Betancourt government experienced its first serious uprising on April 20, 1960, when a military faction and a small group of followers attempted to seize control of a military garrison in the state of Táchira.

In addition to the military problem from the political Right, President Betancourt also experienced dissension from the younger members of *Acción Democrática*. The youth of AD had ideological differences with the older party leadership regarding the direction the party should pursue. After all, it had been the party youth who led the AD underground within Venezuela during the Pérez Jiménez regime, and by 1960 they had become disenchanted with the resumption of power by the older party leaders, such as Rómulo Betancourt, Gonzalo Barrios, and Raúl Leoni.

The final blow to the strained relations between the older and younger members of *Acción Democrática*, however, developed over a series of articles in *La Esfera*, the party's unofficial newspaper. Angered by the articles, the party leadership had the young authors—Domingo Alberto Rangel and Américo Martin—brought before the party leadership, who sanctioned them for their writings. The AD youth almost unanimously signed a petition in support of Rangel and Martín, and, in response to the petition, the party leadership expelled the majority of the signatories, a move that alienated even more of the party youth.

The expelled group initially called itself *Acción Democrática de Izquierda* (Democratic Action of the Left), but later changed its name to the

Movimiento de Izquierda Revolucionaria (Movement of the Revolutionary Left) (MIR). The MIR leaders admitted to being influenced by the success of the Cuban Revolution and criticized the older *Acción Democrática* leadership for abandoning a popular strategy of economic development. The MIR contained a broad spectrum of members that ranged from ultra leftist to mildly leftist, and it recruited many of its members from the student population, at both the university and secondary levels. As members of *Acción Democrática*, the *miristas* (members of the MIR) had worked underground with the communist youth during the Pérez Jiménez regime. By 1960, however, they proclaimed their new party to be Marxist-Leninist and judged the Communist party as too conservative.

The Cuban version of Marxism (formulated by Fidel Castro, Ernesto "Che" Guevara [1928–1967], and Régis Debray) that so influenced the MIR promoted three basic principles: (1) the countryside was the main area of the revolution; (2) in a *guerrilla* war, the rural insurgents could defeat a regular army; and (3) it was not necessary to wait for a revolutionary environment to occur, but, rather, the proper conditions could be created. That a revolutionary situation can be *created* by armed *guerrilla* warfare centered in the rural areas is what sets Castroism, or Castro-communism, apart from other revolutionary doctrines and Marxist interpretations. The Cuban model argues that the *guerrilla* is the creator of the revolutionary situation.

CASTRO-COMMUNIST INSURGENCY

The Castro-communist insurgency erupted in Venezuela on October 19, 1960, following the arrest of the editors of the MIR newspaper, *Izquierda*, in which an editorial appeared that called for a "popular revolution" against the Betancourt government. Riots broke out in the streets of Caracas in protest of the closing of the newspaper and the jailing of the three editors. Most of the demonstrators were students from the Universidad Central de Venezuela. In response to the civil unrest in early November, the campus experienced a shoot-out between students and federal troops. The October street demonstrators lacked leadership and were dispersed rather easily by the police. In response to the demonstrations against the government by the students and the parties of the Left, the government staged a well-attended counter-demonstration to show its massive base of support. The demonstration, on November 1, 1960, in the *El Silencio* area of Caracas, had been organized by the trade and peasant unions.

Having been defeated in their recent insurgency efforts, the extreme Left faced a dilemma as to the most advantageous course to follow. One aspect of the early insurgency efforts, by both the *Partido Comunista de Venezuela* (Venezuelan Communist Party) (PCV) and MIR, was that they lacked direction. The failure of the October-November 1960 demonstrations convinced the Left that a formal insurgency plan would be needed. The PCV and MIR, united by the demonstrations in Caracas, began to formulate a plan to overthrow the democratic regime of President Betancourt. One group of insurgents advocated a strategy of protracted rural *guerrilla* warfare (along the general lines proposed by Mao Zedong [1896–1976] and Che Guevara), while another faction argued for a strategy that promised a rapid victory to the insurgent cause. The united insurgents chose the latter agenda.

The older communists had avoided revolutionary tactics in their initial efforts to overthrow President Betancourt and, influenced as they were by Mao Zedong, continued to attempt to win the support of the population with a long-term program of persuasion. They utilized their union positions as propaganda outlets, as Chairman Mao had claimed that *guerrilla* warfare would fail if its political objectives did not coincide with the aspirations of the people. By January 1961, however, the Communist party had changed its direction and started to promote a "non-peaceful path" to bring about the desired political change.

Throughout 1961, the leftist insurgents followed their "Plan for Rapid Victory." The tactics the leftists employed were generally minor annoyances, primarily because neither the communists nor the *miristas* had prior experience in urban insurgency beyond protesting and street rioting. There was also a shortage of arms for the insurgents and a lack of experienced personnel who knew how to use weapons or make bombs. Starting in 1961, however, Venezuelan youth began to travel to Cuba to receive training in rural and urban insurgency tactics. The Cubans also provided the Venezuelan revolutionaries with manuals on sabotage and *guerrilla* warfare tactics, although it appears that the Cubans did not send arms until later. In response to the assistance that Cuban leaders had given to the insurgents, President Betancourt officially broke diplomatic relations with the Castro government on November 11, 1961.

By the beginning of 1962, the revolutionaries had abandoned street rioting and adopted urban terrorism almost exclusively. Terrorist activities included robbing banks, burning warehouses, killing policemen, and kidnapping. Part of the justification for the switch to terrorism was the inability to get the Venezuelan public involved in the riots, which the Left had hoped to do. It was also during this period (1961–1962) that the insurgents began the rural *guerrilla* tactics against the government, even though it is unknown exactly when their training camps were established.

In late January 1962, the armed forces had begun to find evidence of *guerrilla* training camps and supplies, and soon thereafter, some MIR and PCV leaders went to the Venezuelan mountains and organized the first rural *guerrilla* groups. The failure of the rural insurgency efforts led to an increase in the number of urban terrorist activities. From a low of 2 urban incidents in February, when the rural phase was the major emphasis, the number rose to 30 by September. September and October 1962 were very stressful for the fragile democracy. The extreme Left had increased its insurgency activities aimed at fostering the overthrow of the Betancourt government. In addition to over 200 civilian arrests, the government also placed over 20 members of Congress under "house arrest." Newly revised urban terrorist activities in September 1962 included the bombing of a bus station in Caracas, setting fire to oil pipelines in Maracaibo, and attacking the Coca-Cola plant in Caracas. The strategy clearly had changed from simple rioting in the streets to the destruction of lives and property.

Leftists within the navy also attempted two uprisings in 1962. On May 4, approximately 450 marines and 50 national guardsmen revolted and seized the naval base in Carúpano. Within two days, however, troops loyal to Betancourt crushed the uprising with minimal fatalities. The second leftist naval faction struck on June 2, 1962 at Puerto Cabello. The commanders of the revolt drew support from over 1,500 marines, soldiers, and civilians. The fighting lasted for three days, but finally the insurgents were defeated.

The defeat of the various *guerrilla* insurgency acts during 1962 illustrated to the communists and the *miristas* that the Plan for Rapid Victory could not be carried out without some adjustment. With the defeat of the June 1961 revolt in Barcelona, troops loyal to the government thwarted the last major right-wing attempt to overthrow President Betancourt. The leftist insurgents understood, by the end of 1962, that new and more organized plans were needed if they were to succeed in their attempt to oust the government. The Left learned that the task of seizing power from Betancourt would be more difficult than previously anticipated.

The year 1963 became one of the most violent in the often turbulent history of Venezuela. The new philosophy of the *Partido Comunista de Venezuela* and the *Movimiento de Izquierda Revolucionaria* became evident when their leaders, along with extremist elements of both the *Unión Republicana Democrática* and the military, officially formed a unified insurgent organization. With the formation of the *Fuerzas Armadas de Liberación Nacional* (Armed Forces of National Liberation) (FALN) and the *Frente de Liberación Nacional* (National Liberation Front) (FLN), a systematic and cohesive plan of direction for the insurgency effort became possible.

For its followers, the armed struggle by the FALN/FLN was seen as the only vehicle capable of achieving the emancipation of the Venezuelan people. The FALN coordinated the separate *guerrilla* bands operating in the Venezuelan countryside and received its political direction from the FLN. The emphasis placed on the armed struggle transformed the FALN into the dominant partner in the FALN/FLN organization. However, with the failure of the insurgents' earlier Plan for Rapid Victory (1960–1963), the FALN/FLN leadership had to reevaluate its options. The group, however, decided to again follow a rapid victory program, because it believed that a prolonged war (following the Chinese model) would allow Betancourt the opportunity to transfer power to an elected successor. If the elections were to take place in December 1963, as scheduled, the chances of a Castro-communist takeover would be greatly reduced. A PCV strategy paper at the time stated that the electoral process would deepen the electoral illusions of the people and contribute to the stability of the government. As a consequence, the FALN came to realize that a significant revolutionary juncture in Venezuela would be the 1963 electoral campaign.

The primary area of importance for the FALN was the urban *guerrilla* or terrorist, with special emphasis placed on Caracas. The *Comando Nacional Guerrillero* (National *Guerrilla* Command) provided the direction and leadership for the urban-based insurgents. These urban terrorists had originally been organized into small units and were to support the rural *guerrillas*, since the early leaders believed that the rural *guerrillas* were the most important battle front, following the example of the Cuban revolution. After the switch to emphasize the role of urban *guerrillas*, the urban units were reorganized into two types: one performed most of its acts within the city of operation, and the other traveled to outlying areas to perform its acts and then returned to the city for safety. These larger units were subdivided into smaller bands that specialized in a particular type of insurgency (e.g., arson or bank robbery), although all of the groups assisted in intelligence gathering and recruitment.

With the failure of the leftist military uprisings at Carúpano and Puerto Cabello, and also of the rural *guerrilla* units, the FALN saw no other alternative than a full-scale, two-stage urban push of violence. The first stage consisted of terrorism, sabotage, arson, and robbery, and, if by late 1963 President Betancourt remained in power, the second stage would follow. The second stage included an increase in the frequency of the events in the first stage, plus street violence, sniper attacks, and bombing attacks in major cities. The FALN used urban terrorism to disrupt society, discredit the government, antagonize the military, and create conditions for a *golpe*.

In January 1963, the government discovered an FALN radio installation that contained equipment capable of establishing contact with Cuba and transmitters powerful enough to relay information to all parts of Venezuela. Much of the propaganda from Cuba was sent via Radio Havana, which had begun service in May 1961. The youth of Venezuela had joined the youth of many of the other Latin American nations in receiving support from Cuba. Estimates for 1962 indicated that over 200 Venezuelan youth traveled to Cuba for *guerrilla* training. It is also probable that Venezuela acquired communist literature and military assistance from Cuba during this time. The United States Central Intelligence Agency believed that Cuba had been involved in Venezuelan subversion since 1959.

In an attempt to curb the insurgency movement, the Venezuelan government began to regulate constitutional guarantees. The magazine *Momento* published a letter it received from Interior Minister Carlos Andrés Pérez, which ordered the censorship of the press, in accordance with the May 4, 1962, suspension of constitutional guarantees. The letter stated that publications were forbidden to release information related to "the public order" without first consulting with government officials. In this regard, the *Hispanic American Report* noted that the government had placed official censors at each major newspaper office. On October 8, 1962, President Betancourt suspended constitutional guarantees for the fourth time, in reaction to subversive activities by the insurgents. One week later, Betancourt announced that Minister Pérez had formally delivered to the president of the Venezuelan Supreme Court the government's request to outlaw the *Partido Comunista de Venezuela* and the *Movimiento de Izquierda Revolucionaria*.

The FALN leadership attempted to achieve its immediate goal of stopping the democratic process prior to the December elections. As part of their strategy, the FALN continued to utilize both urban insurgents and rural *guerrillas* in an attempt to persuade residents to withdraw their support of the Betancourt government. The urban insurgency actions were well prepared, and multiple plans were ready in advance so that actions could be carried out with only minimal notice. By mid-1963, street riots were seldom used, while sabotage and terrorism had become the most popular insurgent activities during the desperate months leading up to the election.

One of the most significant acts of mass terror was the killing of national guardsmen on a passenger train en route from Caracas to El Encanto in September. The terrorists shot the soldiers while the train was passing through a tunnel and then tossed the wounded men from the train. The train, also carrying women and children, did not contain first aid kits because the terrorists had previously removed them. Within a week of the incident, organized labor voiced strong support for the government and demanded action against the terrorists. The population now stood solidly behind President Betancourt, and he capitalized on the opportunity for action. In a presidential decree, he ordered the detention and confinement of PCV and MIR activists and other persons who appeared to be involved in any acts of violence and terrorism that threatened major disturbances of public order, or who promoted actions aimed at disturbing the electoral process or impede the upcoming elections. By the end of October, several hundred PCV and MIR party members had been arrested, including PCV leader Gustavo Machado. Lending further support for Betancourt's actions, the government discovered an arms shipment in November that had originated in Cuba. Because of the increased police protection and military support, the mass terrorists were almost completely eliminated in mid-November 1963, when over 700 of them were arrested.

The FALN then began its last-ditch effort to stop the 1963 election. In the three months leading up to the December voting, the FALN carried out 91 acts of violence, which was more than 50 percent of the total for the entire year. These attempts at winning over the population to the insurgent cause actually tended to bring the population closer to the government. It now appeared to the FALN leaders that the only chance of a government overthrow would have to occur in the rural areas of the country.

Despite threats by the extreme Left, plans for the December voting proceeded. Nine major political parties participated in the 1963 national elections; their political ideologies ranged from the constitutional Left to the far Right. President Betancourt had outlawed the far Left, thus eliminating the PCV and the MIR parties from legally participating in the elections. The nine major political parties supported seven candidates. The major candidates and the political parties that supported them in the election were: Dr. Raúl Leoni, *Acción Democrática;* Dr. Rafael Caldera, *Comité de Organización Política Electoral Independiente;* Dr. Jóvito Villalba, *Unión Republicana Democrática, Partido Socialista Venezolano,* and *Movimiento Electoral Nacional Independiente;* Dr. Arturo Uslar Pietri, *Independientes Pro-Frente Nacional* (Independents for a National Front); and Rear Admiral Wolfgang Larrazábal, *Fuerza Democrática Popular* (Popular Democratic Force).

The FALN terrorists fulfilled their pledge of intensifying the violence as the elections drew near; however, despite the increase in violence by the FALN, the electoral process continued. The campaign officially closed on November 30, 1963, with the announcement by Eduardo Arroyo Lameda, president of the *Consejo Supremo Electoral* (Supreme Electoral Council). In his speech two days before the balloting, Arroyo praised the electoral process. Thus, the FALN arrived at the crucial moment not knowing whether it would be successful in achieving its goal of stopping the election. The population, however, appeared to know that the democratic process would proceed. Many Venezuelans had turned from the insurgents' offer of change and toward the government's offer of continued democracy. The September shooting of the national guardsmen, probably more than any other event, turned the Venezuelan people against the FALN, and they demanded that the government put an end to the senseless violence. In the end, the FALN was unable to turn either the urban or rural population against the Betancourt government. After Arroyo closed the electoral campaign, the candidates retired for the weekend. In two days, the candidates would hopefully witness a monumental achievement in Venezuelan history: the popular election of a successor to a president who had also been chosen in another popular election. On the eve of the election, the leaders of the government armed services in a joint radio broadcast pledged to honor the results of the election.

On election day, there were scattered outbursts of violence by the insurgents. Voters disregarded the terrorist threats and began to report to their voting precincts as early as 5:00 A.M. to stand in line. Not quite sure what would happen to them at the polls, 3,107,563 voters cast ballots in the presidential election. By the end of the day, only 1 person had been killed and 13 wounded, but, more importantly, a new and freely elected successor to Rómulo Betancourt had been chosen. Raúl Leoni, the *Acción Democrática* candidate, won the election with 32.8 percent of the votes. The election results can be interpreted as a flat rejection of the insurgent attempts at luring the populace into the undeclared civil war against the Betancourt coalition government. Over 92 percent of the Venezuelan voting population cast ballots on December 1, 1963, and this large voter turnout created a major setback for the FALN/FLN.

SUMMARY

Venezuelan President Rómulo Betancourt brought democracy back to Venezuela. Instituting a plan of administrative austerity, the former exile tackled the severe economic problems that he inherited. He put into practice a series of critical measures, some of them quite unpopular among certain sectors of the population. He survived several assassination attempts, from both domestic and foreign foes. He successfully withstood two splits within his party, even though they created political and social problems for his government. Through it all, however, he was able to complete his constitutional term of office and provide for national elections in 1963.

The success and results of the 1963 elections clearly indicate that the Venezuelan people wanted democracy. They also illustrated a major change in Venezuelan politics. The premier position of *Acción Democrática* was reaffirmed. The Christian democratic COPEI, with its impressive showing, became Venezuela's second major party, and the *Unión Republicana Democrática* dropped to third place among the older political parties of Venezuela. The need for the continuation of a coalition-style government in Venezuelan politics was evident.

NOTES

1. Refer to Juan Carlos Rey, "El futuro de la democracia en Venezuela," *Venezuela hacia el 2000: Desafíos y Opciones* (Caracas: Editorial Nueva Sociedad, 1987), 197.
2. John D. Powell, *Political Mobilization of the Venezuelan Peasants* (Cambridge, MA: Harvard University Press, 1971), 156–157.
3. Refer to Talton F. Ray, *The Politics of the Barrios of Venezuela* (Berkeley: University of California Press, 1969), 85–98.

9

The Institutionalization of Democracy (1964–1973)

An unprecedented event in Venezuelan history took place on March 11, 1964: power changed hands, within a constitutional framework, from a sitting constitutionally elected president to another constitutionally elected president. The ascension of Raúl Leoni and the formation of his *Amplia Base* (Broad Base) coalition also witnessed the free relinquishing of power by the opposition, as COPEI was no longer a member of the governing coalition. President Leoni took possession of the office and governed with broad support, especially with his appointment of several important independent figures to his cabinet.

THE LEONI PRESIDENCY

Although *Acción Democrática* had won the presidency, the party failed to obtain a majority in either chamber of Congress (obtaining 47 percent in the Senate and 37 percent in the Chamber of Deputies). Thus, President Leoni had to continue President Betancourt's practice of governing through a coalition. This time, however, AD and COPEI were unable to work out a mutual program of government, and Leoni looked toward other parties in the Congress. Leoni forged the *Amplia Base* coalition with the center-Left *Unión Republicana Democrática* (URD) and the center-Right

Frente Nacional Democrático (National Democratic Front) (FND). The *Amplia Base* coalition held 106 seats in the Chamber of Deputies (59 percent) and 34 seats in the Senate (68 percent). The social-Christian COPEI, headed by Rafael Caldera, announced in early March that it would not join the Leoni government. The reported reasons for this break were that Leoni had not offered COPEI an appropriate share of the government positions commensurate with the party's popular support, as reflected in the elections. President Leoni and Rafael Caldera had very little contact with each other, which also contributed to the failure of a continuation of the AD-COPEI coalition. By not becoming a partner in the new government, COPEI became the first major political party in Venezuela to assume the role of "loyal opposition."

The *Amplia Base* coalition gave the Leoni government (1964–1969) greater public acceptance, solidarity, and stability. In addition, it diminished the opposition's power, although the FND left the coalition in 1966, and URD withdrew in 1968. President Leoni and *Acción Democrática* drew their most important political backing from the labor sector, particularly rural labor, with whom the party had been closely associated since its foundation. The political viability of the government also depended on the ability of AD to continue to work with its coalition partners. Even though Leoni lacked the dynamism of his predecessor, he had the leadership skills necessary to forge the coalition with URD and FND in order to gain control of Congress.

During his administration, special attention was given to measures designed to further develop the social, economic, and political sectors. In the Guayana region of Venezuela, the steel, hydroelectric, and mining industries were advanced. Moreover, social investment grew considerably during this time, especially in the areas of education, sanitation, and housing. For example, Leoni's government implemented professional training programs for primary and middle school teachers who lacked education degrees. These training programs were executed through the *Instituto de Mejoramiento Profesional* (Institute for Professional Improvement). A new social security law was passed, which extended benefits to include invalids and married couples, and endowed death benefits. A greater importance was given to organized labor unions, even allowing them to operate their own bank, the *Banco de los Trabajadores* (Workers' Bank). Meanwhile, the communication infrastructure required by the country's development was given added priority, especially the roadway system. The Leoni government also expanded the policy of equipping and modernizing the armed forces. In the political arena, *Acción Democrática* experienced another split in its membership.

Similar to the insurgency movement during the Betancourt administration, throughout the administration of President Leoni, Venezuela continued to be a target of left-wing insurgent aggression, which included attempts at overthrowing the president. The United States Central Intelligence Agency reported (1964) that the communist insurgency movement had an estimated 300 *guerrillas* and 500 urban terrorists and that they operated in widely scattered parts of Venezuela. Just as with earlier insurgent groups (as discussed in the previous chapter), students provided most of the manpower for the terrorists.

In a speech to his fellow congressmen, former Interior Minister Carlos Andrés Pérez addressed the issue of the promotion of the insurgency movement at major Venezuelan universities. To illustrate his point, the congressman read to his colleagues several of the slogans students were posting across the campus of the Universidad Central de Venezuela (UCV) as part of a weekly plan of action by the FALN. In 1966, President Leoni ordered troops into the UCV campus to seize rebels who were hiding there. In addition to the arrest of over 800 criminals and terrorist suspects, the government found arms, ammunition, explosives, and terrorist plans. Sending troops into the campus was significant, because the Venezuelan constitution gave the university autonomous status. After Leoni's campus raid, the government removed the school's privileges to ensure the ability to send police into the campus in the event of similar disturbances. In July 1964 the government claimed to have evidence that recent terrorist acts carried out in Venezuela had been ordered by communists, who had pledged to overthrow the Leoni government.

By 1965, the United States Intelligence Board estimated that the insurgency movement, specifically the FALN, had increased its numbers to about 1,500 militants, although many fewer were available at any one time. While the Venezuelan government had long suspected Cuban assistance, proof had not been found until three Cubans were caught at the Muchurucuto beach (on the Barlovento coast) during a joint Cuban-Venezuelan attempt to smuggle arms into the country. This led to a strong response from Carlos Andrés Pérez, the chairman of *Acción Democrática's* congressional caucus. In a speech to his fellow deputies, Pérez stated that Cuban aggression had begun soon after Fidel Castro assumed the presidency (1959), and that Castro had continuously attacked Venezuela in his speeches. Following the rhetorical attack against the Betancourt government, Cuba extended financial support to members of the *Movimiento de Izquierda Revolucionaria* (Movement of the Revolutionary Left) and the *Partido Comunista de Venezuela* (Venezuelan Communist Party) (PCV). Even though the level of terrorism had diminished from that of the 1962–1963 period, the Leoni government continued to be distracted from its duties as it dealt with the insurgency movement.

The PVC had no intention of abandoning its revolutionary program, although the party's central committee and the older communist leaders, such as Gustavo Machado, adopted a policy of legal opposition, which they referred to as a "democratic peace." Eventually, this strategic difference led to a major division between the older Caracas-based leadership and the younger communist *guerrilla* leaders. When the PCV leadership stated its official position that the armed struggle path had been abandoned, the younger leaders, such as Douglas Bravo, expressed their discontent. Thus, the PCV began its generation-based breakup. This event, as would be expected, led to a rift between the older Venezuelan communists and Fidel Castro.

Like President Betancourt, President Leoni also had to deal with problems within *Acción Democrática*. Shortly after his nomination, the party began to undergo serious ideological and policy differences among its members, particularly between the followers of party Secretary-General Jesús A. Paz Galarraga (*pacistas*) and the followers of former President Rómulo Betancourt (*betancuristas*). The level of animosity between the two groups reached its peak over the issue of the 1968 presidential candidate for *Acción Democrática*. The *betancurista* faction supported the nomination of Gonzalo Barrios, while others within the party backed Luis Beltrán Prieto Figueroa, president of the party's executive committee.

Unable to resolve the matter by conciliatory means, the party's interconvention leadership council passed a resolution (in late 1967) that removed from office Prieto Figueroa, Paz Galarraga, and several other members of the party hierarchy. Prieto Figueroa and his followers (*prietistas*) left the party and were joined by the *pacistas*. Thus, within a period of seven years, the party underwent three divisions among its leaders and membership. After his departure from *Acción Democrática*, Prieto Figueroa founded the *Movimiento Electoral del Pueblo* (People's Electoral Movement) (MEP), whose followers became known as *mepistas*.

President Leoni instituted changes in oil industry policy, which allowed the Venezuelan government a greater participation in the fiscal process that regulated the industry. Among his oil policy changes were the promulgation of Decree 187, which assigned to the *Corporación Venezolana del Petróleo* the responsibility of supplying one-third of the national oil market; the increase of benefits originating from a revised system of petroleum-related tax collection; and the reform of the Law of Hydrocarbons, incorporating the legal role of the *contratos de servicio* (service contracts) as a substitute for the system of concessions, with the goal of securing for the nation the maximum benefit possible that could be generated by the oil industry. The price of crude oil remained relatively constant during the administration of President Leoni.

There were four major contenders for the presidency in 1968: Gonzalo Barrios, Dr. Rafael Caldera, Miguel Angel Burelli Rivas, and Luis Beltrán Prieto Figueroa. The splintering of *Acción Democrática* in 1967–1968 proved to be devastating for the party at the ballot box. The final vote count for the presidency was Barrios 28.24 percent, Caldera 29.08 percent, Burelli Rivas 22.27 percent, and Prieto Figueroa 19.32 percent. In the congressional returns, AD received 25.62 percent, COPEI 24.09 percent, URD-FDP-FND 17.17 percent, and MEP 12.97 percent. Dr. Rafael Caldera won the Presidency with a margin of only 31,071 votes (out of 3.1 million votes cast), while *Acción Democrática* remained the largest party in Congress. Caldera thus became the first *copeyano* (member of COPEI) to assume the presidency.

THE CALDERA PRESIDENCY

Caldera had long been active in Venezuelan politics, having founded the *Unión Nacional Estudiantil* (National Student Union) in 1936. During the *Trienio*, he served as attorney general (1945–1946), and between 1946 and 1968, he ran for president four times. The Caldera government constituted itself as a single-party administration and did not formalize an executive-branch coalition with other parties. In Congress, COPEI was in the minority, which demanded extreme care in Caldera's handling of public affairs. His legislative coalition did not include *Acción Democrática*, although COPEI formed congressional alliances with different groups throughout the Caldera presidency. It should be noted, however, that *Acción Democrática* and *Unión Republicana Democrática* remained as loyal opposition during the COPEI administration.

President Caldera's administration (1969–1974) advanced a policy of pre-nationalization, by which the country reserved the right to exploit its natural gas reserves, internal commerce, and control over certain oil industry-related activities. Through the 1971 Hydrocarbons Reversion Law, the state required that all of the foreign-owned petroleum companies' assets within Venezuela revert to the state when their concessions expired. In addition to these measures, greater fiscal pressure was placed upon foreign companies, and the government set out to unilaterally fix oil prices. The government's efforts created a situation in which the oil companies started to allow their equipment to go into disrepair, knowing that they would soon be losing their investments.

President Caldera also renewed the efforts of Presidents Betancourt and Leoni with regard to the country's social development. These efforts included agrarian reform, the expansion of infrastructure, the improvement of the educational system, and the economic development of the southernmost regions of the country. Another area of success was the increase in the scope of labor legislation with regard to farm workers to levels unprecedented by Venezuelan standards. These efforts allowed for a period of internal social mobility and for the expansion of certain public sectors, which would ultimately comprise a bipartisan base of support for Caldera.

In the field of foreign policy, Caldera's administration pursued a policy that proposed Latin American pluralist solidarity and internal social justice programs, both of which were designed to ease tensions between Venezuela and Cuba and, therefore, with the rest of the socialist world. In addition, Caldera rejected the Betancourt Doctrine.

President Caldera's government formalized the pacifist process whereby the radical Left was brought into the institutional political discourse. President Caldera re-legalized the *Partido Comunista de Venezuela* in March 1969 and the *Movimiento de Izquierda Revolucionaria* in March 1973 and offered political amnesty to leftist *guerrillas*, many of whom accepted his offer. One of the most significant actions in this regard was the pardoning of Captain Pedro Medina Silva, ex-commandant of the FALN. Many of the insurgents likely accepted Caldera's offer because of their perception that they were fighting a lost cause. As early as 1965, the United States Central Intelligence Agency reported that several FALN deserters had reported that morale among the group was low and that the field units were short of food and supplies.

The 1973 presidential campaign was well financed, particularly among the two top contenders, Carlos Andrés Pérez and Eduardo Fernández. The Venezuelan magazine *Resumen* noted that *Acción Democrática* and COPEI collectively had spent over 310 million Venezuelan Bolívars ($321 million in 2005 U.S. dollars), with AD reportedly spending 2.5 million Bolívars solely to retain Joe Napolitan, a publicity consultant from the United States. The 1973 campaign signified the first Venezuelan election to be significantly influenced and directed by U.S. strategists and consultants. Their influence was so great that one political leader referred to the Pérez campaign as having been "Made in USA."

Leslie Bethell noted that the 1973 presidential campaign became a popular campaign with songs, fiestas, and beer parties. To take advantage of his youthful image, Pérez wore flashy neckties, had long sideburns, and took well-publicized fast-moving walks through residential neighborhoods. To further enhance his "vibrant" image, Pérez used catchy slogans such as *"democracia con energía"* ("democracy with energy") and *"ese hombre sí camina"* ("that man sure can walk"). The 1973 election was also quite pluralistic. Twelve candidates pursued the presidency, with political ideologies ranging from the far Left to the far Right. The election also included a number of candidates for public office who were supporters of former dictator Marcos Pérez Jiménez. The results of the presidential election were rewarding for *Acción Democrática*. Carlos Andrés Pérez won the presidency with 48.7 percent of the votes—a significant increase (67 percent) over Rafael Caldera's win in 1968. Pérez also managed a 72 percent increase over the results for *Acción Democrática* in the last presidential election. AD obtained a majority in 157 of the nation's 181 municipal councils, and an analysis of state-by-state returns shows that Pérez carried all of the Venezuelan states except Zulia. Clearly, *Acción Democrática*, under the leadership of Carlos Andrés Pérez, was extremely successful in its stated objectives of winning back the presidency and increasing its national membership. In addition, former president Betancourt was responsible for bringing together many former *adecos* (AD supporters) who had left the party in the years since 1958. The reuniting of the party was an important stimulus for regaining support within Venezuela.

Equally significant was the fact that *Acción Democrática* had regained control of both chambers of the national Congress—for the first time since the national elections of December 1958. In the Senate, *Acción Democrática* held 28 of 49 seats; in the Chamber of Deputies, the party held 102 of 200 seats. In contrast, COPEI (Pérez's chief rival) claimed only 13 senators and 64 deputies. Also of importance was the fact that *Acción Democrática* had regained its premier position among the Venezuelan political parties (as determined by popular support). In this regard, not only had Carlos Andrés Pérez regained the presidential sash for his party, but he had also reinvigorated both the party and its supporters.

SUMMARY

This period in Venezuelan history witnessed the institutionalization of the democratic process. National power changed hands from one popularly elected president to another two times during this era, switching not only the person of the president, but also the political party in power. The armed forces remained apolitical, and the majority of the Venezuelan people came to accept democracy—for better or worse—as the only path for national development and political stability. By 1973, another factor emerged in Venezuela that would forever change the political and social landscape: massive petroleum revenue.

10

Venezuelan Boom and Bust (1974–1988)

The years between 1974 and 1988 witnessed both a rapid rise and a decline in the price of crude oil. The price increase and government revenue allowed the presidential administrations of Carlos Andrés Pérez (1974–1979) and Luis Herrera Campíns (1979–1984) opportunities to expand the size and role of the government. The situation also created problems beyond the comprehension of the two leaders. Toward the end of the presidency of Jaime Lusinchi (1984–1989), oil prices plummeted to levels so low that the nation was in dire economic condition by the end of 1988.

THE FIRST PÉREZ PRESIDENCY

When Carlos Andrés Pérez assumed the presidency in March 1974, he attempted to transform himself into the spokesman for Latin America. Utilizing the far-reaching powers in both domestic and foreign affairs that the Venezuelan governmental structure allowed the president, Pérez transformed Venezuelan society and the nation's position within Latin America. Pérez represented a new generation of political leaders in Venezuela; this political shift and the sweeping changes that the Pérez administration effected characterized his first administration.

During Pérez's first term, Venezuelan society underwent profound changes primarily resulting from his economic policy of nationalization of the industries of Venezuela's major natural resources—iron and petroleum—even though opposition parties labeled his measures as having limited reach. Two months into his administration, President Pérez swore in a *Comisión Nacional* (National Commission) designed to study the prompt and complete nationalization of the petroleum industry. The *Consejo Siderúrgico Nacional* (National Iron and Steel Council), also created by Pérez in 1974, studied the acquisition of the iron concessions and the replacement of iron-ore exports with iron and steel products.

The iron industry was the first to be nationalized, in what Pérez described as part of the Latin American strategy to obtain economic independence. In the official nationalization ceremony (January 1, 1975), Pérez commented that the Venezuelan region of Guayana was the "custodian" of the nation's great future, which depended on managing the nation's natural resources. The nationalization of the iron industry voided the concessions to the subsidiaries of the U.S.-owned United States Steel Corporation and Bethlehem Steel. In the settlement, the government paid $101 million ($367 million in 2005 U.S. dollars)[1] as compensation to the two companies. Additionally, the Venezuelan government agreed to negotiate contracts with the two companies under which they would continue to provide the necessary management for the operation of the mines during a one-year period of transition.

Exactly one year later, Pérez presided over the official ceremony marking the nationalization of the petroleum industry. In an elaborate ceremony held on the site of Zumaque I, Venezuela's first commercial oil well, Pérez stated that only by "engaging in this all-out national effort will the country become increasingly autonomous, truly reducing economic dependency along with technological and cultural dependency." Effective January 1, 1976, the government nationalized the 19 oil companies operating in Venezuela (16 foreign-owned and 3 Venezuelan-owned). Of these 19 companies, 3 accounted for four-fifths of the oil produced: Dutch Shell, Creole (an Esso subsidiary), and Mene Grande (a Gulf subsidiary).

As authorized by the nationalization law, which reserved to the state the industry and commerce of hydrocarbons, the president created the *Petróleos de Venezuela* (Venezuelan Petroleum), an organization whose functions included coordinating, programming, and controlling the activities of the oil industry. *Petróleos de Venezuela* (PDVSA) emerged from the *Corporación Venezolana del Petróleo*, which had been created in 1960 by President Betancourt to maximize Venezuela's utilization of its natural resources.

In addition to the $1.16 billion compensation package to the foreign-owned companies, the nationalization agreement authorized the Venezuelan government to enter into contracts with those same companies for technological assistance and equipment. This assistance would be needed for the first few years while Venezuelan nationals received the appropriate training. This stipulation would lead to highly volatile debates within Congress, because many wanted the foreigners completely out of the nation's petroleum business. The petroleum industry was so important to Venezuela that, by 1980, it accounted for 70 percent of the nation's revenue and 26 percent of the total gross national product.

Pérez continued the *Acción Democrática* policy of state-run capitalism and, in fact, involved the government in the economy at a level never before undertaken in Venezuela. The government of Carlos Andrés Pérez spent more money from 1974 to 1979 than had all other Venezuelan governments during the previous 143 years combined. The state was capable of such involvement because the treasury revenue in 1973 was $3.82 billion, and in 1974 it was $9.95 billion. In fact, state-owned companies reportedly spent nearly 25 times more in 1975 than they had in 1960.

In an effort to prevent the economy from being flooded with excess government revenue, thus causing inflation, Pérez established the *Fondo de Inversiones de Venezuela* (Venezuelan Investment Fund), which was designed to "export" between 35 and 50 percent of the new income as loans to other Latin American nations. Venezuela also loaned capital to international lending institutions, such as the Inter-American Development Bank, the International Monetary Fund, and the World Bank. To these three lending institutions, the *Fondo de Inversiones* lent (in 1974) a total of approximately $850 million; to the six nations of Central America, Jamaica, and Perú, the Fund lent approximately $400 million. In addition, the Fund served as its own bank for the large-scale development projects planned for the public sector, such as the expansion of the Venezuelan Shipping Company.

In addition to the nationalization of both iron and petroleum, the government also continued its sizable programs of agrarian reform, agricultural subsidization, large-scale irrigation projects, and the expansion of the hydroelectric industry. Pérez was able to increase dramatically the role of the state in the economy because of the immense resources derived from the rise in oil prices caused by the first worldwide energy crises. The average price per barrel of Venezuelan crude oil increased from $2.05 in 1970 ($10.32 in 2005 U.S. dollars) to $9.30 in 1974 ($36.84 in 2005 dollars). Within a period of five years, prices increased approximately 500 percent. Within one year of the beginning of the Herrera Campíns presidency (1979), the price of Venezuela's Tía Juana Light had increased to $25.20 per barrel

($59.73 in 2005 U.S. dollars). The entire Venezuelan bureaucracy was modified. During his five years in office, Pérez budgeted more than $53 billion toward projects aimed at improving the infrastructure, agriculture, and public health. The production capacity of petroleum, iron, steel, and aluminum was also expanded.

Acción Democrática relied upon the support of the rural population, and so Pérez continued to include significant agrarian projects in his government programs. The Venezuelan Agrarian Reform Law of 1960, initiated under the Betancourt government, strengthened the ties of the agricultural sectors to the required financial capital and multinational enterprises. During the election campaign, Carlos Andrés Pérez condemned the neglect of agricultural interests and declared himself the "President of the Peasants." During his administration, measures were taken to modernize and develop agriculture, such as reconverting and consolidating the agrarian debt; granting supplementary credits for infrastructure and technical assistance; instituting fiscal measures designed to stimulate agricultural production; and freezing prices for the industrial products necessary for agricultural production.

The most outstanding of these measures was the creation of a special fund of approximately $450 million, earmarked exclusively for agricultural development. This fund made possible the concession of numerous credits to small-scale farmers by the *Instituto de Crédito Agropecuario* (Institute for Livestock and Agricultural Credit), and to large-scale farmers through the auspices of the *Banco para el Desarrollo Agrícola y Ganadero* (Bank for Agricultural and Livestock Farming Development).

Overall, Pérez's domestic policies were designed to improve the distribution of Venezuela's oil revenues. In addition to the introduction of price controls, a government funds were allocated to subsidize the prices of food and other commodities. Numerous programs were initiated to expand employment, and the president engaged in government-mandated and government-supported wage increases for many low-paying jobs. In fact, during the five years of his administration, public employment in Venezuela doubled.

Pérez was able to advance these programs quickly because of his broad-based support. Throughout his first term in office, Pérez maintained the legislative support of *Acción Democrática*. In addition to his party holding the majority in both chambers of the national Congress and in the state legislative assemblies and municipal councils, he also enjoyed the support of the labor unions and the private-industry sector of the country. Taking advantage of the AD majority in Congress, President Pérez obtained congressional authorization (May 1974) to govern by decree without judicial or congressional review. In the midst of the administration, columnist David Gordon wrote that President Pérez passed hundreds of decrees a month—or so it seems. In a nine month period, he issued over 100 decrees.

The Venezuelan constitution in force at the time entrusted the president with far-reaching powers in both domestic and foreign affairs, including: the power of appointment and removal of ministers; the authority to submit bills to Congress; the ability to declare a state of emergency and suspend constitutional guarantees; the authority to call special sessions of Congress; and the authority to appoint state governors. A significant prerogative of the chief executive was his ability to adopt necessary regulations to bring laws into effect and such regulations were neither subject to the approval of Congress nor the courts.[2] President Pérez was also authorized to enact economic measures for the public good.

In addition to Pérez's efforts to nationalize Venezuela's natural resources was a move to "nationalize" the nation's human resources. To this end, a scholarship program was created in 1974 that sought to achieve a rapid buildup of the scientific and technological personnel to meet the expected demand that would come with the planned development of Venezuela's industry and agricultural projects. Many of such jobs were presently held by foreigners. In addition to its short-term goal of increasing the industrial workforce, the program also enabled young Venezuelans from disadvantaged socioeconomic backgrounds to gain access to higher education.

In a 1974 speech, President Pérez stated that the Venezuelan youth had a great mission to accomplish by undertaking training as technicians, as well as the specialized personnel that the oil industry required. A few weeks later he announced his plans to create the most ambitious scholarship program ever implemented in Latin America, utilizing the revenue generated by the petroleum industry. These students would attend national and international universities for training. By Decree 132, the scholarship program was created and officially named the *Programa de Becas Gran Mariscal de Ayacucho* (Great Marshall of Ayacucho Scholarship Program). According to the president, the program was charged with the coordination and granting of scholarships to students and professionals who wished to pursue studies in specialized areas primarily related to the oil, iron and steel, and petrochemical industries.

Because of the enormous wealth that the Venezuelan government was now collecting, Pérez planned to not set limitations on the use of the state's petroleum resources, but rather fund students who were willing to further their education in whatever numbers the country's development required. The president remarked that the scholarship recipients would allow nationalism to be more than an empty promise in that the program would equip Venezuelans to take control of their national destiny. In a ceremony commemorating the 150th anniversary of the Battle of Ayacucho, Pérez commented that Venezuelan youth would be trained to fight the battle against poverty, utilizing the advances of science and technology. Even with its positive results, the scholarship program was plagued with problems from the outset. Among the more serious problems was the fact that, as early as 1980, the projected number of qualified personnel for many of the positions would exceed the maximum demand expected. This led to widespread concern about the specializations that were being emphasized within the program. For his part, the president acknowledged that problems existed, and, in an effort to eliminate them, he requested several studies by outside agencies to identify the problem areas and make recommendations on how to solve them. Among those that completed studies were the Center of Policy Alternatives at the Massachusetts Institute of Technology and the United Nations Educational, Scientific, and Cultural Organization (UNESCO). As Pérez pointed out, there had been no precedent for a program of this size, and much of the initial decision-making had been done by trial and error. The UNESCO study reported (1977) that 75 percent of the students selected for the scholarships had come from economically impoverished backgrounds, which was a stated goal of the program. Additionally, the findings showed that 68 percent of the recipients came from rural areas. Overall, the scholarships have funded the successful training of tens of thousands of Venezuelan students, most of who contributed significantly to Venezuela's success in the petroleum and petrochemical fields.

The relative ease with which President Pérez was able to accomplish his domestic agenda gave him the opportunity to improve his image and prestige abroad, particularly within Latin America. This approach worked well for Pérez, who has been described as someone with a propensity for international politics. José A. Silva-Michelena noted that, for the first time since 1850, Venezuela projected itself overseas through a foreign policy of its own. And, as it turned out, this new foreign policy became more aggressive than ever before.

Pérez attempted to change the economic relationship between Venezuela and its trading partners, and he became an avid critic of the economic disparity between developed producer-nations and developing consumer-nations. He remarked that Venezuela aspired to a system of economic security with justice and not privileges but reciprocal respect. He noted that developing nations were forced to sell cheaply what they produced and buy expensively what they consume. Pérez charged that the artificial and unjust divisions within economic relations between nations must cease in order for the creation of a new international economic order. In 1974, in an open letter to United States President Gerald R. Ford (1913–), President Pérez stated that the Organization of Petroleum Exporting Countries (OPEC) had been formed to protect the basic wealth extracted from its members' subsoil because the price of petroleum had never compensated the oil-exporting nations for the high cost of their imports and of the technology needed for their development. The success of OPEC gave Pérez the example he needed to propose a similar approach for Latin America's economic interests, which would become Venezuela's official position to the world. In a later speech to the United Nations General Assembly, Pérez stated that the increase in petroleum prices and OPEC's involvement had allowed Venezuela to be in a position to increase the value of goods and other basic products from developing nations.

Shortly after assuming the presidency, Pérez publicly stated his willingness to work through an international forum to establish a balanced trade relationship between the raw materials produced by developing countries and the manufactured goods and technology produced by developed countries. Keeping with this philosophy, President Pérez and Mexican President Luis Echeverría (1922–) spearheaded the establishment of the *Sistema Económico Latinoamericano* Latin American Economic System (SELA) in 1975, headquartered in Caracas. SELA was established to promote Latin American economic and social advancement and to oppose protectionism by the developed nations.

Two of the surprising moves Pérez made were, in fact, the normalization of relations with Fidel Castro and his attempts to rescind the Organization of American States' sanctions against Cuba. At the center of his warming of relations with Cuba was the belief that the island's behavior was different in 1974 from what it had been in the 1960s. During the earlier administrations of Rómulo Betancourt and Raul Leoni, Cuba had trained and supported Venezuelan insurgents, and part of the time Carlos Andrés Pérez was in charge of the government's efforts to thwart the Castro-supported *guerrillas* operating in Venezuela.

In a 1975 interview for *Business Week,* President Pérez stated that he did not share Castro's ideology nor approve of his system of government, but that Venezuela must accept ideological differences with other nations if they are to join together in a common quest for independent decision-making. In a press conference with Canadian journalists, the president added that Venezuela's relationship with Castro was perfectly normal and based upon an understanding of ideological pluralism. Not only was it possible to maintain relations with non-democratic nations, but it was also feasible to support common policies for the mutual development of the nations in the various regions of the world.

The president's actions toward Cuba and the founding of SELA were not his only international achievements. Venezuela was the first member of OPEC to lend money to the World Bank. Pérez had also placed $500 million in trust with the Inter-American Development Bank for other Latin American nations to borrow in order to help with the increasing prices, particularly in the area of fuel. During the Pérez administration, Venezuela invested $35 million in the Caribbean Development Corporation. The president also traveled abroad more than any other Venezuelan president, including a trip to Moscow in 1976. Pérez also supported Panamá's claims to sovereignty over the Canal Zone.

Despite his relatively wide influence, Carlos Andrés Pérez ended his first term in office with conspicuous difficulties, not only in the exercise of governmental affairs, but also in dealing with his own party. The influence of Rómulo Betancourt on the internal affairs of *Acción Democrática* was of considerable importance at the time, and Betancourt's differences with Pérez were becoming quite evident. Betancourt supported Luis Piñerúa Ordaz for the 1978 presidential candidate. Piñerúa Ordaz conducted an unsuccessful campaign that focused on the recovery of the party's ethical values and criticized the atmosphere of rampant corruption that pervaded Pérez's administration.

The December 1978 elections brought COPEI back to Miraflores, the presidential palace. *Acción Democrática's* candidate, Luis Piñerúa Ordaz, lost to COPEI's Luis Herrera Campíns (1925–) by a little over 3 percentage points. This was a television campaign, with the candidates spending much more time in front of the cameras than previous Venezuelan presidential candidates. Of continued significance, AD and COPEI captured almost 90 percent of the total vote.

THE CAMPÍNS PRESIDENCY

Reflecting the continuation of the growth of the state, the newly elected Luis Herrera Campíns created several new ministries, including Science and Technology, as well as Intelligence Development. He cancelled the price controls imposed by President Pérez on goods and services in an attempt to lower the cost of living through the stimulation of economic competition. This policy earned Herrera Campíns unfavorable criticism, because most observers feared the result would be an increase in the cost of living. In the end, these policies precipitated the process of inflation.

Luis Herrera Campíns's administration brought charges of administrative corruption against the Pérez administration. One of such charges
involved the purchase of six frigates built in Italy by the *Cantieri Navale* for
the Venezuelan National Navy in excess of $60 million. Another important
charge involved the purchase of the presidential airplane, a transaction in
which several high-ranking administration officials had received lucrative
commissions. The third of these notorious corruption charges brought
against the Pérez administration involved the purchase of the refrigerated
ship *Sierra Nevada*, which was a useless purchase, since it did not meet the
requirements of the purpose for which it had been acquired.

Several important political changes occurred during the Herrera Campíns
era. The municipal elections of June 3, 1979, marked the beginning of a
new era in municipal government; from that point forward municipal
councils would be responsible for enacting new municipal administration guidelines (passed by Congress). The national Congress approved
increases in public wages and salaries, the minimum wage, and the pen-
sions for old age, infirmity, and death benefits. These increases had been
introduced into Congress by working-class congressional members in an
effort to counteract the cost-of-living increase brought about by the freeing up of prices.

The oil industry experienced great strides during the Herrera Campíns
administration, owing to the emphasis placed on oil policy and production. As a consequence of the Iranian hostage crisis and the Iran-Iraq war
of 1980, the price of Venezuelan crude oil reached record levels in international markets, up to more than $32 per barrel ($64 in 2005 U.S. dollars).
Such high oil prices naturally led to a remarkable bonanza in oil revenue.
Nevertheless, the foreign debt, which had risen consistently during
President Pérez's tenure, continued to rise unabated.

Other monetary problems for the administration included devaluation
of the *Bolívar* on February 18, 1983, which occurred as a direct result of the
high foreign debt amassed, tremendous domestic and foreign pressures to
pay off such a debt, and the administration's policies that caused revenue
to flee overseas. A preferential dollar exchange rate was put in place for
international mercantile transactions, aimed at benefiting those import-
ers who would make their claims via the *Régimen de Cambio Diferencial*
(Differential Exchange Regime)—an agency that had been established
precisely for the purpose of controlling and administering such claims
and that soon became the most corrupt organization in Venezuela's democratic history.

Notwithstanding the administration's monetary difficulties, there were
several notable cultural achievements during these years. New laws were

passed that had a tremendous influence in the areas of education and culture. The Universidad Pedagógica Experimental "Libertador" ("Libertador" Experimental Pedagogical University) was founded on July 24, 1983, to commemorate the bicentenary of Simón Bolívar's birth. The Teresa Carreño Theater was also constructed during this administration. Perhaps the most highly anticipated building project of the time was the completion of the first phase of the Caracas metropolitan subway system, or *metro*, between the Propatria and Chacaíto stations.

In the areas of labor and industry, the government had mixed results. There was an average decline in the change of real gross domestic product of −1.2 percent between 1979 and 1983, and unemployment averaged about 20 percent throughout the early 1980s. In the area of industrial expansion, a huge coal and steel complex was built in the western state of Zulia; other projects included a new natural gas plant, a new railroad from Caracas to the coast, and a bridge linking Margarita Island with the mainland.

The 1983 electoral campaign was less flamboyant than the previous two presidential elections. *Acción Democrática's* candidate, Jaime Lusinchi, enjoyed an easy victory over former president Rafael Caldera. Lusinchi ran a campaign that emphasized the failings of the Herrera/COPEI administration, and he won the presidency with 56.8 percent of the valid votes cast. The triumph of Jaime Lusinchi and *Acción Democrática* in the national 1983 elections was followed by an impressive win in the municipal elections, obtaining 66.2 percent of the vote, versus 23.7 percent obtained by COPEI.

THE LUSINCHI PRESIDENCY

In June 1984, the Congress approved the *Ley Habilitante* (Enabling Law), which allowed President Lusinchi to combat his foremost concern: the rampant economic crisis. Among the achievements of Lusinchi's economic recovery program were the guarantees of oil industry self-sufficiency; reduction of the national deficit; the achievement of equity in the balance of payments; an increased focus on agrarian and industrial production; the inauguration of the *Complejo Criogénico de Oriente* (Eastern Cryogenics Complex) in Anzoátegui State; and providing stimuli to the agricultural and industrial manufacturing sectors through the auspices of CORDIPLAN, a three-year program to boost productivity.

President Lusinchi's policies aimed at improving domestic companies were particularly evident in the fields of maritime and air transportation, which in turned benefited the tourism industry. He also attempted to increase productivity in the iron, steel, and aluminum industries. His *Pacto Social* (Social Pact) called for the government, industrialists, and workers to join forces in order to reach the common goal of parity with regard to the sacrifices entailed by the reorganization of the national economy.

Lusinchi refinanced Venezuela's foreign debt, which greatly influenced his economic and political policies. He vowed that Venezuela would pay off its foreign debt "until the very last cent," and he took great pride in his debt-refinancing efforts. In December 1986, a new devaluation of the *Bolívar* took place, bringing with it high levels of inflation. Three types of exchange rates were put in place: one of 7.5 *Bolívars* per preferential dollar for basic import transactions; another one of 14.5 *Bolívars* per preferential dollar for certain international mercantile transactions; and yet another of 30 *Bolívars* per dollar for the free money market.

Under President Lusinchi, Venezuela signed the *Declaración de Quito* (Quito Declaration) with the Republic of Ecuador, whereby each nation vowed to combat drug traffic and its use. The Congress passed a law against the use of drugs and narcotics, and the country put forth during a United Nations General Assembly meeting a very well received proposal to control narco-trafficking.

CORRUPTION

The occurrence of administrative corruption was one of the most negative aspects of the presidencies of Carlos Andrés Pérez and Luis Herrera Campíns, and it would become the focal point of their opposition. Although political corruption had been present in Venezuela long before 1974, the drastic increase of fiscal abundance allowed it to reach unprecedented levels during the decade following 1974. Even though *Acción Democrática* generally supported President Pérez on matters requiring votes in Congress, toward the end of his first administration, the AD congressional bloc began to reflect the growing conflict over the issue of public corruption between the followers of former President Betancourt and the followers of President Pérez.

The underlying causes of corruption were found in the weakness of Venezuelan institutions and laws. The drastic increase of funds produced by the exploration of petroleum compounded these causes. Two years into the Pérez administration, it was reported that over 500 cases of maladministration or corruption were being prepared by the Office of the Comptroller General, although it was believed that few would actually go to the courts.

At the end of his first term in office, public denunciations were made against Pérez and his administration regarding the abuses of public funds, the most publicized being the overpriced purchase of the Norwegian refrigerated freighter *Sierra Nevada*. The Venezuelan government purchased the 10,000-ton vessel for $20 million, and it was later learned that the price of the ship was actually $11.9 million. This transaction acquired scandalous proportions and contributed to the initial tarnishing of President Pérez. This type of system—overpayment of contractors, with kickbacks to the contracting officers—was perhaps the most widespread form of graft.

In a joint session of the Senate and Chamber of Deputies, the Congress voted 132 to 106 to declare Pérez politically responsible for the charges simply because they had occurred during his administration. Even though the congressional committee empowered to investigate the charges found the ex-president politically, morally, and administratively responsible, the full Congress did not approve the latter two findings. The congressional report charged that the $8.1 million paid in excess of the actual cost had been distributed among several intermediaries in the transaction and that the Pérez administration was aware of the overpayment. Thus, the Congress found him guilty of fomenting a climate of political corruption but exonerated him from moral and administrative responsibility for any specific charges.

Another example of corruption had to do with a small group of individuals who allegedly utilized their prominent positions for personal gain. Known as the "twelve apostles," several served in the Pérez administration, including Gumersindo Rodríguez (minister of the Central Office of Coordination and Planning), Diego Arria (governor of Caracas and minister of Information and Tourism), and Carmelo Lauría (development minister).

Simón Sáez Mérida claimed that these individuals received payment in corruption, filling their pockets for the millions they had given to the Pérez campaign. Daniel Hellinger noted (1991) that "when the petrodollars began cascading into the national treasury in 1974, these elites found that they had won more than anticipated when they threw in their lot with CAP [Pérez]."

John Martz has noted that most of the Venezuelan government programs were plagued by inefficiency, waste, and corruption, with discussions on the problems appearing almost daily in the press. And few were more vocal and critical than former President Rómulo Betancourt. Most Venezuelan politicians likely held the view that there was nothing wrong with sending government contracts toward individuals who could guarantee support at the ballot box, as long as the contract job was done adequately. In this regard, both *Acción Democrática* and COPEI had utilized petroleum revenue to bolster their political support.

Leslie Bethell asserted the difficulties involved with trying to eliminate corruption while building a political system that, historically, has depended upon patronage and clientelism. However, the simple fact that Venezuelan politics had always been that way could hardly be seen as a justification for the system.

As for the problems associated with administrative malfeasance, when Pérez left office COPEI assumed the presidency. Along with others who opposed Pérez, including competitors within his own party, COPEI spearheaded the investigation into the charges of corruption against the former president. But, as mentioned, when it came down to the vote in Congress, even opposition leaders were unwilling to label Pérez as morally and administratively corrupt. Politically, his administration had abused the system and should have been held accountable. As such, Pérez had not carried through with his responsibility of overseeing his administration.

As noted, Carlos Andrés Pérez was not the only Venezuelan president afflicted with these problems. High-ranking officials in the Luis Herrera Campíns administration were also charged and tried on grounds of administrative corruption following his term in office. Some of the most prominent cases were those of Rodolfo José Cárdenas (ex-governor of the Federal District), Domingo Mariani, ex-president of the *Compañía Anónima de Administración y Fomento Eléctrico* (Electrical and Administration Development Corporation), and of ex-ministers Vicente Narváez Churión, Tomás Abreu Rascanieri, and Bernardo Leal Puche. All of these individuals escaped prosecution by fleeing the country, which led to widespread public indignation.

In general, political corruption by a public official denotes unacceptable deviations from the normal duties of that public official. For Venezuela, the problem also had to do with perception. As long as Venezuela had fiscal resources and the administration got things done, the populace allowed payoffs to individuals who could expedite affairs. Venezuelan politics had always been that way. Today, this explanation seems inadequate, but in the 1980s, it was acceptable. One thing is certain: regardless of whether Carlos Andrés Pérez and Luis Herrera Campíns engaged in corrupt activities, their administrations fostered that behavior.

POLITICAL REDEMPTION

Former President Carlos Andrés Pérez always believed that he was the victim of a witch hunt for having broken the traditional molds of

Venezuelan politics in his effort to introduce new perspectives and ideas. For example, instead of giving high-level government jobs to party favorites, he relied on younger members of *Acción Democrática* as well as non-*adecos*. After the defeat of Piñerúa Ordaz in 1978, a coalition between the Betancourt faction of AD and COPEI sought to link Pérez to some of the most visible cases of political corruption that surfaced during his first administration. Having avoided a political-administrative sanction, Pérez almost immediately began to lay the groundwork for his future recovery.

After overcoming these initial obstacles, Pérez devoted his energy to work within *Acción Democrática* as well as to the formation of a public relations network with some of the most influential and powerful entities in the nation. His efforts to reestablish himself within the AD leadership were so effective that, as early as 1984, the notion of "stopping Carlos Andrés" began to be discussed among many of the older members of *Acción Democrática*.

The undeniable capacity for work that Pérez demonstrated during these years was not limited to parliamentary life, although his actions still tended to focus on Venezuelan politics. As a senator for life, a status formerly given to ex-presidents, Pérez carried out intense activity in Congress, with his primary objectives being to reconquer his political viability with the people and to continue to cultivate and maintain his image as an international leader.

By the middle of 1986, the Venezuelan media once again began to focus on Carlos Andrés Pérez. Some commentators supported him, others despised him, but they were all discussing him. Fully aware of Pérez's political stature, President Lusinchi and others within the *Acción Democrática* hierarchy undertook a campaign designed to ensure that the majority of the votes in the party's internal elections favored a more orthodox candidate, as opposed to Pérez. Such an effort partially achieved its goals, and the orthodox group gained control of the Party's district and regional secretariats. Nevertheless, the question of the presidential candidacy was not resolved, because AD's national leadership remained divided.

Pérez, therefore, found it necessary to go against the party's official pre-candidate, Octavio Lepage. Pérez set in motion a presidential campaign whose objective was to be elected as an "outsider" and to gain an overwhelming majority among the rank-and-file members. It is important to remember that just two years earlier, the party's internal climate showed a clear opposition to Pérez. Remarkably, the 1988 successful candidacy of Carlos Andrés Pérez imposed itself from a regional and grassroots level toward the national level, and from the bases of support toward the centers of party leadership.

Pérez was not an unknown, and his influence reached beyond organizational boundaries. He was not the mere representative of any specific interest group, and, most importantly, he no longer derived his political clout from *Acción Democrática*. Instead, his status came from his own political image. As described in the next chapter, soon after his 1988 reelection, that status would come crashing down.

The national elections of 1988 were remarkable in several ways. First, there were 24 presidential candidates, the most in Venezuelan history. Second, the reelection of former president Carlos Andrés Pérez made him the first Venezuelan to be twice elected president by popular and democratic vote. Third, Pérez—who had been vilified after his first administration—was able to acquire 52.89 percent of the vote with such a large number of opponents. President Pérez also enjoyed an *Acción Democrática* plurality in both the Senate and Chamber of Deputies, with 47.8 percent in the former and 48.3 percent in the latter. This would be the last election in which *Acción Democrática* obtained more than 35 percent in either chamber of the national legislative body.

SUMMARY

The years between 1974 and 1988 witnessed significant changes in the price of crude oil. The nationalization of the iron, steel, and petroleum industries, coupled with oil price increases, provided two presidential administrations with the necessary resources to expand the size and role of the state. In the process, these events also created huge problems. Toward the end of this period, petroleum prices had plummeted to levels so low that the nation found itself in a dire economic condition. These years also created opportunities for political and administrative corruption at levels not seen in Venezuela since the dark days of the Gómez dictatorship.

NOTES

1. Unless otherwise noted, all monetary figures are expressed in U.S. dollars.
2. Lynn R. Kelley, "Venezuelan Constitutional Forms and Realities," in *Venezuela: The Democratic Experience*, John Martz and David Meyers, eds. (New York: Praeger, 1986), 39.

11

Chaos, Futility, and Incompetence (1989–1998)

Since 1958, the Venezuelan political system has required the willing participation of well-disciplined and well-organized political parties and special interest groups. The larger political parties, such as *Acción Democrática* and COPEI, necessarily represented a wide range of social, political, and economic views and positions. On the part of the interest groups, the *Federación de Cámaras de Comercio y Producción* (Federation of Chambers of Commerce and Production), the *Confederación de Trabajadores de Venezuela*, and the *Federación Campesina de Venezuela* particularly stand out. By the 1990s, however, it had become apparent that the old style of doing business in the Venezuelan political arena had run its course. Unfortunately, the transformation to a new set of parameters was not a peaceful one.

THE SECOND PÉREZ PRESIDENCY

On February 2, 1989, Carlos Andrés Pérez received the presidential sash for the second time. His inauguration, held in the Teresa Carreño Theater (instead of the national Congress, like his predecessors), has been dubbed a coronation by many due to the lavishness of the ceremony and the large number of foreign dignitaries in attendance. In his inaugural speech,

President Pérez spoke of hard times ahead that would demand sacrifices from the population. At the same time, he noted that the government would be forced to undertake harsh measures to reorient the national economy. His *Plan de Ajuste Económico* (Economic Adjustment Plan) has become simply known as the Economic Package.

When Pérez assumed the presidency, Venezuela had almost $ 35 billion in foreign debt. As a consequence, a significant portion of Venezuela's revenue was spent on servicing the debt. President Pérez was, therefore, forced to borrow money from the International Monetary Fund, which mandated drastic economic and fiscal reforms, especially in the areas of economic restructuring and the reduction of public spending. The government was forced to allow the *Bolívar* to devalue significantly, decree or allow drastic price increases, reduce state subsidies for public transportation, and increase the price of gasoline.

The president also faced low crude oil prices and the economic consequences therein. In current dollars, the 1989 price of a barrel of Venezuelan oil was about half of what it was when Pérez took office for the first time in 1974. Thus, the country was faced with enormous debt and domestic expenditures and drastically reduced revenue. Pérez's Economic Package mandated increases in the prices of electricity and public services such as telephone, water, and sanitation. The government pursued a policy of industrial reconversion, designed to improve industrial efficiency, so that state industries would become more competitive. In an effort to balance the budget, the administration also undertook the privatization of financially troubled state industries in order to obtain additional fiscal resources and to lower public expenditures.

The adoption of new economic measures signaled that one of the traditional rules of the Venezuelan political system—the creation of a consensus regarding major decisions—was being ignored. Many of the measures adopted by the Pérez administration created a level of inflation not previously seen in Venezuela. Between 1989 and 1991, the accumulated inflation reached an unprecedented 150 percent. Government efforts were unable to control the inflationary forces.

The mere announcement of the austerity measures meant the crumbling of the Venezuelan people's unrealistic expectations that the return of Pérez would mean a return to the abundance of his first administration. Consequently, for many Venezuelans, the catalyst for unrest was the government announcement that harsh economic measures were being implemented at the behest of the International Monetary Fund. These measures, lacking the appropriate political backing, had barely been put into effect when the social unrest broke out.

The Consequences of Change

The Economic Package affected almost all of the Venezuelan population, especially the poor, and provoked a social explosion that ended only after more than 300 people had died at the hands of troops and police. Thus, within days of the second inauguration of Carlos Andrés Pérez, protests occurred that dramatically changed the way Venezuelans regard their nation, its political and economic structures, and even themselves. On this issue, Venezuelan historian and former president Ramón J. Velásquez noted that, since February 1989, Venezuelans have been demonstrating their feelings by taking to the streets. For several days, street violence, protests, and crime reached massive proportions among the poorest elements of Venezuelan society. Subsequent price increases and spending cutbacks have sparked student riots, teacher strikes, and even general strikes by the normally pro-government labor organizations.

In a nutshell, nothing has been the same in Venezuela since February 1989. The populist version of Venezuelan democracy, which had been controlled by *Acción Democrática* and COPEI since 1958, was near extinction. Politics had ceased to be a realm restricted to political parties and special interest groups. Partisan influence over large segments of the population had evaporated, and the traditional political class was disjointed and overwhelmed, without the ability or will to exercise leadership.

Throughout the 1980s, the Venezuelan government allowed domestic social and economic problems to fester without taking effective corrective steps. This inaction gave rise to greater political instability, a radicalization of certain groups, and the fragmentation of political parties and political participation. As a result, social and economic marginalization, extreme poverty, increased unemployment, and social injustice also increased. Electoral absenteeism, social frustration, and changing political attitudes became widespread. This crisis reached its apex in 1989, when unprecedented social conflict was unleashed and the normal models of functioning for both institutional and political protagonists was altered.

As if this were not enough, corruption seemed to have become a permanent fixture of Venezuelan politics. The problem then, as today, was that the country's leadership did not rise to the political occasion. Through misdeeds and financial mismanagement, between 1974 and 1988, more than one billion U.S. dollars were squandered. In addition, political institutions had become weakened to the point of ineptitude and were unable to reform the political system. These events made possible a profound indifference of the population toward its leaders and toward the traditional political class, in general. Thus originated the conditions that would eventually lead to the fall of Carlos Andrés Pérez and the rise of Hugo Chávez Frías. The causes for these events were many. At that time, Venezuelans had witnessed the scarcity of basic necessities among the poorest segments of society, massive hoarding and shortages of food items, a disproportionate increase in public transportation fares and gasoline prices, and police strategies for security that appeared to be based more on repression than on prevention. Added to this list were an institutional inability to prevent widespread abuse and a failure by the government to produce a rapid response to the situation. In fact, from the first signs of street protests until the constitutional guarantees were suspended to allow the armed forces to intervene, approximately 30 days had passed. In addition, communication breakdowns within the government prevented a proper explanation to the general public about why certain harsh—and naturally unpopular—economic measures were being imposed on them. Finally, Venezuelans were experiencing an economic model incapable of generating and distributing wealth equitably as well as radical changes in their political and social attitudes.

All in all, the aftermath of the events of February 1989 was tragic. Many lives were lost, and both the formal and informal mechanisms of the Venezuelan political system were transformed. The government blundered in overestimating President Pérez's personal popularity and conciliatory ability and never expected the high levels of popular discontent. Somewhere along the way, the Venezuelan political parties found themselves profoundly incompetent in tackling the nation's problems. Although, at one time, the mainstream political parties had been able to market themselves as representatives of all social demands and ideals, that was no longer the case. Despite the fact that *Acción Democrática* began to distance itself from the Pérez administration and voiced criticism of his economic adjustment program, the party was unable to rechannel the popular discontent in its favor or reap any sort of political benefit from its own stance regarding Pérez. *Acción Democrática*'s leadership lacked credibility by that point.

After February 27, 1989, Venezuela entered a period of social instability marked by frequent strikes, demonstrations, and student protests. On May 18, 1989, a general strike was called to protest the government's economic policies. In June 1990, violent demonstrations took place in protest against rising gasoline prices; in March 1991, two students died in a confrontation with police in Caracas during demonstrations against the high cost of living; in November 1991, the police killed three people in Caracas during a demonstration; and in December 1991, high school and university classes were suspended as a result of protests that left 10 young demonstrators dead at the hands of the police. By January 1992, renewed demonstrations began to take place across Venezuela calling for the removal of President Pérez from office.

A climate favorable to a *golpe de estado* emerged, and, on February 4, 1992, army forces in Maracaibo, Valencia, Maracay, and Caracas simultaneously moved against the government with 17 military units and battalions. The group of commanders who led the unsuccessful attempt included Lieutenant Colonel Hugo Chávez Frías. Once he saw the defeat of the rebellion he had masterminded, Chávez took advantage of a five-minute television broadcast that would ultimately catapult him to notoriety: He called for his fellow co-conspirators to surrender their arms as he assumed full responsibility for the defeat of the *golpe* attempt. In addition to declaring itself as having come from poor segments of Venezuelan society, the *golpe* leadership sought to gain converts within the military by advancing a credo that emphasized its repudiation of the evils of corruption and misery that politicians had wreaked upon the country. Although the Venezuelan people did not pour out onto the streets to support the *golpe* leaders, neither did they come out in support of the government or the democratic institutions.

Following the February 1992 *golpe* attempt, a presidential consulting commission was appointed, comprised of representatives of various social and political sectors. The objective of the commission was to discuss and implement suggestions, as well as to broaden the governmental base of support. The commission's proposals, however, were neither listened to nor executed with any degree of urgency, which led the public to believe that the politicians, once past the initial shock, lacked the will to enact the changes that were being demanded. Against this backdrop of discontent and frustration, a second *golpe* was attempted (November 27, 1992), this time organized by general officers of the army and marines and by small groups of civilians from the extreme Left. The confrontations involved Mirage, Bronco, OB-10, Toucan, and F-16 fighter airplanes. Both military and civilian targets were bombarded, and broadcast television was used to call for a popular insurrection, which, however, did not come to pass. Once again, the population did not heed the call from *coup* leaders, although it still demanded profound transformations.

Although both *golpes* caused the deaths of innocent people, the November 27 attempt was not a direct result of the February call to arms. These were separate movements that were related only insofar as they were both fueled by the exceptional circumstances brought about by the public's open repudiation of the unpopular Pérez administration. In February,

the *Movimiento Bolivariano Revolucionario 200* (Bolivarian Revolutionary
Movement 200) arose out of the mid-level leadership of the armed forces,
the brainchild of lieutenant colonels, majors, captains, and lieutenants, and
with scant ties to other branches of the military establishment.
The November incident was the brainchild of senior officers from the
marines and air force. Since military principle dictates that lower rank-
ing officers subordinate to their superiors, it was unlikely that the two
rear-admirals and brigadier general who masterminded the November
golpe would have subordinated themselves to the lieutenant colonels who
spearheaded the February 4 rebellion. As such, these two movements
were almost surely unrelated. The commanders of the November uprising tried to avoid the same errors made by their predecessors. This time,
they seized the television affiliates located in the area of Los Mecedores,
but they neglected to control the signal from Channel 10, which allowed
President Pérez to address the nation from Miraflores.

The November uprising seemed to confirm the belief that, the longer
President Pérez remained in power, the more volatile the crisis would
become. It also illustrated that any long-term solution to the economic
and social crises ultimately hinged upon Pérez being removed from office.
Thus, a constitutional procedure to impeach the president was set in motion
that would culminate in his removal from office in 1993. It is important to
point out that multiple interests from several different sources converged
in demanding President Pérez's removal from office. Opposition to his
administration created so many different antagonistic fronts that just dealing with them overwhelmed the administration's capacity to maneuver its
way around such a daunting political mine field.

President Pérez's downfall was not solely the result of his implementation of a severe economic adjustment program, but also of the way in
which he managed to erode his own political base. An arrogant Pérez and
his administration dealt poorly with certain elements of power—a short-
coming that historically has afflicted traditional political parties—and
Pérez ended up encouraging the most diverse political interests to coalesce
against his administration.

A week after the second *golpe* attempt, gubernatorial and mayoral elections were held. Abstention was considerably lower than it was in the previous election, and the decentralization process had begun to take root.
Acción Democrática saw its regional electoral force reduced, and it became
resoundingly clear that the party machine was much less influential than
it had been in previous years. The political leaders thus had to come to
terms with the fact that the two-party system (*Acción Democrática* and
COPEI) had deteriorated.

This two-party system had been the backbone of modern Venezuelan politics. *Acción Democrática* and COPEI were originally created as disciplined and unified entities that sought the common goals of their respective members. While there was little room for dissenters or internal tendencies, the political parties saw themselves as the mechanism to penetrate and control other social organizations. The gubernatorial election of December 1989 clearly illustrated the realities of these political changes. First, the election marked a major shift in presidential authority, because prior to the 1989 election, state governors were appointed by the president. Second, the results of the balloting document three significant changes: a high rate of absenteeism, a loss of regional support for *Acción Democrática* and COPEI, and an increase in support of several minor political parties, such as *Causa Я* (Radical Cause) and *Movimiento al Socialismo* (Movement toward Socialism).

Impeachment

The opposition to Pérez during his second administration included a desire to settle old scores. Pérez's opponents had made it their common cause to carry out a discrediting campaign centered around the mismanagement of the *"partida secreta"* funds, and their common goal was the removal of Pérez from the presidency. The *Causa Я*, a political party made up of leftist elements, facilitated a joint effort with journalist José Vicente Rangel with the hope of denouncing the mismanagement of the funds on the part of the president, the minister of interior relations, and the minister of the secretariat to the presidency.

The campaign unleashed against Pérez was through a conglomerate of opponents—the mass media, various private sectors, and COPEI—and was aided by the aloof stance of his own *Acción Democrática* party. Collectively, they weakened the Pérez presidency to the point that they created a constitutional crisis, with the "justification" for this crisis being the alleged mishandling of the "secret fund." It is possible, however, that these opposition groups were attempting to derail the process of economic modernization at the very expense of the stability of constitutional democracy.

At the end of 1992, the Supreme Court received the request for a trial. Months later, in March 1993, the public prosecutor, Ramón Escobar Salom, taking advantage of the ever acute political and social crisis brought about by the popular anti-Pérez demonstrations occurring throughout the country, presented to the Supreme Court the case regarding the mismanagement of the *partida secreta* funds. In May 1993, the Supreme Court decided that, in light of the existing evidence, a trial would be ordered against President Pérez and his closest collaborators.

On May 21, 1993, the Venezuelan Congress voted unanimously to suspend President Pérez from office, thus opening the way for the Supreme Court to prosecute him on charges of administrative corruption. On August 31, Congress voted to bar him from returning to power, even if the investigation were to find him innocent. Pérez supporters charged that the essence of the current problems of the ex-president stemmed from the formation of his new economic program. Repeatedly (especially since early 1992), the anti-Pérez forces called for his resignation, but the president refused. The anti-Pérez alliance gained strength, and his adversaries formed a coalition that maneuvered the demands for his suspension by order of the Supreme Court. Thus, the act of political revenge had been accomplished through a *golpe de estado* by the national Congress.

In his final speech as president, Carlos Andrés Pérez's words reflected a harsh introspection and a certain disenchantment common to those times when a politician faces defeat. With Pérez's departure from office, the impetus for a reform process came to a halt. In February 1994, former president Rafael Caldera took office for a second term and immediately adopted economic control measures and halted the decentralization process. These measures were designed to paralyze the reformist plan started by Pérez.

After having served the prison term imposed by the Supreme Court and after Congress had successfully rallied to strip him of his status as senator for life, Pérez rebuilt his political leadership. History has begun to bestow upon him a certain degree of recognition, since his government and his national development plan created the foundations upon which Venezuela may now build its future development and participate in global transformations. However, another chapter of this dramatic history remains to be written.

THE SECOND CALDERA PRESIDENCY

New presidential elections were held in December 1993, with 18 candidates running for the office. Receiving only 30.5 percent of the votes, former President Rafael Caldera regained the presidency. A persuasive orator able to depict whichever reality best suits his political aspirations, Caldera was able to play the political game of ambiguity and justify the revolts and *golpes* of 1992. Taking advantage of the situation, Caldera broke the golden rule of democratic discourse and abandoned his defense of civility. Caldera became every bit as manipulative and politically opportunistic as any other mundane politician in addressing the Venezuelan people as an innocent party. However, he also showed himself to be singularly ruthless in severing his loyalty to the party he had founded—COPEI—after it refused to nominate him for the presidency. Instead, Caldera sought the quickest coalition that could get him elected. His new popular base was an alliance of 17 political parties (many of them from the extreme Left) and his new *Convergencia* party.

When Caldera assumed the presidency for the second time in February 1994, the country had been engulfed in political crises for several years. During the two years before his inauguration, the country had witnessed two *golpes* and the impeachment of a sitting president on charges of corruption. Venezuela was also in the midst of severe economic and social woes, despite the much-needed, yet unpopular, reforms of former President Pérez.

No political party obtained a majority in either chamber of the Congress, although President Caldera's *Convergencia* movement won the presidency of the Senate, while *Acción Democrática* won the presidency of the Chamber of Deputies. Although Caldera called for a "national consensus" to deal with Venezuela's problems, achieving that consensus proved to be extremely difficult. Instead of the traditional two-party system that had dominated Venezuelan politics since 1958, the 1994 Congress had five different organizations that gained significant numbers of seats. In the Chamber of Deputies, *Acción Democrática* held 27.9 percent of the seats, COPEI held 26.9 percent, the alliance between *Convergencia* and the *Movimiento al Socialismo* held 25.4 percent, and the *Causa Я* held 19.9 percent. In the Senate, AD controlled 34.6 percent of the seats, COPEI held 28.8 percent, the Convergencia–*Movimiento al Socialismo* alliance held 19.2 percent, and the *Causa Я* held 17.3 percent.

President Caldera had to face perhaps the worst economic crisis in Venezuelan history, which included high inflation, economic contraction, and the collapse of several major banks. To deal with the continued social unrest, the Caldera administration suspended several constitutional guarantees. According to Human Rights Watch, the Caldera administration claimed that the crisis of the financial system, exchange market instability, and speculation mandated that the administration suspend guarantees that, among other things, protected against arbitrary searches and arrests, protected the freedom of movement, the expropriation of property without compensation, and the right to engage in any legal economic activity. The suspension of these rights began a wave of human rights violations.

Another matter that Rafael Caldera dealt with upon his inauguration was the release of Hugo Chávez Frías from prison in 1994, suspending all charges against him—an act that further alienated him from a large percentage of the population. The communication media has alleged that Caldera's 1993 election was the result of obscure back-room negotiations, but such dealings among opposition leaders remain unsatisfactory in explaining President Pérez's removal from office. The active role of the Venezuelan mass media may have been partly to blame, because they undertook a program of demystifying the role of political parties and reducing their overall public relevance. As such, the media fostered the ongoing schism between the social bases and the organizational leadership of the political parties.

Both the political Left and the Right coalesced in a sort of blind alliance against President Pérez. Their tremendous national prestige and influence on the media influenced public opinion against the Pérez administration. By most accounts, their opposition to Pérez was political and not ideological. In April 1992, a televised interview took place in which Arturo Uslar Pietri made known his views of the political situation. He stated that the situation had become compounded by several crises that had been accumulating and that the government lacked the proper will to effectively confront them. He argued that the events of February 4, 1992, had taken place amid a maelstrom of widespread public discontent, nonconformity, and repudiation of the political system. The government's credibility was so deeply compromised, he claimed, that the only viable way out would be the resignation of President Pérez. Those of a mindset similar to Uslar Pietri argued that the president had lost his authority and it was his duty to facilitate change in order to restore legitimacy to the office of the president.

Despite his inability to recognize any collective virtues in the Venezuelan people, Uslar Pietri was the epitome of the national conscience at that moment in Venezuelan history. Perhaps a result of being a man without democratic convictions or perhaps because he had not been able to come to terms with the events of October 18, 1945, the reality was that Uslar Pietri mounted an extremely firm opposition to the government. For example, amid the turbulent political scene of 1992, he published a book suggestively titled *Golpe y Estado en Venezuela* (Coup and State in Venezuela).

HUGO CHÁVEZ FRÍAS

After Hugo Chávez was released from prison, he became a symbol of the opposition to the 1958 Venezuelan political model. Chávez promised to dissolve the national Congress and convene a constituent assembly to reorganize the country and its laws. Aided by the popular discontent within

Venezuela about declining standards of living and widespread political corruption among government officials, Chávez won the 1998 presidential election with 56.2 percent of the valid popular vote. His nearest rival was Henrique Salas Romer, a coalition candidate, with 39.97 percent of the votes.

SUMMARY

With the passage of time, the issue of partisan discipline in Venezuela became a retaliatory instrument at the service of those who controlled the party machine. Against their own better judgment and experience, party leaders became highly dependent upon the resources of power. The popular crusade was abandoned, and an ever greater distancing took place between the party leadership, militancy, and its civilian base of support. In short, the party system abandoned its core values and degenerated into self-serving and counterproductive electoral machines, which ultimately succeeded only in alienating the populace. The popular rejection of the two-party system became evident by the alarming rise of apathy and absenteeism, the disappearance of partisan identities, and the proportionate rise of "independent" voters.

The Venezuelan people blamed the two main parties (*Acción Democrática* and COPEI) for the profound social and economic inequities; the extreme poverty; the lack of access to basic health care services, education, security, and housing; the erratic distribution of resources; the high rates of unemployment and under-unemployment; and chronic and generalized corruption. In short, people did not believe that the parties worried about their welfare, and they doubted the parties' capacity to solve Venezuela's problems and effect a positive change. Consequently, the people came to question one of the primary original objectives of the political parties: their role in channeling society's interests and transforming them into efficient political strategies. As a result, the parties saw their legitimacy severely eroded, which in turn caused them to become overwhelmed and at a loss for answers. They were without credible programs and, worst of all, without an effective will to amend and correct their errors and deficiencies. The loss of prestige suffered by the political parties had been so alarming in those last few years that the most effective form of political discourse had been that of anti-politics. This sentiment is still strong today in Venezuela. This situation started, in the opinion of some observers, when the parties became unable to continue distributing donations or fulfilling their promises. The political crisis was, thus, associated with the decrease in state resources.

12

The Bolivarian Revolution (1999–2005)

When Hugo Chávez Frías became president, a new style of political discourse emerged that completely broke with the Venezuelan democratic traditions created in 1958. This new and revolutionary model found its voice in a new group of leaders, eliminating the traditional AD-COPEI axis, and is based on an attempt to guarantee that no single political party will dominate the political process by assuming full control over the public's participation in it. A prime example of this new political ideology was reflected in the convening of a national Constituent Assembly to create a new government in which the traditional power players would have little or no role.

A new and highly conflicted relationship was thus established between the new populist ideology and the old political and social protagonists. These protagonists were the traditional political parties, the Church, the labor unions, and the middle class, all of which had been deemed politically irrelevant in the new populist age by President Chávez. Thus, Venezuela's competitive democratic tradition of over 40 years has been systematically dismantled.

Former *golpista* Hugo Chávez Frías campaigned for the presidency in 1998 with the promise to represent the poor, dissolve the national Congress, convene a Constituent Assembly, eradicate corruption, and distribute the nation's resources more equitably. To the nation's poor, his words brought hope; to the middle and upper classes, his rhetoric brought anxiety. When the December 1998 election was over, the former *golpista* won the presidency with 56.2 percent of the valid popular vote.

THE CHÁVEZ PRESIDENCY

Following his election, President Chávez began to prepare for the drafting of a new constitution for Venezuela. New elections were held for a Constituent Assembly, which drafted a new set of laws in 1999. After the new constitution was promulgated in December 1999, Chávez was once again elected president (July 2000) with 59.76 percent of the votes, thanks to the support of Venezuela's poor. It should be noted that the assembly that drafted the new constitution consisted of 131 elected individuals, all but six of whom were associated with the Chávez movement. In the new unicameral National Assembly that replaced the bicameral Congress, Chávez's *Movimiento Quinta República* (Fifth Republic Movement) and the pro-Chávez *Movimiento al Socialismo* parties won 55.8 percent of the seats in the 165-member legislature.

Almost immediately after his election, anti-Chávez forces begin to express their opposition to his socialist and pseudo-socialist ideas and agenda. The same year as his re-election, Foreign Minister José Vicente Rangel claimed that the government had uncovered a plot to kill the president. Business leaders assailed the policies of the Chávez government, and the president became more and more aggressive toward the middle and upper classes. In December 2001, *Fedecámaras* called for a one-day strike in protest against Chávez's controversial economic reforms.

Another area that President Chávez needed to gain control of in order to further his revolution was the petroleum industry. In February 2002, he appointed a new board of directors for *Petróleos de Venezuela* (PDVSA) in a move to gain greater control of the agency. This possibly illegal move was opposed by PDVSA executives, and, in April, trade unions and *Fedecámaras* declared a general strike in support of the PDVSA dissidents. Approximately 500,000 people rallied on April 11, 2002, in support of the general strike and the PDVSA protest. National guardsmen and pro-Chávez thugs clashed with the protesters, killing more than 15 people and injuring over 100 more. In a move to minimize public knowledge of events, Chávez shut down the national media coverage of the violence.

In response to the uncontrolled violence, the military high command rebelled and demanded that Chávez resign. Army and national guard leaders announced on April 12 that Chávez had resigned and had been taken into military custody. Military leaders named Pedro Carmona, one of the strike organizers, as head of a transitional government. In a bizarre chain of events, Chávez returned to power two days later with the support of the air force. In an effort to restore peace and social stability in Venezuela, a tripartite group—with representatives from the Organization of American States, the United Nations Development Program, and the Carter Center—was formed in August to facilitate a dialogue between the government and the opposition.

Despite the mostly unsuccessful efforts by the tripartite group, dissatisfaction with the Chávez administration led to a general strike in early December 2002. As before, the protesters called for the resignation of President Chávez. On December 4, 2002, the petroleum sector joined the strike and was followed by other sectors of the economy. In effect, the Venezuelan economy was shutting down. These moves only further antagonized President Chávez, who ordered the military to raid warehouses to seize food and supplies and distribute them free to the poor. The oil strike eventually led to fuel shortages.

As 2003 began, Venezuela found itself in the continued throes of a general strike by oil industry management intent upon ousting President Chávez. The country's exports of oil and oil derivatives dropped steadily, with daily losses averaging 2.8 million barrels per day. Chávez responded to the attack by replacing upper management in PDVSA and dismissing 18,000 employees on grounds of mismanagement and corruption. PDVSA board members filed a lawsuit, charging that the dismissal was illegal and politically motivated. The court upheld the charges and ordered the immediate return of management and workers to their former posts. Alí Rodríguez, the new CEO of PDVSA, and Rafael Rodríguez, Chávez's Minister of Energy and Mines, indicated that the government would ignore the ruling. The economic ousting of the president did not work. By May, the oil industry recovered, and the opposition began to focus on political strategies to remove Chávez.

In May 2003, representatives of the government and the opposition signed a deal brokered by the Group of Friends, organized by the Organization of American States. The Group of Friends included Brazil, Chile, Spain, Portugal, Mexico, and the United States. Of particular importance in the agreement was the establishment of a framework for a referendum on President Chávez's continued tenure in office.

In the meantime, the president began to shore up his constituency through a series of *misiones* (missions) or programs, supposedly created to eradicate poverty and illiteracy in Venezuela. Most of the programs are part of an education/medicine-for-oil exchange program with Cuba and are deemed an underhanded means of spreading socialism by the opposition. There are seven *misiones*. *Misión Barrio Adentro* (Inside the Barrio) began in March 2003, during the country's economic woes. The government-sponsored program, designed to provide free health and dental care to the poor, began in the *Barrio Libertador* of Caracas and then spread to the rest of the country. It employed 15,000 Cuban doctors who were paid approximately $250 per month, more than their Cuban salaries and less than Venezuelan doctors. The *Federación Venezolana de Medicina* (Venezuelan Medical Federation) filed a lawsuit to prevent the Cuban doctors from practicing medicine in Venezuela, but without success.

As oil revenues increased, new missions were implemented, many of them under the Ministry of Energy and Mines. In October, *Misión* Robinson (named in honor of Simón Rodríguez, Bolívar's teacher and mentor, who often used the pseudonym Samuel Robinson) began a series of programs designed to eradicate illiteracy. While illiteracy is relatively low in Venezuela, it is a large factor in poverty. *Misión* I employed Cuban literacy experts to train teachers to educate students in an accelerated program based on numbers, and *Misión* II prepared teachers to bring their students to a sixth-grade literacy level in only two years.

Misiones Ribas and *Sucre* were aimed at secondary and university educa-tion. The *Ribas* program was designed to bring high school dropouts up to graduation level in two years and put them in the workforce with either PDVSA or CADAFE. *Mission Sucre* gives students U.S. $100 per month toward a university education.

A food distribution network known as *Misión Mercado* established gov-ernment supermarkets that offers food at slightly below market rates. This concept was a result of the 2002 general strike that shut down food distri-bution. *Misión* Miranda is perhaps the most controversial program. Using government monies, Chávez created a military reserve of 100,000 men by the end of 2003. The government claimed it was employing thousands of unemployed ex-military personnel at minimum wage. The opposition grew fearful that the *mirandistas* would become a parallel army, loyal to Chávez.

Much of the fear stemmed from the August 2003 referendum drive that presented the *Consejo Nacional Electoral* (National Electoral Council) (CNE) with 3.2 million signatures to oust the president. Based on a 1999 Venezuelan law under the new constitution, offices filled by popular vote were subject to revocation, including that of the presidency. Recall votes had to equal or exceed those that elected the official. Despite CNE's rejec-tion of the initial signatures, a government "rapid reaction" squad raided

CNE offices and, according to reports, "punished" many of those who signed the petition.

In November 2003, a second petition with 3.6 million names was presented to the CNE. The majority of the council rejected the petition because of some disputed signatures. The nation erupted in riots, and the petitioners appealed to the Electoral Chamber of the Venezuelan Supreme Court. The court reinstated some of the disputed signatures, which gave the opposition 2.7 million valid signatures, 300,000 more than were needed to begin a referendum. A week later, under pressure from the government, the Constitutional Chamber of the Supreme Court overturned the ruling on the grounds that the Electoral Chamber did not have jurisdiction in the case. Names of petition signers were publicly posted, and many government workers were fired or "laid off" in retaliation.

Despite the setbacks, the CNE set aside five days in May 2004 to give persons whose signatures were disputed the opportunity to verify them. Although there were some forged signatures, the number of verified signatures reached the level necessary for a referendum, and the recall vote was set for August 15, 2004.

As the referendum was underway, the government announced that it had captured a number of Colombians near the property of Cuban exile and opposition leader Roberto Alonso. The government claimed the men were paramilitaries hired by the *Bloque Democrático* (Democratic Bloc) to form a 3,000-man militia and that testimony given by captured Colombians corroborated their story. Alonso fled to the United States, where he awaits extradition by the Venezuelan government.

Despite government interference and voter intimidation, the recall election began as scheduled. A record number of votes were cast, and polling hours were extended in some cases up to eight hours. The vote returned with 59.25 percent in favor of the president remaining in power. The election was observed by former President Jimmy Carter and by the Secretary-General of the Organization of American States, César Gaviria. After a review of the tabulations, the Carter Center endorsed the results, claiming that, even with the dismissal of a number of votes, the majority was still in favor of the president. Although the results were confirmed in an audit by the European Union, the opposition continues to claim, with some merit, electoral fraud. Chávez won the referendum but not the country. The margin of victory was slim and questionable, and no peaceful political reconciliation ensued.

After re-establishing his presidency, Hugo Chávez undertook more stringent methods of establishing democratic socialism by enforcing land redistribution. In 2001, the government's *Plan Zamora* used Venezuela's

Ley de Tierras (Land Law) to enact radical land reform. In general, it taxed unused landholdings and expropriated unused private lands with compensation for small farmers and collectives. *Plan Zamora* was sketchy and questionable since about 90 percent of Venezuela's population is urban. The *Misión Mercado* (Market Mission) scheme seemed more sensible to outside observers. The government's rationale was food security, an idea reinforced in 2002 by the general strike. Working on this premise, the land redistribution efforts at the beginning of 2005 initiated forced seizures of land against the provisions of the *Ley de Tierras*. Forced redistribution has further strained Venezuela's political stability.

More recent acts by the Chávez government include efforts to seize a portion of the central bank's international reserves to spend on social programs, and the seizure of land to redistribute to the poor.

Petroleum

Despite resolutions to diversify its economy, Venezuela remains heavily dependent on oil. Aware of the dependency, Chávez has become a price hawk in OPEC, pushing for higher prices and lower production quotas. He intends to continue his reputation as a petro-populist, using oil revenues to maintain his political support within Venezuela. To that end, he has brought PDVSA under the direction of the Ministry of Energy and Mines. He has also attempted to raise oil funds by increasing the percentage of royalties on joint extraction contracts and has recently explored the sale of some or all of Citgo's assets. (Citgo is a Venezuelan state-owned oil company.) Chávez's funneling of oil revenues for short-term social programs is risky. Even his supporters acknowledge that true social development may take several decades and that the country's oil revenues may be depleted before then.

Foreign Policy

Equally risky are Chávez's international politics. Despite ongoing domestic problems, Chávez has initiated several foreign policy programs to strengthen his international position. The president and his *Movimiento V República* support what he calls Latin American integration. This includes the creation or the extension of presently held joint ventures among Latin American nations. He continues to support Venezuela as an associate member of the *Mercado Común del Sur* or *Mercado Comum do Sul* (South America's Economic Common Market), also known as *Mercosur* or *Mercosul*, formed in 1995.

In 2005, Chávez announced the creation of *Telesur*, or *Televisión del Sur*. *Telesur* is to be jointly owned by several Latin American countries, although Venezuela owns 51 percent of the venture. Although this shores up his promises of Latin American integration, it is also part of a number of government-owned organizations that Chávez is establishing to counterbalance private corporations owned by his political opponents. The anti–U.S. *Telesur* is intended to offset U.S. cable news and *Venevisión*, presently Venezuela's largest TV station, which is owned and operated by media mogul Gustavo Cisneros. Under Cisneros's direction, *Venevisión* used cartoons to oppose Chávez during the attempted coup in 2002. Fearing nationalization and censorship, Cisneros has become more subdued and has moved 80 percent of his operations to the United States.

Venezuela's government also plans a bilateral trade relationship with Brazil and another oil-for-expertise exchange with Cuba. Plans for a pipeline through Colombia were almost destroyed because of an international incident involving Rodrigo Granda, the foreign minister of the *Fuerzas Armadas Revolucionarias de Colombia* (Colombian Armed Revolutionary Forces) (FARC). Arrested by Venezuelan forces near Caracas, Granda was returned to the city of Cúcuta and turned over to Colombian authorities. A media circus resulted in heightened diplomatic tensions, and Colombia questioned Venezuela's lack of cooperation and true intentions regarding the FARC. In February 2005, Chávez met with Colombian president Alvaro Uribe to resolve tensions. With the help of mediators from Cuba, Perú, and Brazil, the two nations agreed to resolve similar issues through diplomatic channels rather than through the media. The pipeline deal was re-established.

While Chávez supports Latin American integration, he is a vocal opponent of other nations and international programs. In particular, he is a strong critic of the United States. Part of this opposition is because of political alignment with other socialist countries, especially Cuba, North Korea, and the People's Republic of China. Other acts, however, seem to be deliberately antagonistic toward the United States. In addition to his continued relationship with Cuba, he has also established relationships with Iran and Libya. The former *golpe* leader against President Carlos Andrés Pérez has made numerous public statements against U.S. foreign policy, including the U.S.-assisted ousting of Jean-Bertrand Aristide in Haiti and the 2003 invasion of Iraq. Chávez continues to claim, without proof, that the United States is planning to assassinate him, and he has threatened to stop oil exports to the United States if it took action against his country.

The United States has consistently remained opposed to the left-wing administration of President Chávez. It has funded the democratic efforts of his opposition and continues to refer to Chávez as a negative force in the Western Hemisphere. Recently, the administration of President George W. Bush requested support from other South American countries to help isolate Chávez and his efforts to export his socialist ideas throughout Latin America. Chávez maintains that he is the Fidel Castro of South America and that petro-populism will find victory in its Third Way to democratic socialism.

FINAL THOUGHTS[1]

No one wishes to see an irreparable breakdown of the Venezuelan democratic process. While the current government of President Hugo Chávez Frías bases its legitimacy on the sheer numbers of votes it received, his opposition continues to demand that the constitutional mechanisms meant to regulate the exercise of power by inept or ineffective administrations be reinstated. In order to fully assess the current rift between Venezuela's government and people, the lessons of April 2002 must be put into proper perspective.

President Chávez's Fifth Republic should rectify its policies and bring back the institutions and mechanisms that the current constitution makes provisions for in order to properly moderate the government's reach. The current administration cannot afford to continue postponing the task of governing responsibly, nor can it afford to continue to rely on a seemingly unlimited petroleum resource. If Venezuela's destiny remains tied to the fortunes of high petroleum prices, it will be virtually impossible to build a durable political model that will survive the test of time.

If it is indeed democracy that Venezuela's leaders follow as their guiding principle, then it will also become essential to articulate a proper balance between the government and its opposition. Conversely, it will be necessary to do away with the pervasive and undemocratic mind-set that compels some leaders to be under the mistaken notion that governing at the expense of a consensus is somehow a viable option. President Chávez must ultimately comprehend that the so-called legitimacy afforded him by sheer numbers of votes is not enough to warrant an irresponsible exercise of power. Indeed, the events of the 1970s and 1980s clearly illustrated that democracy demands a legitimacy of governance that can only be afforded to those who exercise their power efficiently, responsibly, and with a considerable measure of administrative honesty.

The opposition, on the other hand, must take responsibility to build a viable alternative model to that of the Venezuelan Fifth Republic. Such an administrative alternative should be modeled upon mechanisms and policies that would eradicate power structures that could potentially lead to administrative injustice and corruption. The opposition must also regain the people's trust and avail itself of the full use of the advantages of the mass communication media. However, mass media exposure alone will not be sufficient to earn the people's trust. Efforts must be made by the opposition leaders to articulate a clear message and a program of social projects that will inspire, revive, and attract Venezuelans' fidelity. Lastly, the opposition must take this message to the streets and give it a popular voice.

It is crucial to understand the basic fact that civil society cannot pretend to substitute a party system without ceasing to be civil. One of the responsibilities of a free and competitive party system is to actively contribute to the creation of a civic mind-set, and to give people the opportunity to fully participate in articulating their own political destiny.

Venezuela needs another truly effective "democratic revolution." Such a revolution, as experienced on January 23, 1958, would have to genuinely transfer power back to the people. The revolution must also curb the uncontrolled growth and reach of the state's bureaucracy. At the same time, the government must end the paternalistic cycle through which many Venezuelans view their government as society's redeeming savior. In reality, the Venezuelan people are the government's savior.

NOTE

1. These comments are based upon correspondences between Micheal Tarver and Professor Luis Loaiza Rincón, at the Universidad de Los Andes (Mérida, Venezuela).

Notable People in
the History of Venezuela

Barrios, Gonzalo (1902–1993), Venezuelan attorney and politician. Cofounder of the *Movimiento de Organización Venezolana* (Movement for Venezuelan Organization). Most significantly, he's one of the cofounders of *Acción Democrática* (AD) in 1941. Lost a narrow electoral bid in 1968 to the COPEI candidate, Rafael Caldera. Barrios was president of the Venezuelan Congress from 1974 to 1979, as well as president of his own party, AD. Although forced to live in exile throughout a good part of the twentieth century, he nevertheless carried out an extremely active role in the advancement of democratic ideals in his native country.

Bello, Andrés (1781–1865), Venezuelan humanist, poet, lawmaker, philosopher, educator, and philologist. His writings and translations won him early renown, and his travels with Alexander von Humboldt helped broaden his intellectual scope. He was one of Simón Bolívar's teachers. Among his most famous poems are his *"Alocución a la poesía"* and *"Silva a la agricultura de la zona tórrida."* He was the author of landmark works in jurisprudence and of a *Gramática de la lengua castellana destinada al uso de los americanos.* Bello's humanist work helped shape the Americanist consciousness of the newly independent American nations.

Betancourt, Rómulo (1908–1981), politician, orator, cofounder of Venezuela's *Acción Democrática* (AD), provisional president (1945–1948), president (1959–1964), and one of Venezuela's most important and controversial political figures. His administration was known for an extensive agrarian reform program, a renegotiation of royalty-sharing with oil companies, and the firm establishment of democracy in Venezuela. His administration was plagued by insurgency both from the extreme Left and the extreme Right.

Blanco, Andrés Eloy (1896–1955), Venezuelan politician, orator, and poet. He was a member of the Generation of 1928 and cofounder of *Acción Democrática*. Among his greatest works are *"Canto a España,"* for which he won first prize in an international competition sponsored by Spain's Spanish Language Academy in 1923. This prestigious prize brought Blanco world renown. It was as a result of his struggles under the oppressive regime of Juan Vicente Gómez that Blanco found his unique voice, made patently evident in works such as *"Barco de Piedra"* and *"Malvina Recobrada."* In Blanco's work, Venezuelan poetry reached full maturity with a unique tone. Andrés Eloy Blanco was one of the greatest masters of metaphor and imagery in the Spanish language.

Bolívar, Simón—also known as *el Libertador* ("the Liberator") (1783–1830), Venezuelan essayist, military leader, and liberator of South America. Bolívar also worked alongside Francisco de Miranda and other members of a pro-independence group called the *Sociedad Patriótica* to further revolutionary ideals. He fought successfully in a series of key military campaigns that won the freedom of Nueva Granada, Venezuela, and Ecuador and held a historic meeting in Guayaquil, Ecuador, with General José de San Martín to contemplate the liberation of Perú. His *Proclama de Guerra a Muerte* at the outset of his *Campaña Admirable* to invade and seize control of Venezuela became the turning point of Venezuela's independence. Bolívar's literary output includes such landmark works of South American thought as the *Manifiesto de Cartagena*, the *Carta de Jamaica*, and the *Discurso de Angostura*. He died in Santa Marta, Colombia in 1830.

Bonpland, Aimé (1773–1858), French physician, botanist, naturalist, and explorer of Venezuela, South America, and the Caribbean. Cowrote the landmark work *Personal Narrative of a Journey to the Equinoctial Regions of the New Continent*, with Alexander von Humboldt.

Caldera, Rafael (1916–), attorney, politician, head of Christian democratic movement in Venezuela, cofounder of the *Comité de Organización*

Política Electoral Independiente (COPEI) party, twice president of Venezuela (1969–1974 and 1994–1999), and unsuccessful candidate in his electoral bid in 1983. The highlight of his first administration was the joining of the Andean Pact common market by Venezuela in 1973. Prior to his second administration, he broke ranks with COPEI and formed a political party called *Convergencia Nacional*. The priorities of his second administration focused on reinstating national harmony after the destabilizing effects of the two *golpes* in 1992 against then president Carlos Andrés Pérez and on the ensuing judicial trial against Pérez.

Carreño, Teresa (1856–1917), Venezuela's most celebrated pianist and composer. Born in Caracas, Carreño spent most of her life abroad, in Europe and the United States. In her honor, the main cultural complex of Caracas is named Teatro Teresa Carreño.

Castro, Cipriano (1858–1924), military *caudillo* and president of Venezuela. He was the first of four military rulers from the Andean state of Táchira. His administration (1899–1908), which centered on the *Revolución Restauradora,* had little success in the way of domestic reform or progress. The highlight of his administration was probably the Venezuelan debt controversy of 1902, which led to a joint Anglo-German-Italian blockade of Venezuela. While away in Europe undergoing medical treatment, Cipriano Castro was deposed by his vice president, Juan Vicente Gómez.

Chávez Frías, Hugo (1954–), military officer and left-wing populist president of Venezuela since 1999. A former lieutenant colonel, his policies, allegedly inspired by the ideals of Simón Bolívar, have gained the overwhelming support of Venezuela's impoverished majority while being denounced by the middle and upper classes. His tenure in office has withstood a failed *golpe* in 2002 and a failed recall referendum in 2004.

Cosa, Juan de la (1460–1510), Spanish navigator and cartographer who accompanied Christopher Columbus in his first two voyages of discovery, as well as Alonso de Ojeda in 1499, and created his historic *mappa mundi* in 1500, the first world map to include the American continent, including Venezuela.

Crespo, Joaquín (1841–1898), military *caudillo* and president of Venezuela on two occasions (1884–1886 and 1894–1898). During his second administration, Venezuela was engaged in a boundary dispute with Great Britain. When he chose his successor, revolts occurred, and Crespo was killed in the fighting.

Delgado Chalbaud, Carlos (1909–1950), Venezuelan engineer, military officer, minister of defense. He participated in the Revolutions of October 1945 and November 1948. Headed the *Junta Militar de Gobierno* (1948–1950) until his assassination in November 1950. The circumstances surrounding his death have been the cause of great controversy.

Falcón, Juan Crisóstomo—also known as *el Gran Ciudadano* ("the Great Citizen") (1820–1870), military leader and president of Venezuela, 1863–1868. He was the leader, along with Ezequiel Zamora, of the movement in the 1860s that pitted federalists against centralists for control of Venezuela's political future. After the triumph of the *Revolución Azul*, he was forced into exile. Was honored with the rank of marshal of the republic and given the honorific title of *Gran Ciudadano*.

Gallegos, Rómulo (1884–1969), writer, educator, politician, and president of Venezuela (1948). He is Venezuela's most renowned twentieth-century author. He was elected president in 1948 as the *Acción Democrática* party candidate. His efforts at wide-ranging land reform and his reduction of the role of the military alienated many of his powerful contemporaries. On November 24, 1948, he was overthrown by the military and sent into exile. Among his most celebrated literary works are *Doña Bárbara* and *La Trepadora*.

Gómez, Juan Vicente—also known as *el Benemérito* ("the Meritorious one") (1857–1935), military general, dictator, and president of Venezuela. He seized power while President Cipriano Castro was out of the country. In the 27 years of his rule (1908–1935), Gómez presided over seven different constitutions, each of which increased his control over Venezuelan affairs. His administration witnessed the modernization of Venezuela as a result of the revenue generated by the processing and exporting of crude oil. Gómez's domestic agenda, called the *Rehabilitación*, was constitutional in appearance and dictatorial in practice. Gómez was referred to as *el Benemérito* by his supporters and *el Bagre* (the Catfish) by his detractors.

Guzmán Blanco, Antonio—also known as *el Ilustre Americano* ("the Illustrious American")—(1829–1899), physician, prototypical *caudillo*, and president of Venezuela. He was leader of the *Partido Liberal Amarillo*. He became president of Venezuela in 1870 through a movement called *Regeneración*, which began the process of modernization in Venezuela. He was president of Venezuela on three occasions, 1870–1877, 1879–1884, and 1886–1887. His administrations emphasized public works, universal education, and the modernization of Caracas as the national capital. A grand master of Venezuelan masonry, Guzmán Blanco significantly reduced the role of the Church in state affairs. Following his third administration, he moved to Paris, where he spent the rest of his life.

Hojeda (Ojeda), Alonso de (1466–1516), Spanish navigator, *conquistador*, and discoverer of large portions of the Venezuelan coast. His discoveries helped define the Venezuelan coastline in Juan de la Cosa's historic *mappa mundi*.

Humboldt, Friedrich Heinrich Alexander von (1769–1859), German geographer, naturalist, and explorer considered the founder of scientific geography. He carried out extensive geographical, geological, and naturalistic investigations in Venezuela, South America, and the Caribbean. Simón Bolívar called him the "scientific discoverer of the New World." Among von Humboldt's most important works are *Personal Narrative of a Journey to the Equinoctial Regions of the New Continent* and *Cosmos: A Sketch of the Physical Description of the Universe*.

Larrazábal Ugueto, Wolfgang (1911–2003), naval admiral and president of the *Junta de Gobierno* (1958). Assumed executive power after the January 23, 1958, revolution, which ousted the dictatorship of Marcos Pérez Jiménez. He was an unsuccessful candidate for president in the democratic elections of December 1958.

Leoni, Raúl (1905–1972), Venezuelan politician and president of Venezuela (1964–1969). His administration reached out to the opposition to form an *Amplia Base*, or broad-based, coalition. One of his biggest challenges was the constant threat of armed insurrection and *guerrilla* warfare. His careful maneuvering allowed for the reestablishment of political stability in the country, by allowing for the reintegration of the *Movimiento de Izquierda Revolucionaria* (Movement of the Revolutionary Left) and the *Partido Comunista de Venezuela* (Venezuelan Communist party) into the democratic process. Thus, President Leoni laid the groundwork for his peace initiative, thereby adding a much-needed measure of security, confidence, and stability to Venezuela's fledgling democracy. His *Ley de Conmutación de Penas*, or Law of Commutation of Penal Sentences, allowed more than 250 armed insurrection detainees to be set free. During his administration, oil production maintained a boom of record productivity and stability, the iron and steel industrial complex was strengthened and revitalized, unemployment was kept at record lows, and agrarian reform as well as the agroindustrial complex enjoyed record gains.

López Contreras, Eleazar (1883–1973), military officer, minister of war, and president of Venezuela (1935–1941). He served in the governments of Cipriano Castro and Juan Vicente Gómez. His administration is known for making the successful transition from dictatorship to democracy, although some limits still existed on civic and political freedoms. During his administration, the army was modernized and gained respect among the Venezuelan people.

Losada y Quiroga, Diego de (1513–1569), one of the first *conquistadores* of the Darién region, explorer of the region of Venezuela, and founder of the city of Santiago de León de Caracas in 1567.

Márquez Bustillos, Victorino (1858–1941), provisional president of Venezuela and ally of Juan Vicente Gómez. He served as provisional president from 1915 to 1922, during which time Gómez served as president elect and commander in chief of the army. Márquez Bustillos was provisional president during World War I.

Medina Angarita, Isaías (1897–1953), military officer, minister of War, and president of Venezuela (1941–1945). He was elected president by the Congress in 1941. He restored civic and political liberties, allowed political parties to publicly function again, granted suffrage to women, and granted the freedoms of speech and of the press. Medina Angarita led Venezuela through World War II and into membership in the United Nations. On October 18, 1945, President Medina Angarita was overthrown in a military *golpe*, ending a 46-year period of Táchira-born rulers.

Miranda, Francisco de—also known as *el Precursor*, or *el primer criollo universal* ("the first universal Creole") (1750–1816), Venezuelan intellectual and revolutionist. He is considered the "precursor" of South America's independence to distinguish him from Simón Bolívar, who is known as the "*Libertador*." He also took part in the American Revolutionary War and in the French Revolutionary War. With foreign assistance, he led an unsuccessful expedition to the Venezuelan coast in 1806. After the start of the revolution in 1810, he returned to Venezuela and took a commanding position leading the patriotic forces. After a series of misfortunes, he surrendered to the Spanish in 1812. Angered by his surrender, Bolívar and other patriots turned him over to the Spanish, who deported him to Spain and imprisoned him in Cádiz, where he remained until his death.

Monagas, José Gregorio (1795–1858), military leader and president of Venezuela. Along with his brother, he was a firm defender of Gran

Colombian unity, in opposition to Páez's efforts of Venezuelan secession. He was president from 1851 to 1855, succeeding his brother, José Tadeo. José Gregorio Monagas abolished slavery in Venezuela in 1854.

Monagas, José Tadeo (1784–1868), military leader and president of Venezuela. He was a commander during Venezuela's independence movement and was president of the Republic of Venezuela on two occasions, 1847–1851 and 1855–1858. In 1848, he ousted the conservatives from his government and sent former President Páez into exile, initiating 11 years of dictatorial rule with his brother, José Gregorio. Ten years after being ousted from power, Monagas headed a successful counter-revolution known as the *Revolución Azul,* but died that same year. His remains lie in the Panteón Nacional.

Páez, José Antonio (1790–1873), military hero and first president of Venezuela. He was commanding general at the decisive Battle of Carabobo in 1821, for the liberation of Venezuelan territory from Spain. In 1829–1830, he led the movement for the separation of Venezuela from Gran Colombia, thus establishing the independent Republic of Venezuela. Páez was president of Venezuela on three occasions: 1830–1835, 1839–1843, and 1861–1863. He was leader of the conservative movement in Venezuela. In 1863, he was exiled from Venezuela and took up residence in the United States until his death in 1873.

Pérez, Carlos Andrés (1922–), politician and president of Venezuela on two occasions: 1974–1979 and 1989–1994. Pérez sought to make oil a tool of leverage and negotiation to be used by Third World nations to improve their world standing and seek a fairer playing field in the world economy. Pérez sought the nationalization of the oil and iron industries to improve the standard of living of Venezuelan workers and the redistribution of riches. In Pérez's second term in office, economic conditions worsened considerably following the global collapse in oil prices. Pérez's harsh economic policies led to widespread discontent among the public. Amid such dire economic conditions and unpopular feeling, the stage was set for two unsuccessful *golpes* in 1992. The Senate impeached President Pérez on the grounds of malfeasance and misappropriation of funds for illegal activities. This marked the first time a Venezuelan president had been impeached from office.

Pérez Jiménez, Marcos (1914–2001), military officer and president of Venezuela (1952–1958). He participated in the 1945 October Revolution, which brought to power the *Acción Democrática* party. He was a member of the three-man *junta* that overthrew President Rómulo Gallegos in 1948. He appointed himself president in 1952 and led a corrupt dictatorship marked by extreme anticommunism and repression. His government became notorious for its lavish expenditures to refurbish the Venezuelan highway system and the country's tourism industry, making Caracas a flashy showplace of his administration. He was ousted by the January 23 Revolution in 1958. He lived in exile in Miami, Florida, until 1963, when he was extradited to Venezuela. He was imprisoned in Venezuela from 1963 to 1968 and, after his release, lived in exile in Spain until his death.

Raleigh, Walter (1552–1618), naval officer, man of letters, and favorite protegé of Queen Elizabeth I of England. In 1595, he sailed up the Orinoco River toward the Guayana region in search of the mythical land of *El Dorado*, a mission he later recounted in his book *The Discoverie of the Large, Rich, an Bewtiful Empyre of Guiana*, published in 1596.

Rodríguez, Simón (1769–1854), Venezuelan philosopher and educator. He was Simón Bolívar's most influential mentor and instilled in him the loftiest ideals of justice and freedom. His long intellectual mentorship and association with Bolívar aided in shaping Bolívar's awareness of a Hispanic American identity. Simón Rodríguez was responsible for many treatises on subjects as varied as colonial instruction, botany, agriculture, conservation, and colonization. Rodríguez also chronicled the exploits of Simón Bolívar during the *Libertador's* independence campaign.

Sucre, Antonio José de—also known as *Gran Mariscal de Ayacucho* (Grand Marshal of Ayacucho) (1795–1830), Venezuelan military leader and one of South America's most illustrious independence leaders. He was one of Simón Bolívar's most trusted friends. In 1811, he joined the battles for American independence from Spain. After defeating Spanish forces at Boyacá in 1819, he was given the rank of brigadier general. Bolívar put him in charge of the campaign to liberate Quito. He won a decisive victory at the Battle of Pichincha. Two more victories followed against the Spaniards in Perú, notably on August 6, 1824, and at Ayacucho on December 9 of the same year. The latter was a decisive victory against the Spaniards, capturing most of the Spanish troops and command, including the viceroy. Sucre was elected president of the newly created nation of Bolivia in 1826, but after becoming disenchanted with political conflicts, he resigned and moved to Quito. In 1829 and at Bolívar's request, the Congress of Gran Colombia named him president of that nation. Once the plot to divide Gran Colombia into separate nations was underway, Sucre headed to Quito to attempt to stem the rising secessionist tide but was assassinated en route. The Bolivian city of Sucre was named after him, as well as the former Sucre (currency) of Ecuador.

Urdaneta, Rafael—also known as *el Brillante* ("the Brilliant") (1788–1845), Venezuelan general and hero in the independence of Colombia and Venezuela. In Bogotá and after the Declaration of Independence of 1810, Urdaneta joined the patriotic forces in the revolutionary war against Spain. He later became Simon Bolívar's key advisor and general of the Patriotic Army. Having served as secretary of the military and of defense and as congressional Senator on numerous occasions, Urdaneta died in Paris in 1845.

Villalba, Jóvito (1908–1989), Venezuelan politician, orator, and educator. Founder of the *Unión Republicana Democrática* party and unsuccessful presidential candidate on numerous occasions.

Glossary of Selected Terms

adeco: supporter of *Acción Democrática* (AD).

aduana: colonial institution in charge of the deposit, inspection, and collection of domestic and foreign commercial import and export taxes.

alcabala: Spanish colonial sales tax.

alcantarista: supporters of Francisco Linares Alcántara.

andino: person from the Andean region of Venezuela.

Arahuaco (Arawak): Amerindian ethnic group native to the Caribbean region and northern South America. They are found in Venezuela's Guayana region. The name also refers to their language.

asentamiento: rural settlement.

asiento: settlement or commercial contract granted by the Spanish Crown to individuals or companies.

audiencia: royal court of justice in colonial Spanish America, which also had some administrative powers.

Betancourt Doctrine: political philosophy of the Venezuelan government that refused to recognize any regime that came to power by military force.

betancurista: follower of Rómulo Betancourt.

cabildo: town council.

cacique: local political boss; historically, referred to Indian tribal chief.

Campaña Admirable: military campaign encompassing the liberation of colonial Venezuela from Spanish rule.

Glossary of Selected Terms

Campaña del Sur: military campaign encompassing the liberation of the subequatorial Andean territories of South America from Spanish colonial rule.

campesino: peasant.

capitán general: military commander of a captaincy-general administrative unit.

capitanía general: large subdivision of a viceroyalty headed by a military leader known as a captain-general.

caraqueño: resident of the city of Caracas.

Carib: largest Amerindian group in Eastern Venezuela at the time of the arrival of the Spaniards.

Carta de Jamaica: name given to the correspondence written to British subject Henry Cullen by Simón Bolívar in Kingston, Jamaica, in 1815, and in which Bolívar lays out his vision for the future of Latin America.

caudillismo: system of governing headed by a *caudillo.*

caudillo: a military leader; especially significant to nineteenth-century Venezuelan history.

cédula: decree.

chavista: supporter of Hugo Chávez Frías.

chicha: historically, an Andean corn liquor made by Native Americans; in present-day Venezuela, a nonalcoholic rice drink.

Círculos Bolivarianos: civilian groups supported by President Hugo Chávez's partisans, who often used force to discourage outspoken dissent from opposition groups.

Compañía de Caracas or Real Compañía Guipuzcoana de Caracas: trade society created in 1728 in San Sebastián, Guipúzcoa, Spain, in order to regulate Spanish commerce with colonial Venezuela.

Congreso de Angostura: assembly convened by Simón Bolívar in Angostura, Venezuela, in 1819 to promote his vision of a Gran Colombia—to be comprised of the territories of present-day Ecuador, Colombia, and Venezuela—and in which Bolívar was elected provisional president. A constitutional project that called for the union of Venezuela and Colombia was also approved for the Republic of Colombia, but it never came to pass.

conquistador: Spanish explorer.

consulado: merchant council.

copeyano: supporter of the *Comité de Organización Política Electoral Independiente* (COPEI).

CORDIPLAN (*Oficina Central de Coordinación y Planificación*): national office responsible for the coordination and implementation of plans for national development.

Correo del Orinoco: newspaper founded by Simón Bolívar in Angostura to propagate revolutionary doctrine.

criollo: person of European descent born in the New World.

El Dorado: mythical South American kingdom of gold and riches that fueled the greed of many conquistadors and was believed to be located in what is now Colombia's Bogotá *meseta* or in Venezuela's Guayana region near the Orinoco River, according to conflicting Amerindian tales.

encomendero: holder of an *encomienda* grant.

encomienda: system of tributary labor established in colonial Spanish America.

Fedecámaras (Federación de Cámaras de Comercio y Producción): Venezuelan Federation of Chambers of Commerce and Production.

fueros: special privileges granted by the state; generally granted to the Church and the military.

Generation of 1928: group of Caracas University students who, in 1928, founded an academic movement against the oppressive dictatorship of Juan Vicente Gómez. Many of the students who participated in this movement later became the progressive leaders of democratic reform in Venezuela.

gobernación: provincial government.

gobernador: governor; head of a gobernación.

golpe de estado: violent seizure of political power. In French, the concept is known as *coup d'état.*

guajiro: Arawak-speaking Native American from the Guajira Peninsula of Venezuela. Historically distinguished from other Amerindians in that they were pastoral.

guerrilla: literally "little war;" in contemporary Venezuelan history, the term refers to the left-wing groups that attempted to overthrow the democratic governments of the 1960s.

guzmancista: supporters of Antonio Guzmán Blanco.

hacienda: large landed estate.

hato: livestock ranch.

Intendencia de Ejército y Real Hacienda: colonial institution of political and economic jurisdiction, brought to Spain and to its overseas empire as part of the Bourbon Reforms.

intendiente: head of an *intendencia.*

junta: literally, a group. Politically, the term refers to the group of individuals who head the government.

Junta Revolucionaria de Caracas or *Junta de Caracas: junta* created after the Revolution of April 19, 1810. The *junta* was very active in seeking other Venezuelan *cabildos* to join the revolutionary cause and form similar revolutionary *juntas* in their own jurisdictions. It was also active in enlisting foreign support for the revolutionary cause.

latifundio: land tenure pattern characterized by large land holdings by individuals, especially hereditary estates that produced agricultural or commercial cash crops.

Glossary of Selected Terms

latifundista: holder of a *latifundio.*
Leyenda Dorada or *Leyenda Blanca:* legend that sought to aggrandize the prestige of Spanish colonial rule.
Leyenda Negra: legend that sought to discredit and tarnish the prestige of Spanish colonial rule.
liga: (see *sindicato*).
limpieza de sangre: absence of any Moorish, Jewish, or heretical ancestors from one's family tree.
llanero: rancher or cowboy from the Venezuelan *llanos.*
llanos: vast tropical grasslands or savannahs of the Orinoco basin and the Guiana highlands, north of the equatorial forest of the Amazon basin.
lopecista: supporter of Eleazar López Contreras.
medinista: supporter of Isaías Medina Angarita.
mepista: supporter of the *Movimiento Electoral del Pueblo* (MEP).
Mercosur or *Mercosul* (*Mercado Común del Sur* or *Mercado Comum do Sul*): free-trade zone among Brazil, Argentina, Uruguay, and Paraguay founded in 1995. Bolivia, Chile, Colombia, Ecuador, Peru, and Venezuela have associate member status.
mestizo: person of mixed heritage descended from European and Native American ancestry.
minifundia: land division or distribution in small plots, frequently allowing only for subsistence agriculture.
mirista: supporter of the *Movimiento de Izquierda Revolucionaria* (MIR).
Movimiento 23 de enero: civic and military movement that overthrew the dictatorship of Marcos Pérez Jiménez on January 23, 1958.
Movimiento Bolivariano Revolucionario 200 (MBR-200): revolutionary movement started by a group of junior military officers, including Hugo Chávez, on July 24, 1983, the 200th anniversary of the birth of Simón Bolívar. Leaders are initiated through a Masonic-style ritual, held at a historic site, where they pledge their lives to the movement. Active primarily in neighborhoods, the barracks, and universities, the movement has recently organized itself among the nation's poor.
mulato: person of mixed heritage descended from European and African ancestry.
Nuevas Leyes de Indias: set of laws issued in 1542 that reformed Spanish colonial administration with regard to the *encomienda* system.
octubrismo: ideals of the October Revolution of 1945.
Pacto Andino: free-trade accord signed by the Andean nations of Bolivia, Colombia, Chile, Ecuador, and Perú in 1969 that sought to foster economic development and lay the foundations for a unique common market. Venezuela joined in 1973. Chile and Perú abandoned it in 1976 and 1992, respectively.
Pacto de Punto Fijo: accord proposed by Rómulo Betancourt among Betancourt, Caldera, and Villalba after the overthrow of Pérez Jiménez

to reach a compromise among AD, COPEI, and URD that would allow them to cogovern. The pact was signed on October 31, 1958, at the Quinta "Punto Fijo" property of Rafael Caldera.

pardo: (see mulato).

PDVSA (Petróleos de Venezuela, S.A.): Venezuelan organization that is responsible for the planning, coordination, and supervision of the national oil industry. Created in January 1976.

peninsular: person of European descent born in the Iberian Peninsula.

Proclama de Guerra a Muerte: proclamation of war to the death issued by Simón Bolívar against all Spaniards in 1813, at the onset of his *Campaña Admirable.*

rancho: shanty town or squatter settlement on the periphery of a major town or city.

Real Cédula de Gracias al Sacar: decree that stipulated that *pardos* could buy their way to "white man" status and gain some measure of equality with the *criollos.*

RECADI *(Régimen de Cambios Diferenciales):* government office responsible for instituting a preferential currency exchange rate for U.S. dollars during the 1980s.

Recopilación de las Leyes de los Reynos de las Indias: compedium of laws compiled by Juan de Solórzano in 1681 to organize the institutions that controlled colonial society and administration.

Regeneración: liberal movement of modernization that initially brought Antonio Guzmán Blanco to power.

Rehabilitación: name given to General Juan Vicente Gómez's domestic policies.

Revolución Azul: armed liberal movement that overthrew the presidency of Juan Crisóstomo Falcón in 1868.

Revolución Legalista: armed insurrection from "legalist" factions led by General Joaquín Crespo, firm believers in the constitution of 1881, against the supporters of President Raimundo Andueza Palacio, who favored constitutional reform.

Revolución Libertadora: revolutionary insurrection among large landholders against President Cipriano Castro.

Revolución de Octubre: revolutionary movement that overthrew the presidency of Isaías Medina Angarita in October 1945.

Revolución Reivindicadora: political and military movement from 1878 to 1879 that sought to return Antonio Guzmán Blanco to power after the death of President Francisco Linares Alcántara.

Revolución Restauradora: military invasion of Venezuela (1899) led by Cipriano Castro's forces to seize power, constituting the first instance of massive *andino* participation in national politics.

Sagrada, La: popular name given to the military police of Juan Vicente Gómez.

Glossary of Selected Terms

sindicato: trade union.

Sociedad Patriótica: revolutionary propaganda organization active in Caracas and other Venezuelan towns during the First Republic, cofounded by Simón Bolívar, Francisco de Miranda and other revolutionary leaders in 1810.

superbloque: large, multistory apartment housing constructed for the urban poor by the Marcos Pérez Jiménez government.

tepui: elevated vertical rock formation with a flat top common in the Guayana region of southeastern Venezuela.

Tierra Firme: name given to the Caribbean coast of the South American continent, between Margarita Island and the Darién region of Panamá.

Trienio: the three years from October 1945 to November 1948, during which Venezuela experienced democratic governments.

uerredista, urdista, or *urredista:* supporter of the *Unión Republicana Democrática* (URD).

Welsers: German banking family that took part in the sixteenth-century conquest of Venezuela by a grant awarded by Holy Roman Emperor Carlos V (King Carlos I of Spain).

zambo/sambo: people of mixed heritage descended from African and Native American ancestry.

Bibliographic Essay

For those who wish to do further research on Venezuela, there are a number of general English-language overviews on Venezuelan history, including Edwin Lieuwen's classic *Venezuela* (London: Oxford University Press, 1965, reprinted 1985); Guillermo Morón, *A History of Venezuela* (London: George Allen & Unwin, 1964); and John V. Lombardi, *Venezuela: The Search for Order, The Dream of Progress* (New York: Oxford University Press, 1982). Several notable reference works also should be consulted: Donna K. Rudolph, *Historical Dictionary of Venezuela* (Metuchen, N.J.: Scarecrow Press, 1971); John V. Lombardi and Damos Carrera, et al., *Venezuelan History, A Comprehensive Working Bibliography* (Boston: G.K. Hall, 1977); and D.A.G. Waddell, *Venezuela* (Santa Barbara, Calif.: ABC-Clio Press, 1990).

Other suggested works that explore a variety of specialized topics are Daniel H. Levine, *Religion and Politics in Latin America: The Catholic Church in Venezuela and Colombia* (Princeton, N.J.: Princeton University Press, 1981); Arlene J. Díaz, *Female Citizens, Patriarchs, and the Law in Venezuela, 1786–1904* (Lincoln: University of Nebraska Press, 2004); Elisabeth J. Friedman, *Unfinished Transitions: Women and the Gendered Development of Democracy in Venezuela 1936–1996* (University Park: Pennsylvania State University Press, 2000); Betilde V. Muñoz, "Where Are the Women? The Role of Women in the National Political Process in Venezuela" (University of South Florida M.A. Thesis, 1999); Elizabeth Alvarez, "Professional Women in Venezuela: Changing Gender Roles in a Changing Economy" (Colorado State University M.A. Thesis, 1992); Winthrop R. Wright, *Café con Leche, Race, Class and National Image in Venezuela* (Austin: University of Texas Press, 1990); William Roseberry, *Coffee and Capitalism in the Venezuelan Andes* (Austin: University of Texas Press, 1983); Robert Loring Allen, *Venezuelan Economic Development: A Politico-Economic Analysis* (Greenwich, Conn.: Jai Press, 1977); Michael J. Enright, Antonio Francés, and Edith Scott Saavedra, *Venezuela, the Challenge of Competitiveness* (New York: St. Martin's Press, 1996); John D. Powell, *Political Mobilization of the Venezuelan Peasants* (Cambridge: Harvard University Press, 1971); Juan Carlos Rey, "El futuro de la democracia en Venezuela," *Venezuela hacia el 2000: Desafíos y Opciones* (Caracas: Editorial Nueva Sociedad, 1987); Talton F. Ray, *The Politics of the Barrios of Venezuela* (Berkeley: University of California Press, 1969).

Good sources on Venezuela's pre-Columbian and colonial periods include John V. Lombardi, *People and Places in Colonial Venezuela* (Bloomington: Indiana University Press, 1976); Neil L. Whitehead, *Lords of the Tiger Spirit: A History of the Caribs in Colonial Venezuela and Guayana 1498–1820* (Providence, R.I.: Foris Publications, 1988); José de Oviedo y Baños, *The Conquest and Settlement of Venezuela* (Berkeley: University of California Press, 1987); Norma Graffon, *El Dorado: Lands of Gold: Opposing Viewpoints* (San Diego: Greenwood Press, 1990); Cornelis Christiaan Goslinga, *Dutch in the Caribbean and on the Wild Coast 1580–1680* (Assen, The Netherlands: Van Gorcum, 1971); Robert J. Ferry, *The Colonial Elite of Early Caracas: Formation and Crisis 1567–1767* (Berkeley: University of California Press, 1989); P. Michael McKinley, *Pre-Revolutionary Caracas: Politics, Economy and Society, 1777–1811* (New York: Cambridge University Press, 1985); Roland Dennis Hussey, *Caracas Company, 1728–1784: A Study in the History of Spanish Monopolistic Trade* (London: Oxford University Press, 1934); and Allan J. Kuethe, *Military Reform and Society in New Granada, 1773–1808* (Gainesville: University Presses of Florida, 1978).

Information on race relations in Venezuela can be found in James King, "Negro Slavery in the Viceroyalty of New Granada" (University of California, Berkeley, Ph.D. Dissertation, 1939) and Henry Williams Kirsch, "The Pardo in Venezuelan Society, 1759–1812" (University of Florida M.A. Thesis, 1965). The independence period can be explored through Christian Archer, *The Wars of Independence in Spanish America* (Wilmington, Del.: Scholarly Resources, 2000); John Lynch, *The Spanish American Revolutions 1808–1826* (New York: W.W. Norton, 1973); and Jay Kinsbruner, *The Spanish-American Independence Movement* (Hindsdale, Ill.: Dryden Press, 1973).

For works on the life and thought of Simón Bolívar, see David Bushnell, *Simón Bolívar: Liberation and Disappointment* (New York: Pearson Longman, 2004); Vicente Lecuna and Harold A. Bierck, *The Selected Writings of Bolívar* (New York: Colonial Press, 1951); Daniel Florencio O'Leary, *Bolívar and the Wars of Independence* (Austin: University of Texas Press, 1970); and Gerald E. Fitzgerald, ed. *The Political Thought of Bolívar: Selected Writings* (The Hague: Martinus Nijhoff, 1971). Those who wish to explore the lives of other leaders should see Karen Racine, *Francisco de Miranda, A Transatlantic Life in the Age of Revolution* (Wilmington, Del.: Scholarly Resources, 2003) and Stephen K. Stoan. *Pablo Morillo and Venezuela 1815–1820* (Columbus: Ohio State University Press, 1974). *Sir Robert Ker Porter's Caracas Diary, 1825–1842* (Caracas: Editorial Arte, 1966, reprint) provides an excellent first-hand account of Venezuela during the Páez years.

General works about the history of the nineteenth century are Judith Ewell, *Venezuela: A Century of Change* (Stanford, Calif.: Stanford University Press, 1984) and Fernando López-Alves, *State Formation and Democracy in Latin America, 1810–1900* (Durham, N.C.: Duke University Press, 2000). Other topics on the nineteenth century include William L. Harris, "Venezuela: Wars, Claims, and the Cry for a Stronger Monroe Doctrine," in Thomas M. Leonard, *The United States–Latin American Relations, 1850–1903* (Tuscaloosa: University of Alabama Press, 1999) and Robert L. Gilmore, *Caudillism and Militarism in Venezuela, 1810–1910* (Athens: Ohio University Press, 1964).

Recommended works that explore the twentieth century include John Martz and David Myers, *Venezuela: The Democratic Experience* (New York: Praeger, 1977); Jennifer L. McCoy and David J. Meyers, *The Unraveling of Representative Democracy in Venezuela* (Baltimore: Johns Hopkins University Press, 2004); Michael J. McCaughan, *The Battle of Venezuela* (New York: Seven Stories Press, 2005); Jorge I. Dominguez and Michael Shifter, *Constructing Democratic Governance in Latin America* (Baltimore: Johns Hopkins University, 2003). For examinations of the petroleum industry, see Jorge Salazar-Carrillo and Bernadette West, *Oil and Development in Venezuela during the 20th Century* (Westport, Conn.: Praeger, 2004); Aníbal R. Martínez, *Chronology of Venezuelan Oil* (London: Allen & Unwin, 1969); Jason Feer, *Petróleos de Venezuela, S.A.* (New York: Energy Intelligence Group, 1999); Robert Loring Allen, *Venezuelan Economic Development: A Politico-Economic Analysis* (Greenwich, Conn.: Jai Press, 1977); Rómulo Betancourt, *Venezuela, Oil and Politics* (Boston: Houghton Mifflin, 1979); Gustave Coronel, *The Nationalization of the Venezuelan Oil Industry from Technocratic Success to Political Failure* (Lexington, Mass.: Lexington Books, 1983); Juan Carlos Boué, *Venezuela: The Political Economy of Oil* (Oxford, England: Oxford

University Press, 1993); and Stephen G. Rabe, *The Road to OPEC: United States Relations with Venezuela, 1919–1976* (Austin: University of Texas Press, 1982).

For readers interested in learning more about the controversial Hugo Chávez Frías, see Steve Ellner and Daniel Hellinger, *Venezuelan Politics in the Chávez Era: Class, Polarization, and Conflict* (Boulder, Colo.: L. Rienner, 2003); Olivia Burlingame Goumbri, *The Venezuela Reader: The Building of a People's Democracy* (Washington, D.C.: EPICA, 2005); Richard Gott, *Hugo Chávez and the Bolivarian Revolution* (New York: Verso, 2005); and Richard Gott, *In the Shadow of the Liberator: Hugo Chávez and the Transformation of Venezuela* (London: Verso, 2000).

Index

Abreu Rascanieri, Tomás, 135
Acción Democrática (AD), 12, 85,
    88–107, 112–21, 125–26, 130,
    132–33, 135–37, 139, 141–42,
    144–145, 147, 149, 151
Adeco. See Acción Democrática
Admirable Campaign, 52
Adriani, Alberto, 86
Agrarian Reform, 54, 89, 91–94,
    103–5, 120, 125–26, 132
Ajaguas, 22
Alcantaristas, 70
Altiplano, 3
Amplia Base Coalition, 115–16
Andean Federation, 58–60
Andes, 3, 11, 15, 19, 21–22, 40, 51,
    54, 56, 58, 60, 67, 80. See also
    Mérida; Táchira; Trujillo
Andino. See Andes
Andrade, Ignacio, 71, 78
Andueza Palacio, Raimundo, 71

Angostura, 54–55, 59
Aparicio, 13
Arahuacos, 9, 21–23, 32
Araque, Carlos Luis, 99
Arawaks, 9, 21–23, 32
Ardás, Diego de, 27
Arévalo Cedeño, Emilio, 83
Armed Forces (includes National
    Guard), 44, 50–55, 60–62, 77,
    80, 85, 90–91, 93, 95–96, 98–99,
    101, 106–7, 109, 111, 113, 116,
    121, 131, 142–44, 152–54
Arria, Diego, 134
Arroyo Lameda, Eduardo, 112–13
Audiencia de Bogotá, 32, 35–36
Audiencia de Caracas, 37
Audiencia de Santo Domingo, 34–36
Ayamanes, 22

Banco Agrícola y Pecuario, 104
Banco de los Trabajadores, 116

Banco para el Desarrollo Agrícola y Ganadero, 126
Baralt, Rafael María, 8
Barquisimeto, 2–4, 9, 40
Barrio, 105, 154
Barrios, Gonzalo, 90, 106, 118–19
Bastidas, Rodrigo de, 37
Bello, Andrés, 1, 7, 50
Berrio, Antonio de, 28, 33
Berrio, Fernando de, 28, 32
Betancourt, Rómulo, 83, 86–87, 90, 92–93, 99, 101–13, 115–18, 120–21, 124, 126, 129–30, 133–34, 136
Betancourt Doctrine, 106, 120
Betancurista. *See* Betancourt, Rómulo
Blanco, Andrés Eloy, 8
Bloque Democrático, 155
Bogotá (Santa Fe de Bogotá), 27–28, 32, 35–36, 54, 58–60, 62
Bolívar, Simón, 1, 7, 10, 13, 16, 45–47, 49, 50–63, 70, 132, 154
Bonaparte, Napoleon, 48
Boves, José Tomás, 52
Bravo, Douglas, 118
British Guiana, 28, 72, 79
Burelli Rivas, Miguel Angel, 119

Cabildo, 35, 37–38, 45, 47
Cacao, 1, 37, 39–45 passim, 64, 82
Caldera, Rafael, 94, 97, 112, 116, 119–21, 132, 146–48
Campaña Admirable, 52
Campesino, 91–92, 96, 104–5
Canal Zone, 130
Cannibalism, 32
Canuco farming, 22
Captaincy-General, 36, 75
Capuchins, 38. *See also* Catholic Church
Caquetíos, 22
Caracas, 1, 3–4, 7, 10–11, 13, 23, 27, 33, 35–55 passim, 59, 63–66,

69–71, 75, 78, 83, 86, 90, 96, 98, 99, 102–3, 107–11, 118, 129, 132, 134–35 142–43, 154, 157
Cárdenas, Rodolfo José, 135
Caribs, 21–24, 28, 31–33
Carlos I, King of Spain, 27
Carlos II, King of Spain, 36, 42
Carlos III, King of Spain, 36, 43, 75
Carlos IV, King of Spain, 48
Carlos V, Holy Roman Emperor, 27
Carnevali, Alberto, 96, 100
Carreño, Cayetano, 10
Carreño, José María, 62
Carreño, Teresa, 10, 132, 139
Carta de Jamaica, 53
Carta de Lafond, 56
Casa León, Marquis de, 51
Casas, Juan de, 48–49
Castro, Cipriano, 71, 74, 77–79, 83, 86, 96
Castro, Fidel, 102, 107–8, 117–18, 129, 158
Castro, Julián, 67
Castrocommunism, 107, 110
Catholic Church, 6, 11–12, 34, 37–39, 50, 52, 58, 89, 93–94, 99, 151
Caudillismo, 61, 63, 65, 67, 69, 71, 73, 75, 78, 84. *See also Caudillo*
Caudillo, 7, 60–62, 65–67, 69–71, 73, 78–80. *See also Caudillismo*
Causa Radical, 145, 147
Central Intelligence Agency (CIA), 17, 111, 117, 120
Centro Criogénico de Oriente, 132
Chávez Frías, Hugo, 14, 16, 142–43, 147–48, 151, 155, 158; and February 1992 *Golpe de Estado*, 143–48 passim; and 2004 Recall Referendum, 153–55
Chibchas, 21, 27
Chirino, José Leonardo, 46

Church. *See* Catholic Church
Círculo Valenciano, 78
Cleveland, Grover, 72
Coffee, 2–4, 9, 40, 64, 70, 80, 82–83
Colombia, 3, 13, 27, 45–46, 51–52,
  54–55, 57–62, 78–79, 96, 155,
  157. *See also* Gran Colombia
Colonial administration, 34, 45
Colonization, 27–29, 34, 38
Columbus, Christopher, 19,
  24–26, 46
Columbus, Fernando, 25
Comando Nacional Guerrillero, 110
Comisión Nacional, 124
*Comité de Organización Política
  Electoral Independiente* (COPEI),
  85–86, 91, 94, 99, 101, 112
Compañía Guipuzcoana de Caracas,
  41–42
Concepción, David, 13
*Confederación de Trabajadores
  de Venezuela* (CTV), 91, 96,
  105, 139
Congreso Admirable, 59
Congreso de Angostura, 54–55, 59
Congreso Nacional, 50, 52, 54–55,
  59–60, 65, 69, 72, 88, 90, 93–94,
  99, 104, 109, 115–17, 119, 121,
  125–27, 131–36, 139, 146–48,
  151–52
Conquistador, 12, 27–28, 33–35
Consejo Nacional Electoral (CNE),
  154–55
Consejo Siderúrgico Nacional, 124
Consejo Supremo Electoral, 112
Consulado, 37, 172
Convergencia, 147
Copeyano. See *Comité de
  Organización Política Electoral
  Independiente*
Coro, 3, 9, 13, 22, 26, 36–39, 46–47,
  50, 69
Corporación Venezolana del Petróleo
  (CVP), 106, 118, 124

Corruption, 58–59, 65, 68, 78,
  87, 89, 92, 98, 102, 130–31,
  133–37, 141, 143, 146–47,
  149, 152–53, 159
Council of Cádiz, 48–49
Coup d'état. See *Golpe de Estado*
Crespo, Joaquín, 70–71, 78
Criollo, 35, 39, 41, 44–47,
  51, 66
Cruz Diez, Carlos, 10
Cuba, 81, 102, 107–8, 110–12, 117,
  120, 129–30, 154–55, 157
Cubagua, 26–27, 34
Cúcuta, 51, 55–56, 157
Cuibas, 22
Cumaná, 4, 13, 33, 35–36, 38,
  42, 52
Cumanagotos, 24

Debray, Régis, 107
Declaración de Principios, 101–2
Declaración de Quito, 133
Delgado Chalbaud, Carlos, 90,
  95–96
Delgado Chalbaud, Román, 83
Democratic Socialism, 155, 158
El Dorado, 1, 27–28, 31–32
Ducharne, Horacio, 83

Echeverría, Luis, 129
Elections (includes campaigns
  and results), 16–17, 35, 58–59,
  61–64, 71, 79, 88–90, 93–94, 97,
  99–102, 105, 110–26 passim,
  130–32, 136–37, 141, 144–49,
  152–55
Encomendero, 44
Escobar Salom, Ramón, 145
*Escuela de Aplicación de
  Artillería*, 97
Escuela Militar de Venezuela, 96
Escuela Superior de Guerra, 97
La Esfera, 106
España, José María, 46

Falcón, Juan Crisóstomo, 68–69
Federación Campesina de Venezuela
    (FCV), 91–92, 104, 139
Federación de Cámaras de
    Comercio y Producción
    (Fedecámaras), 139
Federación de Estudiantes de
    Venezuela (FEV), 87
Federación Venezolana de Medicina
    (FVM), 154
Federal District. See Caracas
Federalism, 61–77 passim, 85
Federal War, 64–68, 71–75
Felipe II, King of Spain, 33
Felipe IV, King of Spain, 38
Felipe V, King of Spain, 36, 42
Fernández, Edmundo, 90
Fernández, Eduardo, 120
Fernández de Serpa, Diego, 35
Fernando V "The Catholic," King
    of Castile and León (Fernando
    II of Aragón), 26
Fernando VII, King of Spain,
    48–49, 52–55
Fondo de Inversiones de Venezuela
    (FIV), 125
Foreign Debt, 27, 78–80, 103,
    131, 133, 140
Franciscans, 33, 38
Frente de Liberación Nacional
    (FLN), 109
Frente Electoral Independiente
    (FEI), 97
Frente Nacional Democrático
    (FND), 116
Frente Universitario (FU), 98
Fuero, 50
Fuerza Democrática Popular
    (FDP), 112
Fuerzas Armadas de Liberación
    Nacional (FALN), 108–13,
    117, 120
Fuerzas Armadas Revolucionarias de
    Colombia (FARC), 157

Gabaldón, José Rafael, 83
Gallagher, Matthew, 7, 39
Gallegos, Rómulo, 1, 8, 87–88,
    93–95
García Ponce, Guillermo, 98
"Generation of 1928," 83
Gil Fortoul, José, 8
Golpe de Estado, 49, 88, 90, 92,
    94–96, 98, 102, 110, 143–44,
    146–48, 157; of April 1810, 49;
    of October 1945, 88, 90, 92,
    148; of November 1948, 94–96;
    of January 1958, 98, 102; of
    February 1992, 143–44, 146–48;
    November 1992, 143–44,
    147–48
Gómez, Juan Vicente, 63, 77–96
    passim, 100, 104, 137; and
    Rehabilitación, 79–83
González, Juan Vicente, 8
Gran Colombia, 13, 51, 54–59,
    61, 66, 167–69, 172. See also
    Colombia
Gran Consejo Militar, 96
Guahibos, 5
Guajiros, 21
Gual, Manuel, 46
Gual, Pedro, 67–68, 71
Guaraúnos, 24
Guayana, 2, 5, 9, 24, 28, 32–41
    passim, 67, 69, 72, 79, 116, 124
Guerra, Cristóbal, 26
Guerra, Luis, 26
Guerra de los Cinco Años, 65
Guerra Federal, 65
Guerra Larga, 65
Guerrilla, 52, 54, 110–11, 117, 120,
    129
Guiana. See Guayana
Guzmán, Antonio Leocadio, 64
Guzmanato, 69, 70, 71. See also
    Guzmán Blanco
Guzmán Blanco, Antonio, 7–8,
    10–11, 68–71; and the Bienio,

69; and the *Quinquenio*, 69–70; and the *Septenio*, 69–70. See also *Guzmanato*
Guzmán Otero, Andrés, 93

Hernández, José Gregorio, 12
Hernández, José Manuel, 71
Herrera Campíns, Luis, 123, 125, 130–35
Hojeda, Alonso de, 26
Hyslop, Maxwell, 53–54

Independence Movement, 7–8, 10, 13, 37, 45–60, 66–69, 72–75, 124
Independientes Pro-Frente Nacional (IPFN), 112
Indigenous Cultures, 5–6, 9, 19–33 passim, 44, 46, 50, 58, 75
Instituto de Crédito Agropecuario, 126
Instituto de Mejoramiento Profesional, 116
Intendencia, 36
Intendiente, 36
International Monetary Fund (IMF), 125, 140
Iron-Steel Industry, 116, 124, 126–27, 132–33, 137
Isabel I "The Catholic," Queen of Castile and León, 26

"Jamaica Letter," 53
Jesuits, 38. See also Catholic Church
Jiménez de Quesada, Gonzalo, 29, 35
Jirajaras, 22
Junta, 47–49, 51, 90, 92–100; *Junta Militar de Gobierno* (1945), 95, 96; *Junta Revolucionaria de Gobierno* (1945), 90, 95–96; *Junta Militar de Gobierno* (1948), 95; *Junta Patriótica* (1957), 98;

Junta Militar de Gobierno (1958), 99–100

Keymis, Laurence, 28
Kirora, 21–22

Lairet, Germán, 98
Lake Maracaibo, 2–3, 6, 15, 21, 82. See also Maracaibo
Lamas, José Angel, 10
Lamb, James, 7, 39
Landaeta, Antonio José, 10
Landaeta, Juan José, 10
Larrazábal Ugueto, Wolfgang, 99, 112
Latifundia, 66, 78
Latifundista, 66, 78
Leal Puche, Bernardo, 135
Leftist Insurgency, 88, 107–110, 120, 145
Leoni, Raúl, 83, 90, 106, 112–13, 115–20, 129
Lepage, Octavio, 136
Ley de Tierras, 156
Ley Habilitante, 132
Linares Alcántara, Francisco, 70
Llaneros. See *Llanos*
Llanos, 2, 4–5, 9, 11, 22, 24, 28, 40, 50, 52, 54–55, 60, 64, 67
Llovera Páez, Luis Felipe, 95–96
Lopecista. See López Contreras
López, Juan Pedro, 10
López Contreras, Eleazar, 85–89, 92, 100
Lovera, Juan, 10
Lusinchi, Jaime, 123, 132–33, 136

Machado, Gustavo, 87, 112, 118
Manifiesto de Cartagena, 51
Mano y Metate, 21
Mantuano, 45, 66
Mao, Zedong (Tse-tung), 108

Maracaibo, 2–3, 11, 34–37, 41, 47, 69, 109, 143. *See also* Lake Maracaibo

Margarita, 13, 26, 28, 32, 34–37, 41–42, 53, 132

Mariani, Domingo, 135

Mariches, 23

Martín, Américo, 98

Marxism, 94, 107, 110

Medina Angarita, Isaías, 85, 87–90, 92, 100

Medinista. See Medina Angarita

Mepista, 118

Mercado Común del Sur or *Mercado Comum do Sul* (Mercosur or Mercosul), 156

Mérida, 3–4, 13, 21–22, 27, 37–39, 45, 51, 68

Meso-Indians, 20

Mestizaje, 31, 48

Mestizo, 43, 46, 53, 66

Michelena, Arturo, 1, 10

Military Coup. See *Golpe de Estado*

Miranda, Francisco de, 7, 10, 13, 46–47, 50–52, 60, 63

Mirista. See Movimiento de Izquierda Revolucionaria

Misiones (anti-poverty programs), 154, 156

Moleiro, Moisés, 98

Monagas, José Gregorio, 64–65

Monagas, José Ruperto, 69

Monagas, José Tadeo, 64–65, 69

Monroe Doctrine, 72

Morillo, Pablo, 53–55

Motilón, 21–22

Movimiento al Socialismo (MAS), 145, 147, 152

Movimiento Bolivariano Revolucionario 200 (MBR-200), 144

Movimiento de Izquierda Revolucionaria (MIR), 107, 109, 111, 117, 120

Movimiento de Organización Venezolana (ORVE), 86–88

Movimiento Electoral Nacional Independiente (MENI), 99, 112

Movimiento Electoral del Pueblo (MEP), 118

Movimiento Quinta República (MVR), 152, 156

Movimiento 23 de enero, 99

Mulato, 43

Municipal Council, 94, 99, 105, 121, 126, 131

Napoleonic Wars, 54

Narváez Churión, Vicente, 135

Neo-Indians, 20–21

Niño, Pedro Alonso, 26

Nolasco Colón, Pedro, 10

Nueva Cádiz, 26–27

Nueva Granada, 34–35, 45, 51–55, 62

Nuevas Leyes de Indias (1542), 44

Oficina Central de Coordinación y Planificación (CORDIPLAN), 132

Oidor, 34, 37

Ojeda, Alonso de, 26

Ojeda, Fabricio, 98

Olney, Richard, 72

Olney Declaration, 72

Onotos, 21

Organization of American States (OAS), 129, 153, 155

Organization of Petroleum Exporting Countries (OPEC), 15, 106, 129–30, 156

Orinoco River and Delta, 2, 4–6, 9, 19, 21, 23–25, 27–29, 31–33, 54, 72, 79

Otomoacos, 24

Oviedo y Baños, José de, 7

Pacista. See Paz Galarraga
Pacto Social, 133
Paecista. See Páez
Páez, José Antonio, 54–56, 58–68
    passim, 95–96
Palacios y Sojo, Pedro, 10
Palenques, 23
Paleo-Indians, 19–20
Pardo, 44, 47, 50, 53
Pardo, Isaac, 93
Parra, Teresa de la (aka Ana
    Teresa Parra Sanojo), 8
Partida Secreta, 145
Partido Comunista de Venezuela
    (PCV), 85, 87, 91, 93, 97, 99,
    108–9, 111, 117, 120
Partido Democrático Nacional
    (PDN), 86, 88
Partido Republicano Progresista
    (PRP), 87
Partido Revolucionario Venezolano
    (PRV), 87
Partido Socialista (PS), 99
Partido Socialista de Trabajadores
    (PST), 99
Partido Socialista Venezolano
    (PSV), 112
Paz Galarraga, Jesús A., 118
Pearls, 25–27, 29, 31
Pemón, 5, 21, 24
Peninsular, 44, 47
Peñaloza, Juan Pablo, 83
Pérez, Carlos Andrés, 15, 111, 117,
    120–21, 123–31, 133–37, 139–48,
    157; and First Administration,
    120–21, 123–31, 133–34; and
    Impeachment, 145–47; and
    Second Administration,
    136–37, 139–48
Pérez Jiménez, Marcos, 95–100,
    102, 105–7, 121; and the
    Seguridad Nacional, 97, 100
Petróleos de Venezuela
    (PDVSA), 124

Petroleum, 1, 2, 5, 7, 11, 14–17, 77,
    80, 82–83, 86–89, 91, 98, 100,
    103, 105–6, 109, 118–19, 121,
    123–29, 131–33, 135, 137, 140,
    152–54, 156–58
Piapocos, 25
Piaroas, 5
Picón Salas, Mariano, 86
Picornell, Juan Bautista, 46
Piñerúa Ordaz, Luis, 130, 136
Píritus, 24
Plan de Ajuste Económico, 140
Plan Zamora, 155–56
Plaza, Salvador de la, 87
Pocaterra, José Rafael, 8
Porter, Robert Ker, 63–64, 75
Presidencia, 34
Prietista. See Prieto Figueroa
Prieto Figueroa, Luis Beltrán, 90,
    118–19
Proclama de Guerra a Muerte, 52
Programa Mínimo de Gobierno, 102

Quevedo, Pedro José, 99

Raleigh, Walter, 28, 31–32
Rangel, Domingo Alberto, 106
Rangel, José Vicente, 145, 152
Real Cédula de Gracias al Sacar, 47
Real y Pontificia Universidad de
    Caracas, 39
Recall Referendum (2004), 153–55.
    See also Chávez Frías
Régimen de Cambio Diferencial
    (RECADI), 131
Revolución Azul, 69
Revolución de las Reformas, 66
Revolución de Octubre (1945), 88,
    90–93, 95, 100, 104, 119, 148.
    See also Golpe de Estado; Trienio
Revolución Federal, 65
Revolución Legalista, 71
Revolución Libertadora, 78
Revolución Reconquistadora, 69

Revolución Reivindicadora, 70
Revolución Restauradora, 74, 78
Riego Revolt, 55
Rodríguez, Alí, 153
Rodríguez, Gumersindo, 134
Rodríguez, Rafael, 153
Rodríguez, Simón, 134
Rodríguez del Toro, María
    Teresa, 46
Rojas, Pedro José, 67–68
Rojas Paúl, Juan Pablo, 71
Romerogarcía, Manuel, 8
Roosevelt, Theodore, 79

Sáenz, Manuela, 57–58
Sáez Mérida, Simón, 134
La Sagrada, 80
Sambo, 44
Sanabria, Edgar, 99
San Martín, José de, 56–57
Santander, Francisco de Paula,
    54–59
Santo Domingo, 26, 34–36, 38
Santo Tomé de Guayana, 29,
    32–33
Sedeño, Antonio de, 39
Seminary of Santa Rosa
    (Caracas), 39
Sierra Nevada, 131, 134
Sistema Económico Latinoamericano
    (SELA), 129
Slavery, 24–27, 44–46, 50, 54, 58,
    62, 65
Sociedad Patriótica, 51
Sosa, Arturo, 99
Soto, Jesús, 10
Soublette, Carlos, 62–64
Suárez Flamerich, Germán, 96
Sucre, Antonio José de, 56–60
Superbloque, 105

Táchira, 3, 15, 27, 39, 68, 74, 80, 86,
    88, 90, 92, 96, 106

Tachirense, 80, 86, 88, 92. See also
    Táchira
Tamanacos, 23
Tepui, 6
Teques, 23
Tierra Firme, 29, 38, 48
Timotocuicas, 22–23
Toro, Elías, 93
Torre, Miguel de la, 55
Tovar, Manuel Felipe, 67, 71
Tovar y Tovar, Martín, 10
Trienio, 90–95, 100, 103–4, 119. See
    also Golpe de Estado; Revolución
    de Octubre
Trinidad, 5–7, 25, 27–29, 32–36, 39,
    42, 47–48, 52, 79
Trujillo, 3, 13, 27, 37, 51, 55, 68

Uerredista. See Unión Republicana
    Democrática
Unión Nacional Estudiantil (UNE),
    119
Unión Patriótica Militar (UPM), 97
Unión Republicana Democrática
    (URD), 91, 93, 99, 101, 109, 112,
    114–15, 119
Unions, 91–97, 107–8, 116, 126,
    151–52. See also Confederación
    de Trabajadores de Venezuela;
    Federación Campesina de
    Venezuela
United Nations, 128–29, 133, 153
United States of America, 12–13,
    15–16, 46–48, 63, 71–72, 74,
    81–82, 98, 111, 117, 120, 124,
    129, 153, 155, 157
Universidad Central de Venezuela
    (UCV), 83, 96, 107, 117
Universidad Pedagógica
    Experimental "Libertador," 132
Urdaneta, Rafael, 60
Urdista. See Unión Republicana
    Democrática

Urredista. See *Unión Republicana Democrática*
Uslar Pietri, Arturo, 8, 112, 148

Vargas, José María, 62, 64
Vargas, Mario Ricardo, 90
Velásquez, Ramón J., 141
Viceroyalty, 34–36, 45, 54
Villalba, Jóvito, 83, 93, 97, 112
Villalobos, Marcelo de, 34

Waraos, 24, 25
Welsers, 35, 39

World War One, 2, 15, 81–82
World War Two, 5, 15, 88–89

Yanomami, 5, 21, 24–25
Yanos, 24
Yaruros, 24

Zambo, 44, 46, 176
Zamora, Ezequiel, 67, 164
Zea, Francisco Antonio, 54
Zona en Reclamación, 72
Zulia, 11, 67, 121, 132

Printed in the USA
CPSIA information can be obtained
at www.ICGtesting.com
LVHW020924131124
796374LV00002B/259